# SENTIENT LANDS

Piergiorgio Di Giminiani

# SENTIENT LANDS

*Indigeneity, Property, and Political Imagination in Neoliberal Chile*

THE UNIVERSITY OF
ARIZONA PRESS
TUCSON

The University of Arizona Press
www.uapress.arizona.edu

We respectfully acknowledge the University of Arizona is on the land and territories of Indigenous peoples. Today, Arizona is home to twenty-two federally recognized tribes, with Tucson being home to the O'odham and the Yaqui. Committed to diversity and inclusion, the University strives to build sustainable relationships with sovereign Native Nations and Indigenous communities through education offerings, partnerships, and community service.

© 2018 by The Arizona Board of Regents
All rights reserved. Published 2018
First paperback edition published 2025

ISBN-13: 978-0-8165-3552-1 (cloth)
ISBN-13: 978-0-8165-5534-5 (paper)
ISBN-13: 978-0-8165-3911-6 (ebook)

Cover design by Leigh McDonald
Cover photo by Pablo Trincado

Publication of this book is made possible in part by the proceeds of a permanent endowment created with the assistance of a Challenge Grant from the National Endowment for the Humanities, a federal agency.

Library of Congress Cataloging-in-Publication Data
Names: Di Giminiani, Piergiorgio, author.
Title: Sentient lands : indigeneity, property, and political imagination in neoliberal Chile / Piergiorgio Di Giminiani.
Description: Tucson : The University of Arizona Press, 2018 | Includes bibliographical references and index.
Identifiers: LCCN 2018014009 | ISBN 9780816535521 (cloth : alk. paper)
Subjects: LCSH: Mapuche Indians—Land tenure—Government policy—Chile. | Mapuche Indians—Chile—Government relations. | Mapuche Indians—Chile—Politics and government. | Mapuche Indians—Chile—Social conditions. | Mapuche Indians—Legal status, laws, etc.—Chile. | Reparations for historical injustices—Chile.
Classification: LCC F3126 .D49 2018 | DDC 323.1198/72083—dc23 LC record available at https://lccn.loc.gov/2018014009

Printed in the United States of America
♾ This paper meets the requirements of ANSI/NISO Z39.48-1992 (Permanence of Paper).

In memory of a great teacher,
Liscán Contreras Ñiripil

# CONTENTS

*List of Illustrations*     ix
*Acknowledgments*     xi

Introduction: Sentient Lands     3

## Part I. People and Land

1. Historical Debts: Race, Land, and Nation Building in Southern Chile     33
2. Being from the Land: Place, Memory, and Experience     57
3. Working the Land: Environmental Anxieties, Care, and the Quest for Endurance     85
4. Owning the Land: Entitlement, Assimilation, and Other Dilemmas of Property     112

## Part II. Land Claims

5. Mapping Ancestral Land: The Power of Documents in Land Claims     141
6. Negotiating Ancestral Land: Claimants, Bureaucrats, and the Realpolitik of Sacredness     163
7. The Future of Ancestral Land: Uncertainties of World Making in a Reclaimed Territory     187

*Glossary*     205
*Notes*     207
*References*     217
*Index*     237

# ILLUSTRATIONS

| | | |
|---|---|---|
| 1. | Road cutting through Comunidad Contreras | 6 |
| 2. | Traiguen and surroundings | 25 |
| 3. | The center of Traiguen at the beginning of the nineteenth century | 41 |
| 4. | Meeting held at the community center with local authorities and candidates during the campaign for municipal elections | 56 |
| 5. | Street in Traiguen | 75 |
| 6. | Fields within an Indigenous community | 77 |
| 7. | Plantation of young eucalyptus trees near Traiguen | 97 |
| 8. | Crossing the Quino River by log bridge | 99 |
| 9. | Cereal harvest, or trilla | 103 |
| 10. | School in Comunidad Contreras | 123 |
| 11. | Map of land division | 130 |
| 12. | CONADI headquarters in the center of Temuco | 146 |
| 13. | Map of the Título de Merced 18-B | 152 |
| 14. | Sit-in at regional government building (Intendencia Regional) in Temuco | 167 |
| 15. | Community members signing a land transference agreement | 179 |
| 16. | A ceremony held to celebrate the land property transfer | 190 |

# ACKNOWLEDGMENTS

THIS BOOK RAISES NO REPRESENTATIONAL CLAIM ON MAPUCHE SOCIety. It would have made no sense to pursue such a goal, given the vast heterogeneity of the Mapuche population. My condition of being *winka* (non-Mapuche) makes even more evident the absurdity of attempting to define what a Mapuche theory of geography, environment, and land is. Developing a satisfactory knowledge of Mapuche philosophy takes a lifetime even for Mapuche people; imagine how long it takes for someone who is, on top of that, a foreigner in Chile. Rather than venturing into sketching an Indigenous theory of land connections, this book offers the reader ethnographic, historical, and theoretical observations of the ambivalent relations in which Mapuche claimants and non-Indigenous Chileans find themselves embroiled in the context of land politics. I am interested in the uncertainties and controversies concerning how and when lands could act as sentient in the lived world of Indigenous rural Chile vis-à-vis historical processes of land encroachment and formalization. This book is first and foremost about relations. Its long gestation has been a life-changing experience grounded in many different encounters I have had the privilege of getting involved with. Of course, the fact that the arguments I raise stem from multiple relations does not clear me of any possible errors in recounting events and concepts that I have been exposed to. Responsibility is solely mine.

The reader will soon realize that one relation in particular occupies a central stage. It is the long-term collaboration with members of one Mapuche settlement, Comunidad Contreras, with whom I share numerous stories and experiences during a fraction of their prolonged struggle for land restitution. As soon as our relationship began in 2007 as part of fieldwork research for my doctoral project, it was clear to the people of Comunidad Contreras that my work could and should serve as a testimony for their fight and possibly inspire other Mapuche groups in the area, often restrained by political apathy and a history of paternalism by state institutions. In being granted the honor and burden to recount the struggle of Comunidad Contreras, I hope that this work does justice to the expectations of friends and acquaintances. My deepest gratitude goes to the late Liscán and his son and daughter, Miguel and Francisca Contreras. Their house became a home in Chile and they cared for me as a family member, "a more gringo-looking Contreras," making fieldwork in southern Chile the richest learning experience of my life. The late Francisca Contreras and Arturo Huaiquilao hold a special place in my heart, as food, jokes, and conversations were never short in their house. I am indebted to *werken* Jose Contreras for first inviting me to visit his community and his close relatives—his mother, Quinturay; his wife, Flor; and his siblings, Juana, Filomena, Juanita, David, Oliver, and Lucho Inaipil. I also wish to thank Ruby Huenchuñir, Carlos Vasquez, *lonko* Nelly Cheuque, Luisa Gineo, Segundo Queupumil, Enrique Cheuquelao, Arturito Huaiquilao, Gabriel Contreras, Berta Queupumil and his family, Juan Rivera, Nolo Contreras, Elsa Calabrano, Pato Contreras, and Luly Huaquilao. Too many are the people from Comunidad Contreras that I would like to personally thank for their generosity. I apologize for shortcomings of my memory and note-taking, in case some names are not mentioned here, but please rest assured that my gratitude goes first to all members of Comunidad Contreras, whether currently residing in this settlement or living elsewhere. Also thanks to the late Lipin Contreras and his family in the town of Victoria for the many visits to their houses. *Chaltu may!!!*

In Traiguen, I would like to acknowledge the late Rigoberto Osses, who during his tenure as mayor was a firm ally of Comunidad Contreras, and the late Julian Schneider, another person sharing his friendship with this community. I also wish to thank all Mapuche and chilenos living around the town who agreed to be interviewed. In Temuco, I would like to thank all CONADI (Consejo Nacional de Desarrollo Indígena, or National Corporation for Indigenous Development) officers who allowed me to participate in their meetings with members of Comunidad Contreras and to interview them individually. I thank Maria Eugenia Quepumil, who assisted me during archival research at Archivo General de Asuntos Indígenas (AGAI) of CONADI. Figures 11 and 13 were reproduced with the permission of AGAI, for which I thank Joaquin Bizama. Many thanks also to the staff members of Lonko Kilapang who were active between 2007 and 2008, in particular Mauricio Huenchulaf, those of the Fundación Instituto Indígena, and Elicura Chihuailaf for our conversations. For my initial stint of fieldwork, I was an affiliate researcher at the Instituto de Estudios Indígenas of Universidad de la Frontera. I thank its former director Alejandro Herrera, Pato Coliqueo, Sylvia Galindo, Italo Salgado, and, in particular, Ximena Zedan, who, with her husband, Alvaro Maringer, were amazing hosts and friends during my stay in Temuco.

This book grew from my doctoral research at University College London (UCL). I am indebted to my supervisor, Martin Holbraad, for constantly challenging me to realize the analytical potentials of my research, at first beyond my close sight. My gratitude also goes to Allen Abramson and Mukulika Banerjee for many inspiring discussions about politics and land. This book would have not been what it is without the thorough reading of my dissertation by Eric Hirsch and Magnus Course, whom I also thank wholeheartedly for guiding me throughout the years over many issues raised in the following pages. This book has benefited enormously from numerous conversations and seminars at UCL, where I had the chance to share my work with fellow graduate students and lecturers. I wish to thank Emiliano Zolla, Sergio Gonzalez, Sophie Haines, Anthony Pickles, Natasha Beranek, David Cooper, Charles Stewart, Martin Fotta, Michael Stewart, Manuela Pellegrino, Rafael Schacter, Janine Su, Nico Tassi, Mike Rowlands, Viorel Anastasoaie, Nanneke Redclift, and David Jobanputra, whom I also thank for his careful revision of parts of this work.

I wrote this book as an early career professor at the Pontificia Universidad Católica de Chile. Much of the dedication and energy invested in this book came as a reflection of the most exciting academic project I have been involved in so far in my life, the establishment of a new department in anthropology. Since 2011, the year I joined Universidad Católica, the department grew from a couple of anthropologists to a thriving and diverse group of scholars. Different people at Universidad Católica supported me in writing this book in so many different ways. Thanks to Marjorie Murray, the incredibly generous mastermind behind the birth of anthropology at Universidad Católica, and to Helene Risor, Diana Espirito Santos, Giovanna Bacchiddu, Cristian Simonetti, Joe Feldman, Angel Aedo, Jaime Coquelet, Eduardo Valenzuela, Pedro Morandé, Ingrid Zapata, Pedro Mege, Andrew Webb, Felipe Martinez, Roberto Campbell, Fabian Flores (thanks for introducing me to so many debates in political theory relevant to my work), Pablo Briceño, Martin Fonck, Nicolas Salinas, Julian Moraga, and Paolo Perasso. Throughout my years at Universidad Católica, I was lucky enough to have cultivated an intellectual partnership and friendship with Marcelo Gonzalez and Cristobal Bonelli, whom I thank for being mutual critics of our work and co-designers of antiwitchcraft tactics. Special thanks to Bernardita Galecio for bearing with me during the last stressful stages of writing. *Gracias*!

A big push toward the writing of this book came from a visiting fellowship at the University of Edinburgh in 2014. There I wish to thank Casey High, John Bialecki, Charlotte Gleghorn, Fiona J. Mackintosh, Maya Mayblin, and, in particular, Magnus Course, who acted as a wonderful host at the School of Social and Political Science. I have shared insights from this book over several years in different seminars at the

University of California, Santa Cruz; Universidad de Buenos Aires; University of Edinburgh; Universidad Católica del Norte; and Universidad de Chile; and at conference panels at LASA, EASA, and AAA. I thank organizers and assistants for their comments: Birgit Muller, Nancy Chen, Alberto Arce, Nancy Postero, Manuel Prieto, Florencia Tola, Rolf Foerster, and José Isla. Some of the material discussed in chapters 2, 5, and 6 has appeared in three previous articles published by the *Journal of the Royal Anthropological Institute*, *American Ethnologist*, and *Ethnos*. I thank Matthew Engelke, Angelique Haugerud, Niko Besnier, Mark Graham, and Nils Bubandt for their guidance. Research for this book was made possible by several grants: the Dissertation Fieldwork Grant of the Wenner-Gren Foundation, the Abbey Santander Research Award, the Sutasoma Award of the Royal Anthropological Institute, the UCL Graduate School Research Projects Fund, and the Central Research Fund of the University of London. Further assistance was provided by the CIIR research center (CONICYT/FONDAP/15110006), for which I am wholly grateful. I am indebted to Allyson Carter of the University of Arizona Press, whose relentless support and encouragement through the editorial process has proved priceless. Thanks also to Scott de Herrera for his generous assistance, to the five anonymous reviewers who have read my manuscript and bestowed me with so many valuable comments, and to Alison Stent and Amy Maddox for their dedicated and passionate revision of my work.

Among many things, this book is about reconnecting with one's place in the world. It has been an exciting journey, at times frustrating—one I have undertaken from the south-central Italian countryside to the Chilean one, passing through some other places mentioned earlier. One way or another, Claudia Robles, Marcelo Munch, Natalie Pilato, Riccardo di Pasquale, Almerindo Coccia, Lolita Meco, my dearest late uncle Nico Meco, and my cousins Enrico and Claudia have been companions in this journey. My first and last thoughts go to my family—to my father, Giuseppe, to my mother, Maria Antonietta, and to my brother, Pierpaolo, for giving me love and strength in the most rewarding and arduous moments of this journey. *Grazie dal profondo del mio cuore*!

# SENTIENT LANDS

# INTRODUCTION
*Sentient Lands*

TWO YEARS AFTER SUBMITTING AN APPEAL FOR LAND RESTITUTION, Gabriel Contreras, the elected president of Comunidad Contreras, received a long-awaited phone call from the head office of CONADI. He was informed that a land grant of 365.64 hectares had been approved to his community as compensation for historic land loss. Like the inhabitants of this rural settlement, I received the news during the monthly meeting held at the community building (*sede*).[1] Attendees agreed that this event called for a large celebration to be held at the agricultural estate demanded for restitution, Fundo el Huadaco. One community delegate (*dirigente*) proposed that the event should be celebrated "the Mapuche way" (*a lo Mapuche*), without the presence of CONADI officials, who would otherwise have taken full credit for what was considered an accomplishment of the community. Three weeks later, on an unusually warm winter morning, the residents of Comunidad Contreras congregated around a large metal barn at El Huadaco. For many residents this was the first time they wandered around this property. Only a few middle-aged men knew El Huadaco reasonably well, having been employed as seasonal or casual workers by the former owners, a family of non-Indigenous Chileans.[2] Next to the barn stood a small branch of a canelo (*Drimys winteri*), a tree with a significant role in healing and ritual practices, which had been placed in the ground by community delegates. At one point, lonko Nelly, the ritual organizer of the community, invited all attendees to gather around the canelo branch to perform a *masatun*, a type of dance composed of linear and synchronized movements of alternating lines of male and female dancers. Once the cadenced music of the *pifülka* flutes had drawn to a close, the attendees moved closer to the canelo branch. Speaking in Mapudungun, the Mapuche language,

Nelly began to chant a rhythmic incantation known as *llellipun*. Eventually, she turned to Spanish to continue her speech, since most of the attendees had limited knowledge of Mapudungun. Nelly thanked Chao Dios (god father) for the allotment of El Huadaco. She also appealed for community members to remain united in the coming years, as many challenges, including pending land claims on other sections of their demanded territory, lay ahead.

Nelly's *llellipun* was followed by an *afafan*, a series of screams of acclamation accompanied by the brandishing of *wüño*, wooden sticks commonly used during the *palin*, a Mapuche game resembling hockey. Another round of the *masatun* dance followed, by the end of which a few community members voiced their opinions about the next steps in their long fight for land restoration (*recuperación territorial*). After several speeches, a community delegate invited all attendees to a *misawun*, a large meal typically held after collective rituals. The members of each household gathered around wooden tables that had been carried here by community members for the occasion. Large quantities of grilled beef, soup, soda drinks, sopaipilla (fried bread), wine, and yerba mate, an infused drink common throughout the Southern Cone, were shared around each table. Meanwhile, guests from nearby towns, among them a high-ranking member of the regional government invited by the community board for his support during land negotiations, joined the celebration. In the background, blaring from the stereo of a nearby pickup truck, one could hear recent hit songs by Los Charros de Lumaco, a band of *cumbia ranchera*, the most popular party music in the Chilean countryside. Some people, like myself, began to dance, while others caught up with old friends and neighbors. The celebration went on for several hours. After more than 120 years of ownership by winkas (non-Mapuche people), El Huadaco was once again Mapuche land. Truly, it was a day to remember.

The celebration for the restitution of El Huadaco as part of the "ancestral territory" (*territorio ancestral*) of the community was one of many unprecedented events that I have had the chance to witness in southern Chile. Its novelty is suggestive of some of the profound changes brought by Indigenous politics in Chile over the last twenty years. Since the return of democratic rule in 1990 after seventeen years of Augusto Pinochet's military dictatorship, Mapuche organizations have mobilized in the attempt to reclaim land that they had been dispossessed of in the previous 150 years. In southern Chile, land dispossession was the result of the military invasion of the sovereign Mapuche region at the end of the nineteenth century, which was soon followed by the confinement of the local population within newly founded reservations (*reducciones*) and the territorial expansion by white settlers. Since 1990, governmental responses to Indigenous demands for land restitution and local autonomy have been twofold. On the one hand, mobilization, including occupation (*tomas*) of large agricultural estates owned by white landholders and agribusiness companies, has been repressed through imprisonment of activists and military raids on Mapuche settlements. On the other hand, mounting international criticism of the limited scope of Indigenous collective rights in Chile has pressured postdictatorship governments to design multicultural reforms. In 1993, the center-left government of Concertación de Partidos por la Democracia (Coalition of Parties for Democracy) introduced a land program run by CONADI as part of a major legal reform concerning Indigenous rights. This program was celebrated in the public arena as a first step for the state to pay off its "historical debt" (*deuda histórica*) toward Indigenous groups and build the foundation for a truly democratic and multicultural country. However, many of the promises of restoration made by the land program have failed to materialize. The few successful Mapuche claimants have been relocated to properties other than those claimed for restitution. By transforming the ancestral territory into land with market value, restitution claims have paradoxically introduced new forms of displacement.

The celebration following the restitution of El Huadaco sets the scene for the analysis that I intend to carry out in this book of an overarching tension inherent to all land claims: that between political creativity and the stability of land connections. On the one hand, the ancestral territory is the result of creative actions in the present that have allowed claimants to articulate geographic constructs with the intention of exercising control over indigeneity, a term I use in reference to the proliferation of multiple and sometimes contradictory forms of being Indigenous produced by the intersections of local, national, and global agendas (De la Cadena and Starn 2007, 12). Emerging in the midst of anxieties about ongoing processes of assimilation and migration toward urban areas, the ancestral territory bears promises for the future rather than nostalgic images of the past. On the other hand, the significance of the ancestral territory is built around an idea of land connections as a central element of Indigenous identity. Land claims thus contribute to the articulation of the ancestral territory as an image of historical continuity, which contrasts with the profoundly transformative nature of Indigenous territoriality. For Derrick Fay and Deborah James (2009), the problem is clear: it lies in the fact that "land claims are not indigenous processes, although they attempt to somehow reproduce traditional rights and claims" (15). Claimants are thus compelled to reproduce images of traditional lifestyles that could justify claims over ancestral land in the eyes of national subjects. Yet, paradoxically, they are also forced to prove the consistency of demanded territories as property through technologies of legal documentation, such as deeds of property, archival sources, and maps, initially designed to validate land dispossession (Clifford 1988; Nadasdy 2003). The inescapable contradictions of Indigenous land claims leave us at first with a sense of distrust toward the existence of the ancestral territory as more than a mere image of the past. Among the many questions opened by land claims, one in particular appears central to current debates on the legitimacy of Indigenous demands over land and natural resources. Can ancestral land connections matter today vis-à-vis historical processes of displacement suffered by Indigenous groups? The significance of this question goes well beyond an analytical interest. For Mapuche claimants, proving the resilience of their connections with their native territory is their main chance not only to attain land compensation but also to continue to be Mapuche.

The political and experiential significance of Indigenous land connections is the theme of this book. By looking at the conceptual and practical ramifications of land connections in both dwellers' daily engagement with the environment and the governmental contexts of land claims, I hope to illustrate the salient and transformative nature of the ancestral territory in Indigenous southern Chile. Tracing the historical transformation of the ancestral territory triggered by governmental actions and Indigenous collective action, while acknowledging the ontological depth of land connections at work in Mapuche ideas and practices of selfhood, requires an analytical shift from a focus on land signification to one centered on the mutuality of human/land relations. In the case of Mapuche land claims in Chile, such a shift entails a focus on a key process to which much of this book is dedicated—namely, the mutual constitution of people and land as political subjects. This process is put in motion by the entanglement of Indigenous and legal land ontologies. By land ontologies, I refer to

FIGURE 1 Road cutting through Comunidad Contreras. (Photo by author)

modes, relations, and categories of being that emerge from historically and geographically contingent expressions of land connections. Indigenous land ontologies are predicated upon an intersubjective relation—in other words, a relation between two subjects, land and people, both endowed with sentient abilities. Legal land ontologies, in contrast, are founded upon the principles of property theory according to which land is an object of possession that can be standardized within a regime of value. Indigenous and legal land ontologies are conceptually antagonist and yet deeply entangled in practice. The translation of sentient lands into property can activate new forms of ancestral land connections for claimants, but can also serve to domesticate Indigenous geographies within existing market configurations. A look at this twofold process can shed a light on the destabilizing effects that the incursion of sentient lands in the political arena poses to neoliberal political imagination.

## The Making of People and Land: Politics Beyond Essence and Construction

All across Latin America, the 1990s and 2000s saw a wave of legal reforms aimed at consolidating Indigenous lands (Stocks 2005). Ever since, the increasing weight of Indigenous territorial rights in national politics has activated fierce contestation by private actors and policy makers interested in curtailing them. In Chile, the notion of ancestral territory is under attack from various political standpoints. According to nationalistic and conservative perspectives, the ancestral territories are nothing more than a recent fabrication by a few political radicals with links to left-wing insurgent groups. This argument is built around the suppositions that Indigenous people have been culturally assimilated and that ancestral land occupation is a historically discontinuous process of displacement. Diffusionist theories from the early 1900s, according to which the Mapuche originate from remote areas, such as the Amazonian lowlands, are revived by right-wing political commentators to question the autochthonous status of Indigenous people in the country. From a very different angle, Indigenous rights activists question the participation of rural communities in the state-sponsored program of land restitution as a strategy of co-option. The endowment of small geographic constructs, such as the ancestral territory, subject to claims of entitlement by local population, works to isolate rural settlements in their struggle for land, reduce the geographic extent of legitimate territorial demands, and finally shift public attention away from unresolved aspirations of Indigenous regional autonomy. Despite their opposite agendas, progressive and conservative critiques of land claims agree with the point that the ancestral territory is constructed through political action, whether as the result of identity politics imbuing the land with recent public signification or as the outcome of governmental restructuring of land access and ownership. One of the key motivations in writing this book is the attempt to recognize the transformative nature of the ancestral territory, given largely by the asymmetric encounter of Indigenous politics and state spatial action, while moving beyond the disentanglement of this geographic construct as a mere invented tradition, a point that precludes the possibility of taking seriously claimants' geo-philosophy and their senses of attachment to land. This attempt requires a movement away from two customary explanatory approaches to Indigenous land claims, which I call essentialist and constructivist, to one centered on the intersubjective nature of those relations between human and nonhuman components of the landscape that constitute the ancestral territory. Both models of explanation are relevant beyond questions of ethnographic representation. As a matter of fact, they are key features of postcolonial politics, because they serve as implicit analytical frameworks embedded in power relations between Indigenous people and national society and informing state actions in the context of postcolonial land governance and reparation.

In social sciences, essentialism has come to be understood as the act of reducing complex social phenomena to an essence intended to provide a comprehensive explanation of cultural uniqueness. The predicament of essentialist interpretations is well known in anthropology and is commonly associated with folklorizing representations of nonindustrial societies (Clifford 1988). Essentialism is thus predicated upon the imposition of necessary conditions for a subject to be validly considered part of a collectivity or category. A typical example is the questioning of Indigenous status for all those individuals who are no longer fluent in their native language. In this view, cultural assimilation is an all-or-nothing effect. An essentialist rendering of ancestral land connections presupposes Indigenous territories as the backdrop for a stable set of cultural features inscribed in the landscape. The ancestral territory would thus exist only as the setting for an unproblematic reiteration of past generations in the present. Its significance would be framed in terms of its sacredness, a characterization that is mutually exclusive with profane relations to land, such as agricultural work. Within essentialist approaches, the fact that present-day Indigenous people no longer constitute an enduring record of ancestral lifestyles and yet claim ancestral land connections as a central tenet of their subjectivity remains an insuperable contradiction. Essentialist interpretations of land connections can thus serve to delegitimize claims over ancestral land by imposing standards of authenticity upon Indigenous claimants based on their contiguity with the dwellers of the ancestral territories.

The second customary explanatory approach to Indigenous land claims is constructivism. This term originated as a critique of essentialist interpretations. It refers to the idea that phenomena are necessarily constructed as the result of social signification. Constructivist approaches highlight the highly political and transformative nature of culture, as the construction of social phenomena is a dynamic process in which power relations emerge as the result of conflictive acts of signification. Let us take land as an example. In any society, land is symbolically constructed as an expression of geographic identity and belonging. The symbolic value of land cannot be dissociated from political processes, as in the case of postcolonial contexts, where subaltern groups discursively reinstate their emotional connection with their homeland as part of a broader struggle for cultural survival and self-determination. In contrast to essentialism, a notion that anthropologists have come to fear as a latent threat in any ethnographic account, constructivism has played a more positive and influential part in the history of the discipline. The very notion of culture situates human difference in the field of signification. The consolidation of constructivist approaches to political action is intimately connected to the rise of new social movements in the 1970s. The scholarly debate on these movements represented an attempt by different analysts to develop a framework for the analysis of all forms of collective action—such as those linked to gender and ethnic rights—that have contributed to a historical shift from redistribution to recognition politics (Fraser 1995). The work of sociologist Alberto Melucci (1989) has been particularly influential in fostering a view of politics as the ground for the construction of both social phenomena and social identities. In Melucci's view, collective action allows for the articulation of collective forms of identity among individual actors partaking in social movements from different positions and interests. In Latin America, the rise of recognition politics is most commonly associated with Indigenous and Afro-descendant transnational movements formed since the 1980s (Langer and Muñoz 2003; Van Cott 1994; Warren and Jackson 2002). Indigenous politics have challenged dominant ideologies of ethnic units implicit to discourses of nation building in the region.

Constructivist approaches to recognition politics have helped us to acknowledge the profound intersections between power and culture. They have also drawn our attention to the relational and dynamic nature of identity. Yet I believe that a constructivist approach to Indigenous territorial struggles is not exempt from one particular shortcoming—namely, the idea that semiotic and symbolic constructions of the world arise freely from existing connections among humans and between them and nonhumans. This shortcoming is crucial to the argument I advance in this book. Constructivist approaches are built upon liberal principles, according to which the construction of both collective identities and the object of political action is the implementation of individual intentionality. Implicit to constructivism is the characterization of identity as a discursive form of self-making that transcends the social, ecological, and historical conditions through which different subjectivities are formed. Identity might therefore appear as a collective phenomenon, but it is ultimately constituted by the sum of individual acts of self-determination. In viewing collective action through the lenses of identity politics, one runs the risk of imposing a temporal divide articulated around the *ex novo* construction of new subjectivities and their relations. In doing so, one can also obscure those historical trajectories through which difference has been sustained (Hale 1997, 569). The "now and then" character of constructivism in recognition politics resonates strongly in the analysis of Indigenous land claims. In a constructivist perspective, political action tends to be conceptualized as a process through which new meanings of land connections are formed. In historical struggles over land rights, claimants are able to transform the idea of land into a symbol of Indigenous identity (see Occhipinti 2003). Subjacent to constructivist interpretations of land claims lies a chronological narrative of land connections: we begin with land as a neutral object; then political action erupts as an act of signification; finally, the ancestral territory emerges as a new geographic formation. Constructivist approaches to land claims thus acknowledge the transformative nature of Indigenous geographies at the cost of underestimating those spatial relations and actions that sustain Indigenous forms of life outside the realm of identity politics. Rather than serving as the motivation behind land mobilization, the significance of the ancestral territory is reduced to a symbol for political action.

Territoriality consists of the construction, appropriation, and control of territory, a process that depends on the attempts by multiple national and international audiences to understand and dispute them (Liffman 2011, 1). Ethnic movements in Latin America have highlighted the inseparability of territory and difference, since any territory exists as an expression of unique place making in relation to others (Escobar 2008, 25). Essentialist and constructivist approaches to territorialities fail to grasp that territories are neither prepolitical (that is, spaces where attachment is unaffected by the dynamic formation of new subjectivities and relations through politics) nor postpolitical (in other words, spaces signified exclusively through collective action). Rather, territories undergo continuous cycles of regeneration put in motion by political action as much as embodied experiences in the environment, two actions that are enmeshed since dwelling in specific ways is a political act itself and politics is also made of affects and bodily experiences. Albeit from different points of departure, essentialist and constructivist interpretations of land claims converge on one conclusion: that today ancestral land connections can only exist as an identity trope in line with the incommensurability between the lives of Indigenous claimants and those of their ancestors. The scenarios portrayed by essentialist and constructivist interpretations of land claims clash with the ways in which land connections unfold in Indigenous southern Chile. Here, land connections can be understood as central elements of personhood—without the necessity of thinking about the ancestors as forces determining the present—as if they were the direct and cumulative result of past human actions. The ethnographically informed notion of ancestral territory exceeds its value as a local category to act as a powerful mode of critique against understandings of Indigenous land connections as symbolic constructions. While being Mapuche, an ethnonym meaning people (*che*) of the land (*mapu*), cannot be reduced to life in rural settlements, the ancestral territory plays an active role in processes of self-making. In Mapuche society, places make people as much as people make places. The significance of the ancestral territory lies in the productive relation between two sentient subjects—land and people—that are responsive to both human and nonhuman actions. Therefore, land connections act upon humans while being articulated as a result of human engagement with the local surroundings. Rather than reinstating nostalgic views of the past, land claims work to activate those relational networks, involving humans, sentient beings, and topographic features, through which a person constitutes him- or herself in the Mapuche lived world.

With this book, I hope to move beyond essentialist and constructivist interpretations of Indigenous land demands in order to illustrate one particular process inherent to land claims in southern Chile—namely, the mutual constitution of people and land as political subjects. To think of land connections in terms of mutual constitution requires one to recognize the sentient nature of both land and people. My interest in the politics of sentient lands implies an appraisal of the intricate political ramifications of the notion of sentience. It also implies the acknowledgment of the destabilizing effects of those land connections that openly defy the ontological principles of legal property theories. The potential of sentience in political affairs is far-reaching. For the last forty years, public debates on the value of nonhuman life, such as those concerning animal rights, have centered on the question of sentience, especially in relation to the uncertainties over killable and nonkillable species (Haraway 2008, 89). The politics of sentience are not restricted to debates over universal dignity of nonhuman life, but also include the resilience of those forms of human life built around specific relations with sentient nonhumans. In current debates on multiculturalism, sentience has become an umbrella notion to sustain diverse moral and political claims in defense of those ecological networks on which Indigenous livelihoods depend. Therefore, the very meaning of the term *sentient* is multifaceted and open to continuing redefinitions and contestations. Etymologically, sentience refers to the ability to feel (*sentire* in Latin). Anthropology has a relatively long history of employing the term *sentient* to characterize certain cosmologies, as in animism, where the status of personhood is extended to different categories of nonhuman beings (see Anderson 2000). In particular, the term *sentient landscapes* has been used to refer to the extension of the ability for intentional and affective action to topographic elements observed in numerous societies. Sentient landscapes are defined by the continuing presence of forces embodied in the land that are responsive to human action. Some of these forces are genealogically linked to present-day dwellers, as in the case of Aboriginal Australia (see Povinelli

2016). Others are related to humans in terms of ongoing actions of reciprocity, as in the Andean highlands (see De la Cadena 2015). Asking whether or not rocks (Povinelli 1995) or glaciers (Cruikshank 2005) can listen helps us to abandon metaphorical understanding of land connections in favor of an intersubjective approach to engagement with nonhuman agencies. Such an approach can be read as an attempt to take seriously the life of others represented in anthropological accounts by avoiding the treatment of ontological categories as matters of belief, a movement that entails a priori distinction between truth and falsehood (Viveiros de Castro 2011, 144). Reliance on belief as a methodological tool of analysis jeopardizes from the start any attempt to trace the political and phenomenological ramifications of sentient lands.

Sentient lands concern a type of engagement between two subjects, land and people, which, rather than acting as preconstituted terms of a relation, are made through such a relation. The type of connections elicited by sentient lands presupposes a human ability to feel for the land and a recognition of land's responsiveness to human actions. Engagement with sentient land ultimately unfolds as a relation of affect. Following Gilles Deleuze (1990) in his assessment of Spinoza's work, I view affect not as emotional attachment but rather as the ontological reconfiguration of the subject/object divide whereby the terms of any relation are defined by their mutual influence: "the distinction between power and act . . . disappears in favor of two equally actual powers, that of acting, and that of suffering action, which vary inversely one to the other, but whose sum is both constant and constantly effective" (93). This scenario is certainly not unique to Mapuche society. Everywhere and for everyone, lands have potential to be sentient. However, sentience unfolds differently in distinct lived worlds. This is the reason why in this book I am interested in the particular political implications of human/land connections as sentient. To start with, *sentient lands* is not a local category in the strict sense of the term. Rather, it is an expression that I use to bring together different ideas, practices, and experiences of land connections in Indigenous southern Chile. *Sentient lands* thus works as a translation inevitably troubled with misunderstandings and mistranslation. It is a translation of notions that I have learned from the work of Mapuche writers and the dialogue that I have entered into with friends and acquaintances in my area of study. It is a translation also of the experiences through which residents of Mapuche rural settlements engage with the land as sentient. Finally, it is a translation of my own experience in learning to feel for the land during my and my hosts' combined movement through and engagement with the land during fieldwork. The notion of sentient lands also allows me to align my analytical perspectives with Indigenous claims over ancestral territory as a quintessential part of being Mapuche. In Indigenous southern Chile, some landscape features are recognized as active sentient beings with which different social relations can be established. Hills, forests, watercourses, and ancient sites can perceive human actions and act accordingly, especially in cases when humans fail to behave respectfully (*con respeto*). Some sites, such as ancient burial grounds, hold significance as vivid reminders of past events and facilitate emotional connections between present and past dwellers. Others are associated with master spirits, known as *ngen*, a term roughly translatable as "owner." Some Mapuche people I met during fieldwork were skeptical about the existence of ngen spirits, labeling their mentioning as "superstitious." Others, however, had little doubt about their power and the threat they posed to people who fail to show due respect. Notions of agency do not only concern specific landscape features, but they are also present in broader conceptualization of land. In particular, relation with land is generally framed in terms of reciprocity among Mapuche farmers. Land comprises and is crossed by forces known as *newen*, which mediate all types of relations among humans and with nonhumans.

The sentient character of landscapes in Indigenous southern Chile is embodied by one key notion, that of *tuwün*. This term, roughly translatable as "place of origin," presupposes the existence of the "ancestral territory" as a given element of the Mapuche person. As proposed by several Mapuche writers (Chihuailaf 1999; Millalén 2006; Quilaqueo and Quintriqueo 2010), tuwün refers to the combined effect of environmental conditions and the accumulated influence of past generations on the land itself. Along with genealogical links (*küpal*), tuwün is a quintessential element of being Mapuche. Both act as potentialities of the self, establishing consubstantiality among people sharing genealogical and geographic links, and thus as markers of otherness. Tuwün establishes otherness not only with winkas but also among Mapuche people. The behavior of winkas is indeed unpredictable, since by definition they are removed from any connection with ancestral places and thus remain unaffected by land connections. What makes Mapuche people different from one another is also what makes them different from winkas. By no means does attachment to one's tuwün constitute a necessary condition for self-determination. In Chile, most Mapuche people reside in urban areas, from where they firmly assert their identity. In the countryside, however, migration away from one's tuwün is a source of anxiety, as any rupture in the relation with one's tuwün entails the potential loss of practices and values associated with being Mapuche. While on a theoretical level, tuwün establishes consubstantiality among people with genealogical links with a particular place of origins, land connections cannot be reduced to a mere reiteration of ancestral forces into the present. Indeed, the Mapuche person can be understood as an ongoing process of construction dependent on those social relations that the individual autonomously partakes in (Course 2011). This same process is at work in spatial terms, as engagement with the local environment reframes and activates new relations between present-day dwellers, past generations, and nonhuman elements of the landscape. Ultimately, by situating the individual within unstable networks, landscape experiences contribute to the understanding and determination of the self. In Indigenous southern Chile, land connections defy any deterministic understanding of place. They are not instances of place making as an exclusively human endeavor to give meaning to and represent physical surroundings. Nor are they a form of environmental determinism, whereby present-day dwellers are the unproblematic result of adaptation to a specific environment reproduced over time. Rather, land connections are best understood as an affective relation. Such a relation, as the rest of this book will show, is embroiled with ideas and practices of ownership drawn from legal regimes of property and governmental strategies to govern over sentient lands.

## Property, Attachment, and Other Ontological Questions

In this book, I focus on the deep historical intersections between property and Indigenous notions of place in Mapuche rural settlements. Land claims reveal how the legal language of property is embedded in Mapuche residents' experiences and knowledge of their ancestral territories. However, they also show the limits of the commensuration between ancestral territories and property and the forced translation of the former into the latter inherent to Indigenous land governance. In order to illustrate the entanglement and incommensurability of property and Mapuche notions of place, I refer to two modes of relations with land—namely, Indigenous land ontologies and legal land ontologies. I am aware that these two analytical poles oversimplify the internal diversity of the particular ontological principles behind human/land relations in legal property theory and in Mapuche geo-philosophy. Yet they materialize relationally as opposite ontological arrangements in the context of land claims, where they also acquire a cultural specificity, highlighting the particularities of the Chilean legal culture and lived world of Mapuche rural residents. In referring to legal framework of property as ontology, I also propose a critical movement toward the acknowledgment that law itself works as a particular understanding of being, comparable to others in spite of its political dominance. The key question in property theory is in fact the ontological separation of persons and things, understood as inert and passive objects, first articulated by Roman law. Central to the ontological principles at work in property theory is the transformation of things into essences with a life independent from human engagement. As Roberto Esposito (2015) reminds us, "In order to act on individual cases, the law has to resituate them in a world of ideal essences that are animated by a life of their own. For this reason, the 'facts' that the law addresses are not regarded as such, but rather through a transcendental filter that empties them of their concrete content and projects them into a sort of parallel universe" (66).

In order to acknowledge the simultaneous entanglement and opposition of Indigenous and legal land ontologies, I draw upon three modes of conceptualizing land connections: economic (how land becomes an object with exchange value), phenomenological (how land is constituted as an object of embodied knowledge), and ontological (what kind of being land is). These three conceptualizations are usually associated with three distinct streams of anthropological literature with little communication among them, which the idea of sentient lands necessarily brings together. The economic dimension of land has been a central element of anthropological analysis since the early days of the discipline. Classic works on land tenure (Bourdieu 1990, 147–61; Davis 1973) focused on strategies of inheritance through which kinship groups and individuals could maintain their social status. Attention has also been paid to the impact of colonial reforms that have reframed and, in some cases, dismantled existing forms of land access among colonized groups (Cohn 1996). Given its role as a means of governance, property is a highly contested field in which contrasting notions of legitimacy come into conflict. This phenomenon can also be understood as an unstable set of relations that necessarily vary for different categories of owned objects and owning subjects (Hann 1998; Strathern and Hirsch 2004; Verdery and Humphrey 2004). As Marxist perspectives in anthropology help us not to forget that property consists of power relations among humans (Bloch 1984), so anthropological problematizations of nature/culture divide remind us that property also intervenes in relations with nonhumans (see Strathern 1996). In traditional Euro-American legal theory, property in fact "requires a boundary to be formed, a network of relations to be cut, and the claims of other persons to be severed so that a singular identity can be effected" (Hirsch 2010, 356). Land is a property sui generis, as its highly unstable economic value largely depends on the use of heterogenous inscription devices, such as agricultural technologies transforming land productivity and survey mechanisms, which aim not simply at recording the presence of land as a resource but rather at assembling it as a resource for different actors (Li Murray 2014b, 489).

The phenomenological dimension of land connections concerns the centrality of embodied experiences in the landscape as acts of signification. Anthropological interest in land began as an attempt to provide a cartographic representation of social structure and hierarchy. In this context, land was seen as a neutral stage for the analysis of property relations, with local understandings of the environment demoted to background information (Abramson 2000). Against this perspective, transdisciplinary research on landscape has highlighted how land is imbued with meaning through representations and images that express ideological, moral, and aesthetic values in every society (Cosgrove 1984). Largely inspired by Merleau-Ponty's (1962, 134) collapsing of corporeity and subjectivity, phenomenological approaches to landscape in anthropology have focused on the signification of the local environment as an act of embodiment. By establishing connections within the landscape, bodily activities, such as walking, hearing, and seeing, imbue it with particular meanings (Ingold 2000; Tilley 1994). Landscapes are formed at the intersection of individual experiences of embodiment, which necessarily reflect cultural forms of body use, and collective representations of local surroundings, which antecede individual experiences (Hirsch 1995). Viewing land connections as a form of embodied knowledge about landscape helps us to elude a materialistic reduction of land to an object of ownership. Yet the experiential significance of land cannot be dissociated from the role that property plays in structuring access to and consequently perceptions of the landscapes that humans give meanings to. Knowledge about land ultimately derives from the mutuality of property and embodiment, as two inseparable ways of entangling land connections. Their mutuality highlights the potential ability that the body has to rearrange customary divides between things and persons, such as those upon which property theory is based. Partly a thing, and partly a person, the body is for Esposito (2015) the articulator of all relations between things and persons: "What connects human beings and things is the body. Outside the connection that the body ensures, the two elements are destined to detach from each other in a way that necessarily makes one subordinate to the other" (122). The body is also what allows humans to perceive sentient lands as more than objects of property.

The ontological dimension of land connection stands at the very core of the conceptualization of land as a sentient subject. My use of the term *ontology* is loose. I view this term as the affirmation of what does and can exist. Ontology thus concerns the origins, persistence, and transformation of being. In the social sciences, ontological questions have been raised in relation to the critical reappraisal of the divide between nonhuman objects and human subjects. Attending ethnographically to ontological questions entails a shift of focus from the symbolic elements that constitute a worldview to the practices and ideas imbricated in the ongoing processes of world making (Holbraad 2012). Ontology is thus necessarily multiple and unstable (Mol 2002, 166), which is one reason why it cannot be reduced to a stable and consensual enunciation of what exists. Debates on nonhuman agency have proceeded in two directions. One privileges a view of ontology as the meaningful production of objects and subjects through the enactment of social relations involving humans and nonhumans. This stance is exemplified by Bruno Latour's (2005) Actor Network Theory (ANT), in which society is redefined as an expanding network of associations between humans and nonhumans characterized by a dislocation of agency toward relations among different actors. Here, nonhuman agency is enacted and defined not according to preconceived categories of being, but by relations and movements shifting across different boundaries and scales. The open-ended nature of Latour's networks has been an inspiration for much anthropological research, which has nonetheless departed from some of ANT's universalist aspirations (Goldman 2009).[3] Anthropological research on ontological pluralism has highlighted the conceptual particularism behind different modes of relatedness and categories of being. Differences across societies depend not only on heterogeneous representations of a given reality or nature, but also on those ontological principles that openly defy the nature/culture divide upon which much anthropological analysis has been founded (see Descola 2013; Strathern 1988; Viveiros de Castro 2015). Practices through which worlds are made and sustained thus constitute and depend on modes, relations, and categories of being inherent to specific lived worlds (Scott 2013, 859). Interest in ontological pluralism has tended to privilege the analysis of those phenomena that most directly question dominant ways of thinking about the nature/culture divide, such as the extension of personhood to nonhuman beings and the recognition of agency for objects in non-Western settings. The conceptual potential of these phenomena does not lie in their ability to reduce non-Western groups to coherent and unchanging relational structures, a common critique within anthropology. An awareness of ontological pluralism can prompt a reflexive assessment of anthropology's own ontological premises, primarily based on semiotic understandings of nonhumans as objects of representations. The two directions—one emphasizing enactment as the process through which entities are constituted, the other highlighting the epistemic coherence of nondominant ontologies—are not categorically separated. The first direction allows us to trace movements and exchanges across expanding sets of relation at the cost of underestimating difference in ontological terms. The second helps us to debunk the existence of different ontologies at cost of understating the extent to which different worlds are entangled.

The analysis of ancestral land connections, I believe, offers us an opportunity to reconcile the two opposing scenarios that have characterized anthropological debates on the notion of ontology. Land claims in fact reveal the profound antagonism between the ontological principles of property and those of ancestral territory while also exposing the historical intersections between the two terms. Through property, sentient lands can be reduced to things with which relations of affect are impossible to articulate. In particular, property theories based on Lockean justification of land ownership and development "treats land as wholly passive and merely a commodity. As a result, it cannot recognize the ways that land is active in shaping people" (Kolers 2009, 135). However, in the actions of Mapuche claimants, turning ancestral land into property does not entail the erasure of Indigenous land ontologies. Therefore, questions concerning the entanglement of property and Indigenous geographies cannot be fully answered unless they are phrased within ontological and phenomenological understandings of land connections. It is possible that the plural nature of embodiment can be explained with reference not only to cultural differences in the arrangement of human bodily experiences, but also to the particular ontological configurations that inform and are revealed by relations between humans and other sentient beings specific to different lived worlds. The agential possibilities of sentient lands are acknowledged not because dwellers reproduce ideas drawn from a stable corpus, but rather because perceiving land as sentient necessarily entails engaging in bodily exchanges with it.

Economic, phenomenological, and ontological questions concerning land connections cannot be considered in separation. Bringing these three dimensions together bears a significant implication for the approach to politics that I adopt in this book. The political role that I intend to assign to sentient lands entails a redefinition of politics as a province opened to nonhumans and, accordingly, as the struggle for the coexistence of different worlds. This idea is famously exemplified by Isabelle Stengers' notion of cosmopolitics. For Stengers (2005), the cosmos is "the unknown constituted by . . . multiple, divergent worlds and to the articulation of which they would eventually be capable" (995). The endowment of political agency to nonhumans might at first be interpreted as an attempt to undermine human intentionality. However, what is at stake is the development of a more ecologically sound politics, in which human intentionality is bracketed within a relational and agential world (Bennett 2010, 32). Political conflicts can also be ontological if they originate in the attempts of different worlds to sustain their own existence as they interact and mingle with each other (Blaser 2009, 11). As Marisol De la Cadena (2015) suggests, "Ontological disagreement emerges from practices that make worlds *diverge* even as they continue to make themselves connected to one another" (280). For Sarah Hunt (2014), a Kwakwaka'wakw scholar, the potential of non-Western ontologies to unsettle dominant counterparts can be easily neutralized when the former are reduced to a case study in the comparative analysis of nature/culture arrangement and thereby removed from the broader context of colonial relations. A true recognition of ontological pluralism thus requires an ongoing reflection on domination not only as a form of power within a common reality but also as an action aimed at imposing practically and epistemologically one reality over others (Hage 2012, 302). In Latin America, the current proliferation of environmental and Indigenous territorial conflicts has contributed not only to a radical reappraisal of the limits of liberal modernity (Escobar 2010), but also to the public visualization of those nonmodern forms of doing politics previously overlooked as lacking political rationality (Goldman 2013). Anthropological representations of Amerindian society have not been immune from the purification of politics responsible for the erasure of culturally specific nonhuman agencies from political affairs. Customarily, readers have been exposed to two contrasting images of Amerindian societies: one centered on political action viewed through the lens of identity politics, and the other on more traditional and supposedly apolitical forms of social life, such as kinship and religion (Kelly 2011). In this book, politics concerns not only overt forms of contestation over land but also those very actions and ideas through which the ancestral territory is known and experienced as a sentient subject.

## How to Govern Sentient Lands: Political Imagination under Neoliberalism

The intersections between Indigenous and legal ontologies presented in this book portray a scenario of simultaneous ambivalences and antagonisms in Indigenous/state relations. Any analysis of land claims that posits a straightforward dichotomy between Indigenous groups and the state fails to grasp the complex manners in which state power materializes. Rather than a monolithic entity, the state is commonly understood in social sciences as an ideological project articulating images of unity and cohesion both externally and internally. State actions serve to regulate and reconcile heterogeneous and often conflicting social identities (Corrigan and Sayer 1985, 2) by endowing contradictory practices of governance with an ideal image of coherence and legitimacy (Abrams 1977, 77). Among Mapuche people, the state (*el estado*) is a term embodying everything that is despicable about the winkas. It is seen as a distant bureaucratic entity unsympathetic to the needs and anxieties of Mapuche clients and responsible for land shortage. Yet the state is also a ubiquitous and looked-for entity in rural Chile, where governmental projects targeting small holders and, in some cases, specifically addressing residents of Indigenous communities proliferate. Bonds of friendship between state officials and Mapuche farmers are not uncommon, and many officials are themselves Mapuche. Similarly, Mapuche rural residents, while often suspicious of politicians, may themselves be active supporters of national parties, being divided between right-wing and left-wing positions like the rest of the Chilean population. The subtleties of Indigenous/state relations are further problematized by the ambivalent role that state actors play in the implementation of Indigenous policies. During fieldwork, I had the chance to meet numerous state officials who had relations with residents of Mapuche settlements. Some creatively elided certain state regulations in order to attend to their clients' needs. Others committed infractions in the pursuit of their self-interest. While a few of the functionaries I have met during fieldwork reproduced racist discourses, common among non-Indigenous Chileans, on the indolent nature of Mapuche farmers, many others were clearly sympathetic to Indigenous plights. The profound differences in the orientations of state actors invite us not to reduce them to mere vehicles of official discourses, although their good intentions do not prevent them from acting in ways that reinforce the Mapuche's marginality in Chilean society. Is it possible to avoid simplistic representations of state functionaries while acknowledging their role in the governmental disempowerment of the Mapuche? What kind of anthropological representation is needed to answer this question?

One objective of this book is to develop an analytical framework of state power in postcolonial contexts that is able to account for the subtle and yet oppositional nature of Indigenous/state relations. I use the term *postcolonial* to refer to a broader context of continuity with colonial domination in which colonized groups, such as the Mapuche, have mobilized to revert the effects of colonial encroachment and assimilation typically approached by state institutions through different policies of reparation and reconciliation. As will become apparent in the following chapters, the pervasiveness of state power in postcolonial contexts rests on both explicit state acts of governing Indigenous geographies and the legitimation of state ideology that results from claimants' engagement with the means and rules of the land restitution program. In line with this argument, I treat the postcolonial state as an apparatus of codification inserted into a broader field of intelligibility, which I call political imagination. My intention is to ethnographically delineate the framework of intelligibility through which demands over ancestral land are staked, evaluated, and commensurated. Political imagination concerns the act of identifying with and reacting to political affairs (Comaroff and Comaroff 1999; Spencer 1997) as much as the concrete processes through which the conceptual horizons of social thinking are established, contested, and occasionally subverted. Rather than a work of invention independent from tangible experiences, imagination can be taken as a concrete social process in which multiple power formations produce imaginative capacities directed toward the conceptualization of present and future worlds. Political imagination is necessarily a disputed field of comprehension and communication. Throughout this book, I will situate state actors' actions and intentions within the material and conceptual contexts through which Indigenous geographies are governed. On the one hand, land claims challenge and potentially subvert the boundaries of existing political imagination concerning the right to difference. On the other, in the public arena and in the more circumscribed spaces of state governance, the threatening difference inherent to land claims can be resignified and incorporated within existing boundaries of political imagination.

A focus on the processes of state codification and the political imagination in which they are inserted can reveal the practical and local manifestations of broader ideological constructs. Accordingly, I situate my analysis of the political imagination related to Indigenous land claims within scholarly debates around neoliberalism, the defining ideology of contemporary Chile. Neoliberalism denotes a set of ideas that coalesced during the 1960s as a critique of the Keynesian principles of market regulation and an advocacy for laissez-faire economic policies (Harvey 2005, 20–21). Neoliberal ideology presupposes an ideal type of subject and a theory of human agency based on the principles of self-discipline and individual accountability (Foucault 2008; Hilgers

2011; Rose 1999). These principles have been key factors in the global reconfiguration of statecraft in the last four decades. As pointed out by Elizabeth Povinelli (2011), liberal democracies have for the most part "stopped assessing social programs and actions on the basis of political philosophy and instead restricted themselves to issues of profit and loss, and languages of efficiency, productivity and benefit to gross domestic profit" (22). Rather than a lack of state control, neoliberalism thus engenders a form of governance based on the permeation of market logics into state action (Goodale and Postero 2013, 8). As the rest of this book will show, property and documentation become the privileged languages through which political claims are articulated under neoliberalism (Comaroff and Comaroff 2009). Along with an intensification of privatization processes, neoliberalism has promoted an expansion of proprietorship as a contested field where new entitities are increasingly transformed into property (Hirsch 2010, 357). In line with other anthropological accounts on neoliberalism (Ferguson 2010; Ong 2006), I see this phenomenon as the uneven permeation of a global set of rationalities and values inspired by the financial model into local spaces of production, governance, and relatedness. Neoliberalism is thus pervasive to the extent that its logics adapt to local contingencies. In Chile, a country globally known as a stronghold of neoliberalism, this ideology became entwined with nationalistic and military values promoted by one of the most repressive and extended right-wing regimes in the region. Neoliberalism in fact emerged as the direct consequence of the violent seizure of power by the military junta led by Augusto Pinochet in 1973. Designed by a group of U.S.-trained economists known as the Chicago Boys, a series of economic reforms were introduced with the objective of fostering privatization programs concerning health, education, and natural resource use (Cárcamo-Huechante 2006; Silva 2009; Valdés 1995). Market deregulation in the primary sector led to a swift consolidation of agribusiness companies devoted to transnational exports, such as timber and copper. The growth of the Chilean national economy led Milton Friedman, the main inspiration behind the reform designed by the Chicago Boys, to coin the expression the "Miracle of Chile." Yet behind gross numbers of economic development lay a dramatic rise in vulnerability for marginal sectors of Chilean society (Winn 2004). Furthermore, market deregulation was responsible for the alternation between periods of rapid economic growth and cyclical economic crises. The return of democratic rule in 1990 did not usher in any major structural changes to neoliberal economics. The impact of neoliberalization has been hard felt among marginalized groups, since economic policies favoring the flexibilization of work conditions and the privatization of the healthcare and education sectors have reinforced historically deep patterns of class and racial exclusion (see Richards 2013).

The return to democratic rule did not coincide with the end of neoliberalization. Yet many were the novelties for Indigenous people in Chile as postdictatorship governments introduced unprecedented measures to improve Indigenous rights. These reforms represented a radically discursive shift away from the nationalist agenda of the military junta, in which the Mapuche appeared as an image from the past fully incorporated into a uniform national identity, toward a basic recognition of ethnic diversity (Crow 2013). The introduction of multicultural reforms in Chile reveals the incongruence between the recognition of Indigenous collective rights over natural resources and the ongoing implementation of a neoliberal development model centered on the expansion of international exports and primary resource extraction. The key question is how collective rights for Indigenous people can coexist with processes of market deregulation in the primary sector. This question is clearly not unique to the Chilean case, being a pivotal problem of neoliberal governance in any postcolonial setting. A common response to the impasse between recognition of Indigenous rights and neoliberal reforms has been the design of social policies that attend to the basic needs of Indigenous populations on an individualized basis. In Chile, for instance, reforms mainly consisted in individualized welfare programs focused on housing, agriculture subsidization, and educational financial aid. The emergence of social policies that accommodate the valorization of Indigenous difference within market configurations concerns has come to be known as neoliberal multiculturalism (Hale 2006a; Postero 2007). Central to this phenomenon is the dichotomy between admissible and threatening difference implicit to Indigenous political claims. Inspired by the work of Silva Rivera Cusicanqui, Charles Hale and Rosamel Millaman (2005, 284) have employed the expressions *Indio permitido* (authorized Indian) and *Indio insurecto* (insurgent Indian) to frame this dichotomy. The authorized Indian is an ideal type of Indigenous subject characterized by attachment to traditional values, interest in the development of entrepreneurial skills, and disenchantment from ethnic politics. It is the sort of Indigenous subject that neoliberal multicultural policies envision and reproduce. In contrast, the insurgent Indian stands for all political action that is publicly treated as a threat to national unity and peaceful multicultural coexistence. The categories of insurgent and authorized Indians clearly concern ideal types. Yet these two poles materialize vividly through the dividing line between admissible and threatening forms of indigeneity implicit in many governmental responses to Indigenous demands. As we will see, the identification of admissible difference not only unfolds in the form of public debates on multiculturalism but also depends on concrete processes, such as those put in motion by land claims, that aim to understand radical difference while domesticating it. In exploring the relation between concrete practices of demarcation and verification of ancestral land and public debates on national cohesion and indigeneity, I hope to show the effects of neoliberal political imagination on Mapuche land claims.

## The Setting of This Book

*Sentient Lands* is based on ethnographic research carried out between June 2007 and November 2008, complemented by several shorter visits to southern Chile in the years since. The subjects that appear in this book are Mapuche people and non-Indigenous Chileans residing in the southern region of Araucania.[4] The Mapuche are the largest Indigenous group in the country, estimated at over 1.7 million, roughly 9.99 percent of the total national population.[5] The Araucania region is home to the majority of rural Mapuche settlements in Chile, yet not the majority of Mapuche people. As a consequence of colonial processes of land grabbing and displacement in the last 150 years, countless Mapuche rural residents have migrated to the national capital, Santiago, and to a lesser extent to the mining centers in northern Chile. Especially in urban areas, interethnic marriages are not rare and many Chileans can trace both Mapuche and non-Indigenous genealogies (Valenzuela and Unzueta 2015). With few exceptions, rural residence corresponds with membership in a comunidad indígena, an official territorial unit acting as a legal representative of individuals owning land within a *reducción* (reservation), a term that is today employed in rural areas to indicate a geographic locality. The categories of urban and rural Mapuche are employed in governmental reports and academic texts. However, especially in areas with a large number of Indigenous communities, the Mapuche population cannot be simplistically divided into these two groups given the high degree of mobility between the countryside and local towns for the purposes of employment and education.

The events, conversations, and descriptions detailed in this book mostly took place around the town of Traiguen and in the regional capital of the Araucania region, Temuco (see fig. 2). As with all urban settlements in south-central Chile, Temuco was founded in the aftermath of the forced inclusion of the Mapuche region in the Chilean nation at the end of the twentieth century. Ever since, it has served as a commercial hub for agricultural activities in the region. Today, it is a fast-growing city of roughly three hundred thousand inhabitants and is home to the head office of CONADI and several Indigenous rights organizations. Traiguen, a town of roughly seventeen thousand inhabitants, is located in the fertile central valley between the coastal and Andean mountain range. Known as the granary of Chile (*el granero de Chile*), Traiguen became an important center for cereal production soon after its foundation in 1978. At the turn of the twentieth century, the countryside around Traiguen was subject to intense migratory fluxes of European and, to a lesser extent, Chilean settlers attracted to this fertile area. Land auctions at the end of the nineteenth century resulted in the establishment of large agricultural estates, whose owners became the primary producers of cereals in the country. Despite a gradual decline in the last forty years, the main economic resource in the municipality (*comuna*) of Traiguen remains cereals. Cattle herding and, more recently, the cultivation of monocrops, such as flowers and fruits, for export are also significant economic activities. Timber plantations are common in rougher terrains, where transnational lumber corporations (*forestales*) operate.

The percentage of the Mapuche population in Traiguen is smaller than in nearby municipalities due to the intensity of settler migration to this area in the past.[6] In the countryside surrounding the town, Indigenous communities tend to be engulfed by large agricultural estates. These properties can range from three hundred hectares to over one thousand. Most of them are owned by the heirs of European settlers, mainly French, Swiss, and German. Until the 1960s, local estates were run through the *inquilino* labor system, in which workers were remunerated through housing within these properties and the allocation of basic food supplies.[7] Today, estate workers, either seasonal (*temporeros*) or with stable employment (*asalariados*), are mainly residents of small hamlets known as *aldeas campesinas*. Medium-sized properties are rare in this area given the limited extent of agrarian reforms in the region (1962–1973).[8] Indigenous communities can vary in size from a few hectares occupied by ten households to over one thousand owned by over two hundred residents. Indigenous land reforms in the past have resulted in the division of reservation land into individual land properties so that houses within communities are generally scattered. Land shortage is a widespread source of apprehension among residents of Mapuche settlements, with some houses only owning enough land for their dwelling, a small garden (*huerta*), and an animal enclosure. As a consequence of land shortage, most residents are unable to grow crops for commercial purposes and thus depend on employment on nearby estates for their income. Only those farmers less affected by land shortage or those who have recently attained land subsidies dedicate themselves to subsistence agriculture as their main source of income.[9]

My knowledge of the countryside around Traiguen stems primarily from my involvement with the land claim submitted by Comunidad Contreras. It all started a few weeks into my fieldwork. At that time, I was residing in Temuco in order to carry out interviews on Indigenous rights to natural resources with members of governmental agencies and Mapuche organizations. During one of these interviews I met José Contreras, a member of a Mapuche organization running development projects financed through governmental and international funding schemes. Our conversation soon turned to recent events in his community, Comunidad Contreras, for which he acted as spokesperson (*werken*).[10] I told José that one of my research goals was to write about land claims in the hope of contributing to academic debates and the advancement of Indigenous land rights. My interlocutor assured me that it would be no problem to study his community's land claim, which could only benefit from the

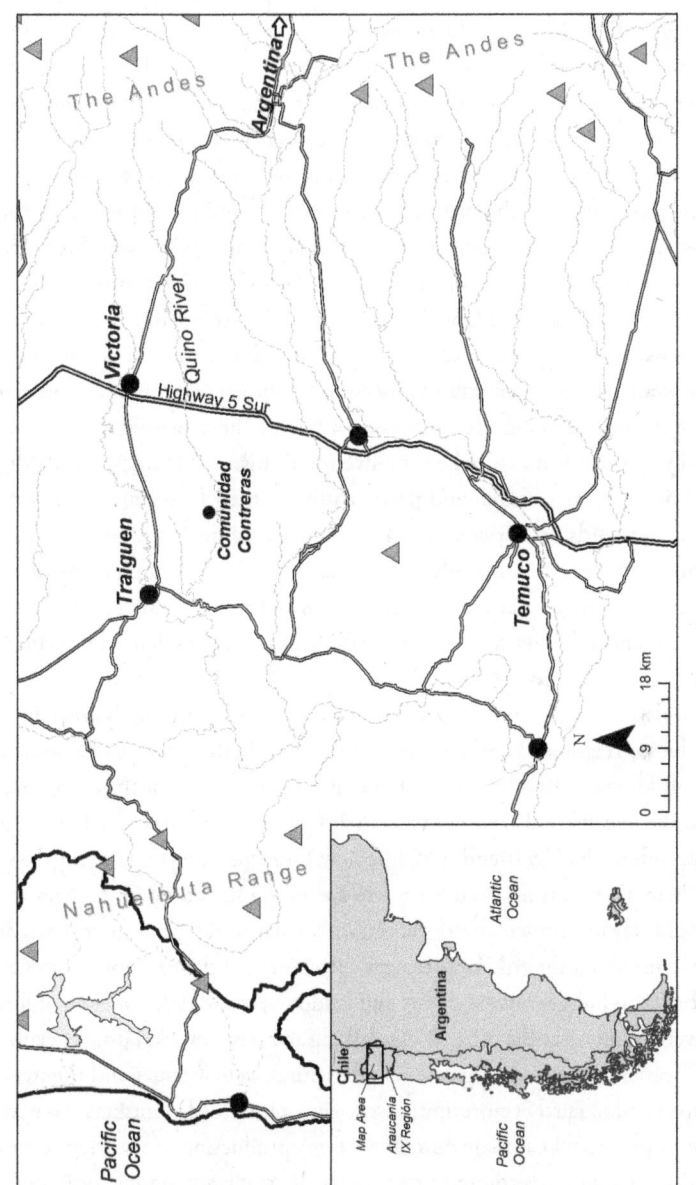

FIGURE 2  Traiguen and surroundings.

presence of an international observer willing to support and document the claim. Upon finishing our conversation, José invited me to join him for the next community meeting. As agreed, on a cold winter Sunday, José picked me up in his car from a street corner in Temuco. After a forty-five-minute drive through the countryside, we reached a field where several people had congregated. It was only later that day that I realized we were standing on land demanded for restitution by Comunidad Contreras. Soon after our arrival, the community delegates began to recap for the attendees some recent events concerning their land claims. As the meeting was coming to an end, the *werken* explained the reason for my presence and invited me to introduce myself to the assembly. *"Marimari pu peñi ka pu lamngen!"* (Greetings brothers and sisters!), I greeted the assembly in Mapudungun before quickly turning to Spanish, a practice common in other Mapuche meetings I had attended. I then went on to explain the reason for my visit. Before leaving, I stated that I would be back in a few weeks. I attended the next community meeting, by the end of which I was invited by Liscán Contreras, José's uncle, to his house for lunch. There, he told me that I could occasionally stay at his house, where he lived with his sons Francisca and Miguel, while carrying out my research and participating in their land claim. This was the start of a firm friendship between Liscán, Francisca, Miguel, and me. Their house became my home for the remainder of my fieldwork. While much of the material presented in this book concerns my experiences in and around Traiguen and Temuco, many of the events I discuss in this book are drawn from my residence in Comunidad Contreras.

Comunidad Contreras is a large Mapuche community of roughly four hundred residents, located eighteen kilometers from Traiguen.[11] In the local area the settlement is commonly known as Reducción Contreras. Residents tend to use the term *reducción* to refer to the locality and *comunidad* to their collective organization. During fieldwork, I was often asked by friends in Chile how I was spending most of my days. For many of them, there was no need for me to spend so much time in the countryside when I could stay in Temuco and travel during the day to carry out interviews. Some also warned me about the risks of getting involved in land claims. News stories about disputes between Indigenous claimants and landowners and the expulsion of foreign activists were common at the time. When talking about fieldwork, I usually explained that my research was an ongoing process of learning, as new issues and themes were appearing every day. Furthermore, my presence in Comunidad Contreras was part of a collaborative process whose main outcome was my production of a written testimony of the political fight of this community, a source of great pride among local residents. In its surroundings, Comunidad Contreras is recognized for its political associativity, as its delegates have close links with grassroots organizations in Temuco and ongoing relations with state officials and local politicians. During fieldwork I often heard from community members that their claim was part of a fight (*lucha*) for land, but they were not willing to take radical action that would cause episodes of violence and instead followed the path of dialogue (*la via del dialogo*).

One of the things that kept me most busy during fieldwork was accompanying the Comunidad Contreras board members to meetings with CONADI officials and intermediaries. My presence was highly symbolic, as it served to show state actors that the community boasted a large network of allies to support their claim. Access to state offices also granted me the opportunity to carry out interviews with officials from different agencies. Although poorly trained in archival research, I also spent time in local archives hunting for information that could be beneficial to both the land claim and my research. My engaged position drew some criticism from acquaintances. I was occasionally told (especially by people with conservative political views) that, as was usually the case with foreigners, my research would be biased and fail to recognize the problems that land disputes were causing to non-Indigenous Chileans. While I recognize that one of the major shortcomings of this book is the marginal place given to the perspectives of non-Indigenous estate owners, I do not consider that rigorous scholarship should be based on the ideal of making two opposite political ideologies equal. This would indeed mask the history of land expropriation and the highly hierarchical race-based relations in Chile. More generally, I have come to believe that rigorous research can indeed coexist with advocacy. As argued by Charles Hale (2006b), political engagement in ethnographic research and cultural critique are not mutually exclusive once we realize that political actions are contradictory and dynamic in the first place. Another factor that further complicates my ethnographic research is the emergence of ethical questions related to the conflictive nature of land disputes. As will be shown later in this book, land claims can bring to light political divisions among claimants dating back to the era of military dictatorship, charges of corruption by state functionaries, and allegations of illegal land grabbing against non-Indigenous land owners. Friends from Comunidad Contreras suggested I should write candidly about everything I heard and observed during fieldwork with no details, including names, dates, and places, omitted. However, it would prove impossible to follow this advice while protecting the privacy of those subjects who could be affected by potentially defamatory information. In particular, this point concerns the numerous people and events outside Comunidad Contreras that my research dealt with. In the end I resolved to use pseudonyms for all individuals except those residents of Comunidad Contreras who expressed their preference to be fully acknowledged.

While engagement with the land claim was an important part of my fieldwork, I spent most of my time doing what residents of rural Mapuche communities do on a daily basis. Throughout my stay, I worked in the agricultural fields with my hosts, Liscán and Miguel, such that by the end of my stay I had graduated from an absolute novice to a decent apprentice. Local farmers do not spend all day in the fields, especially in the winter, when activities are reduced. As in many other rural parts of Chile, domestic life in Comunidad Contreras revolves around conversations with family members, watching TV, and listening to the radio. Visits to neighbors are common, and Mapuche people generally pride themselves for their hospitality, which they see as a further factor that distinguishes themselves from winkas. Visits are not necessarily announced and usually take place in the afternoon. A visitor is generally offered *once*, a light meal comprising eggs, homemade bread, and tea. Sometimes, guests are invited to take some food back to their home, a practice known as *rokin* and most commonly followed during collective events. For me, these visits were a chance to converse with community members as well as my hosts' friends from nearby non-Indigenous settlements. My conversations with Indigenous and non-Indigenous farmers touched on diverse topics, from gossip about neighbors and townspeople to the political and economic differences between Italy (my place of origin) and southern Chile. Conversations were carried out in Spanish, the first language of all my interlocutors. In my area of study, Mapudungun is spoken only by a few residents during public events and rituals. However, conversations in Spanish are frequently punctuated with Mapuche words, especially when referring to phenomena intrinsic to Indigenous culture, which non-Indigenous people, particularly those from other regions of Chile, are likely to ignore.[12]

I am conscious of numerous limitations of my work in offering a comprehensive representation of interethnic relations in southern Chile. Most of these limitations, I believe, depend on the contingencies of my research experience that have necessarily led to a partial depiction of the Mapuche, a large and geographically widespread population. The same can be said about state actors and non-Indigenous Chileans that feature in my research. While the danger of misrepresentation is central to all ethnographic research, I feel that the reader should be aware of at least two contingent factors in fieldwork that have influenced my analytical approach. Firstly, in the countryside around Traiguen, many Indigenous people are identified and self-identify as *awinkados* for several reasons, including an inability to speak Mapudungun. Here, Mapuche identity is understood as a condition caught between two poles of alterity: the "ancient ones," on the one hand, and the winkas, on the other. To be awinkado— that is, to act and think like a winka—is not a future prospect but a condition lamented by many as a current threat to morally valued Mapuche practices.[13] While no area in southern Chile is exempt from doubts and anxieties concerning cultural assimilation, I recognize that my emphasis on being awinkado might resonate less evidently in areas where residents are considered very Mapuche (*bien Mapuche*) by local standards.

The second contingent factor of research limitations is that the ethnographic material I present in this book has inevitably been gathered from a male perspective. This is not to say that in my account female presence is underrepresented, as many of the events and conversations that appear in this book involve women. I also discuss gender relations consistently in relation to issues such as residence, agricultural work, kinship, and participation in political affairs. However, my own ethnographic positionality and the scope of my analysis prevents me from fully exploring issues concerning sexual orientation and power relations between men and women. For the sake of the present discussion, the reader should be aware that racial stereotypes in Chile emphasize the supposedly chauvinist nature of traditional Mapuche marriage arrangements (see Richards 2004). Mapuche writers have challenged this view by emphasizing the double nature of discrimination that Mapuche women face, as both Indigenous and female (Painemal 2008). Racialized views of gender relations in Chile elide the fact that female subjugation is not an ethnic issue but rather a phenomenon permeating all sectors of Chilean society.

## The Rest of This Book

*Sentient Lands* is an attempt to bring together the politics and experiences of land connections. In line with this objective, this book is composed of two parts. The four chapters of part 1, "People and Land," present an analysis of historical processes of displacement and notions of place, environmental values, agricultural practices, and property relations, which are at the very basis of contemporary expressions of ancestral land connections. Chapter 1 offers a review of the historical phenomenon of colonial displacement. Here, I will show how historically rooted discourses on nationhood and race have contributed to contemporary public debates centered on an understanding of Indigenous land as a threat to modernization. By advancing an idea of Mapuche people as poor and traditional Chileans, these discourses have consolidated a logic of disempowering state dependency. In this chapter, I will also discuss some of the critical Mapuche conceptualizations of national identity that reframe the position of Indigenous people within contemporary ideas about national identity. In chapter 2, I explore the relation between Mapuche theories of emplacement and experiences in the landscape that are constitutive of perceptions of the ancestral territory as a sentient subject. The ethnographic analysis of the relation between landscape and places of memory will illustrate how the significance of ancestral land lies not in an unproblematic context of continuity with the past, but is a potentiality in processes of selfhood. The following two chapters illustrate the historical quandary of having to become more like winkas in order to remain Mapuche. This dilemma centers on the protection of the link with one's place of origins as a fundamental element of self-determination, which has historically necessitated the adoption of winka practices often at odds with Mapuche socioecological relations. In chapter 3, I explore the ambivalences of ecological knowledge by focusing on the tension between customary environmental values and the adoption of invasive agricultural practices associated with the winkas. Rather than essentializing Mapuche farmers as ecologically noble or deconstructing their ecological values and concerns as political strategies of representation, this chapter will elucidate the unstable balance between care and exploitation of land implicit to agricultural work in the midst of widespread perceptions of socioecological crisis. Attention will be paid to farmers' engagements with the local environment that produce uncertainties and anxieties concerning humans' relations with other sentient elements of the landscape. Chapter 4 presents some of the long-term consequences of land formalization, in particular the introduction of private properties in the last century. It focuses on the possibilities of self-defense against colonial discrimination engendered by the Mapuche's historical adoption of property technologies and the negative effects of land formalization on existing modes of sociability.

In part 2, "Land Claims," I examine the transformative processes through which the ancestral territories are spatially and conceptually rearticulated in the context of land claims. Some of the issues explored in part 1, including the dilemmas associated with the adoption of winka practices, will be reexamined here in the context of land claims. Chapter 5 focuses on the use of documentation and archival information integral to the process of land demarcation and claim staking. While claimants are able to employ property technologies to frame their knowledge about ancestral land, state power materializes in the endowment of land grants and the codification of Indigenous geographies. In chapter 6, I focus on the controversial interpretations of the role of sacred sites in land claims by state officials. Their approach to land demands reveals a type of interpretative action that I call "understanding by domestication." This type of understanding serves to obviate the ontological principles of Mapuche land connections and to allow for the commensuration of the ancestral territory within the jural language of property. Chapter 7 closes the book by examining some of the consequences of land restoration on claimants' lives and their expectations of the future. Life in the new ancestral territories reinforces some of the ideals associated with neoliberal political imagination, but also helps the projection of futures that are alternative to neoliberal narratives of self-realization and are built around anxieties over environmental destruction, today typically associated with the buzzword *Anthropocene*. Taken together, these three chapters highlight the fine line between assimilation and resistance that Indigenous people traverse in their engagements with dominant legal and bureaucratic frameworks. At stake is the acknowledgment of Indigenous autonomy not only as an issue of cultural rights carved out from existing market configurations but also as a right to world making.

# PART I

# PEOPLE AND LAND

# CHAPTER 1

# HISTORICAL DEBTS

*Race, Land, and Nation Building in Southern Chile*

"TODAY IS A DAY IN WHICH WE CAN LOOK AT OUR FUTURE WITH MORE serenity, because we start paying off all our debts to the Indigenous people, which we have dragged for too long." On January 11, 2016, President Michelle Bachelet, elected two years earlier as the leader of the center-left coalition Nueva Mayoria, publicly announced the launch of a newly drafted bill that, if accepted by the National Congress, could lead to the foundation of a Ministry of Indigenous People, Ministerio de Pueblos Indígenas.[1] Beside journalists and state officials, the crowd gathered at the presidential palace, La Moneda, was made up of members of Indigenous organizations that had participated in the Consulta Indígena (Indigenous consultation), a process consisting of a series of informative meetings and public debates held over three months in different areas of Chile. Bachelet's optimistic tone stressed the importance that dialogue and mutual understanding was meant to have in forging the new relationship between Indigenous people and Chilean society promised by this legislative reform: "The way in which this bill was designed is as important as its content: it is proof that we can mold a new way of working, one in which state organs and Indigenous peoples can sit around the same table" (Gobierno de Chile 2016). Little doubt exists about the novelty of this legislative reform. The new minister would foster the active presence of Indigenous organizations and communities in decision-making through the establishment of a council with elected representatives from each of the nine Indigenous groups officially recognized in Chile. The draft conceptualizes an unprecedented shift from centrally planned development agendas to a participative one. Yet, looked at closely, the promises offered by the bill are not as new as one might initially think. Since the return of democratic rule in the 1990s, Indigenous people in Chile have heard successive governments renewing the promise of paying off historical debts (*deudas historicas*) by facing uncomfortable truths about the past to begin a new phase of reconciliation. An ideal mutual agreement about past injustice and compensation, which pervaded all projects of legislative reforms, reached its apex in 2001, when President Lagos launched the Commission for Historical Truth and New Treatment of Indigenous Peoples (CVHNT). The main mission of the commission, formed by Indigenous and non-Indigenous members of political parties, academics, and representatives of civil organizations, was to provide historically grounded evidence about mistreatment of Indigenous people to be later developed into proposals for social policies and legislative reform. CVHNT was weaved into an "official imaginary of a harmoniously multicultural Chile" (Crow 2013, 193). Yet the content of its final report was far from consensual. Worse, two years after its launch, many of the commission's recommendations were blocked by conservative senators backed by southern landowners (Schlosberg and Carruthers 2010, 28). By excluding voices overtly critical of existing reparation politics in Chile, CVHNT's potential threat to legal and economic frameworks of land ownership and natural resource use in Indigenous territories was ultimately disarmed.

The cyclical nature of governmental promises of restorative justice toward Indigenous people reflects the general complexity of reparation politics. Processes of reparation force us not only to look back at the past but also to engage with questions of historical accountability, such as how nation building should be remembered and by whom (Povinelli 2002, 154). Inherent to restorative justice is the inevitable disagreement over collective responsibility for actions committed by other individuals, in many cases decades earlier. In southern Chile, as in many other countries, current landowners have not been directly involved in dispossession as they might have legally acquired land that was previously expropriated from Indigenous owners. For Janna Thompson (2002, 9), the moral legitimacy of restorative justice is based not on harm inflicted upon an individual in the past but on the intergenerational effects of colonial actions. Restorative justice is thus a process of constant adjustment to assessments of the current effects of historically continuous processes of exclusion and assimilation. Restoration "may be signified but is not exhausted by a particular reparations program or reparative gesture like a public apology" (Walker 2006, 379). Since compensation policies cannot possibly achieve the restoration of living conditions for Indigenous people, constant design of alternative compensatory measures in the fields of housing, education, health, and agriculture becomes necessary. Such a design, not surprisingly, is the key matter of public disagreement in most postcolonial contexts. This is also the case in Chile, where Indigenous restorative justice has followed a global turn toward reparative justice shaped by the language of human rights in the last twenty years

(Nujten and Lorenzo 2009, 205) while being intertwined with the particular national scenario of reconciliation politics in Chile from the 1990s.[2]

Compensation for human rights infringements committed during Augusto Pinochet's military dictatorship (1973–1990) was a key feature of Chile's transition to democratic rule. In the public arena, facing the divisive past of the military dictatorship was justified as a necessary step toward an inclusive model of democracy. One particular image, that of historical debt, has come to signify relations between the state and victims of past mistreatment, a broad category referring to groups as diverse as Indigenous people, residents of informal settlements (*pobladores*), and schoolteachers. Reconciliation in Chile has not been intended to bury the past but rather to cast the past as debt through the deployment of a language influenced by a discourse of human rights as much as by Catholic tradition. As suggested by anthropologist Clara Han (2012), in reconciliation, "An ethical work of the self forges a specific relation to the past as a moral debt" through appeals of pardon (96). Today, the idiom of debt is appropriated and used for political goals by Indigenous groups to effectively ground their demands for cultural and political self-determination. Yet framing reparative justice through the idiom of debt can also restrain Indigenous voices in reconciliation debates. This is because this particular idiom entails an understanding of colonial domination as an event of the past that can be quantified and exhausted through compensation. The payment of historical debts might then be imagined as a new agreement between equal parties—the Mapuche people and national society—in this scenario, but as a result of the debt being quantified, compensation is given form as an increase in housing and welfare subsidies. Thinking of past injustices as quantifiable debt does not overcome history by opening new futures. Rather, it reinforces a bond of dependency between a creditor and a debtor that in this case holds the last word on how and who exactly should be repaid.

In this chapter, I trace the historical roots and current manifestations of the debt owed by Chilean society to Mapuche people. I focus, on the one hand, on the ruptures and continuities of multicultural reconciliation in the present, and on the other hand, on the historical process that, more than any other, has come to define Indigenous/state relations in Chile: the discursive and material transformation of Mapuche people into "poor farmers." This process has been made possible by practical acts of dispossession that forced Mapuche people to become laborers on estates (*fundos*) and in urban centers, and by the discursive inclusion of Indigenous populations into the broader category of peasantry according to an assimilatory narrative collapsing Indigenous marginality into an issue of class inequality. Despite its emancipatory promise, governmental action intending to pay off historical debts to Mapuche people reiterates historically deep understandings of Mapuche people as disempowered objects of development intervention, an idea contested by Indigenous advocacies for self-governance. To trace the trajectory of the historical debt toward Mapuche people, I focus on the disputed formation of Mapuche people as subjects of governance. Subject formation, we have learned from Foucault (1982), is a process spurred by "modes of objectification which transform human beings into subjects" (777). Foucault's notion of subject presupposes the capacity of specific prereflective activities to animate and legitimate a particular horizon of intelligibility in which certain forms of human existence are deemed legitimate over others (Nichols 2014, 14). Subject formation, however, is far from being the ineluctable process of construction imaged in rigid narratives of power-knowledge. Foucault himself (1982) has warned us against the risk of taking subject formation in teleological terms by advocating an empirical approach to this phenomenon: "Rather than analyzing power from the point of view of its internal rationality, [this method] consists of analyzing power relations through the antagonism of strategies" (780). In a similar vein, my review of the historical debt and its current functioning centers on past and present tensions between different understandings of the place that the Mapuche have held within the project of nation building in Chile. A look at the production of conflicting images about the past among Mapuche and non-Indigenous Chileans will show how assimilatory and critical Mapuche perspectives on history are internally diverse and yet diametrically opposed in eliciting incompatible understandings of Indigenous belonging and land connections in the Chilean nation.

## The "Pacification": Contested Memories of Dispossession

The precolonial history of Mapuche people has long been the subject of heated debate. Controversies over interpretation of the archaeological and historiographical record center on land occupation. Current critiques of Indigenous demands are typically built around arguments questioning the autochthony of Mapuche society and the effective use of their territory, a thesis that justified settlers' expansion in the nineteenth century through the argument that there were no legitimate ownership claims before their arrival. The questioning of the autochthonous state of the Mapuche people is largely built around diffusionist theories popularized by early historians of Indigenous societies in Chile at the beginning of the twentieth century. In this diffusionist tradition, data drawn from archival research, museum collections, linguistics, excavations, and folklore were systematized in a speculative thesis on the geographic origins of Mapuche people. Ricardo Latcham (1924), for instance, proposed that the Mapuche were nomadic bands who migrated from Amazonia and settled in the south-central section of today's Chile, replacing a group known as *picunche* (literally, the "people of the north"). Another example comes from Tomás Guevara (1925), for whom Mapuche people were descendants of migrant groups from Peru and Bolivia.

Similar to diffusionist theories, interpretations pointing to lack of ownership claims over land by precolonial Mapuche hold no significance in today's historiography and yet serve to discredit Indigenous demands. As I show later in this book, Lockean arguments justifying land ownership under the sole condition that it can lead to wealth accumulation are commonly deployed to delegitimize Mapuche claims over land. The delegitimation of Indigenous entitlement to land in Chile reflects the rationality of settler nationalism, where the myth of an empty landscape to be developed and transformed is integral to nationalistic narratives of settler expansion (Dalsheim 2011, 60). In contrast with such images of the past, archaeological research has revealed the intricacy of Indigenous territorial arrangements in precolonial times. Complex political and economic structures existed before the arrival of the Spanish army in the Southern Cone in the sixteenth century (Dillehay 2007; Sauer 2015). Mapuche territorial use was likely to follow a semisedentary pattern, with residential communities (ranging from five hundred to eight thousand members) operating on a chiefdom level (Dillehay 1990, 225) and territorial units interconnected by large networks of alliances and commercial exchanges. Residential groups were organized into different levels of aggregation, with the *lof* constituting the basic social unit (Millalén 2006, 31) and the *ayllarehue* serving as a larger political entity bringing together different groups in case of military activities against invaders or other coalitions (Boccara 1999, 429). The sovereign Mapuche region, known as Wallmapu, stretched on both sides of the Andes, with regional differences acknowledged through geographic references such as Puelmapu and Gulumapu, eastern and western lands, respectively (Marimán 2006, 54).[3]

The plasticity of the alliance-based Mapuche organization was key to the successful resistance against the Incan Empire in the fifteenth century. Clashes between Mapuche factions and the Incas coexisted with an intense commercial relationship between the two regions (Sauer 2015, 127). The first incursions of the Spanish army into Mapuche territory date back to 1540, when conquistador Pedro de Valdivia led a military campaign to occupy the region south of Peru known at the time as Nueva Toledo. As for previous attempts at occupation, the Araucanians—the ethnonym given to precolonial Mapuche groups by the Spaniards—formed alliances against the aggressors.[4] In 1553, a coalition led by the *toqui* (war leader) Lautaro, a former Spanish captive, destroyed Tucapel Fort, erected only a few months earlier in the surroundings of what today is the southern town of Cañete. In this battle, Valdivia was captured and later killed (Bengoa 2000, 32). Military raids carried out by both sides continued throughout the sixteenth and seventeenth centuries in what would later be known as the War of Arauco. As it became increasingly evident that the Spanish army could not control the Mapuche territories, the prospect of an agreement with Mapuche war coalitions came to be understood as the only possible exit strategy. In January 1641, under the mediation of Jesuit missionaries, the governor of Chile, Francisco López de Zúñiga, accompanied by army officials and a coalition of Mapuche leaders led by Leintur, met in the valley of Quilín. This meeting resulted in a treaty known as Tratado de las Paces de Quilín, which granted the Mapuche sovereignty over the territory south of the river Bio-Bio in exchange for the liberation of Spanish captives and the free circulation of Christian missionaries in the region (Bengoa 2007). However, the Quilín treaty did not stop confrontations, so that peace talks, known as *trawün* or *parlamentos*, were regularly held to articulate new agreements while also allowing Spanish vigilance over Mapuche territories (Dillehay and Zavala 2013). The major consequence of the Quilín treaty was the consolidation of the Bio-Bio border and the consequential emergence of feelings of ethnic belonging. The term *Mapuche*, or "people from the land," was increasingly used to differentiate Native people from colonizers, eventually replacing the more common category of self-identification *reche* or *che*, "real people" or "people" (Boccara 1999). Like all borders, the Bio-Bio River was far from impermeable. Spaniards imported Mapuche produce while south of the Bio-Bio, the adoption of European goods and technologies contributed to the expansion of cattle and sheep husbandry as the main source of subsistence. The settlement of Christian missionaries, mainly Jesuit, in the Mapuche region gave way to a broad process of conversion of the Mapuche people but did not erase Indigenous religious practices and notions. Ever since the earliest instances of evangelization, Christian features have been incorporated into Mapuche religious practices (Foerster 1993), a phenomenon that I explore in detail in the remainder of this book.

Despite ongoing skirmishes across the Bio-Bio River border, the Mapuche successfully retained their independence throughout Spanish rule in the Southern Cone. This scenario changed dramatically in the nineteenth century, a time that saw the rise of independence movements against Spanish crowns. Chile became an independent republic in 1810. Clashes between independent and royal troops involved Mapuche groups only marginally, as they unfolded largely outside the Mapuche region (Bengoa 2000, 139). Yet the foundation of the Chilean republic was to prove a turning point in Mapuche colonial history. For Chilean political and economic elites, modernization could only be achieved through full control over its national territory, a spatial formation referring to everything lying west of the Andean range, including, of course, the sovereign Mapuche region (Pinto 2003). In the public arena, military action was mainly justified as a much-needed intervention to bring political stability to the Mapuche territory, or La Frontera as it was known in Chile at the time, which was increasingly reached by speculators and settlers with a consequent proliferation of land disputes. The idealistic image of patriots resisting against the Spanish army, which permeated early independentist discourses, was thus replaced by representations of

Mapuche people as a threat to national development. With the exception of a few critical voices, especially among the Catholic clergy, public support for the military invasion grew in the buildup to the war. Media outlets of the time, such as the major conservative newspaper *El Mercurio*, gathered support for the military campaign by proliferating images of the Mapuche people as "savages" attacking peaceful Chilean settlers (Crow 2013, 41). South of the Bio-Bio River, the Mapuche population was aware of the prospect of war, as more and more Chilean settlers were entering their territory. During this period, regional alliances were strengthened in preparation for the imminent attack.[5]

The military occupation officially began in 1866, when General Cornelio Saavedra was assigned the role of general commander in the south. In that same year, the Chilean Senate approved a bill named Ley del 4 Diciembre 1866, which declared the Mapuche region state-owned land (*terrenos fiscales*) in its entirety. This law followed the principle of *terra nullius*, a keystone of colonial rule around the globe in the nineteenth century that designated certain areas as no-man's-land—in other words, as lacking any effective sovereignty or ownership claim (Moran 2002). General Saavedra's plan came to be known in the media as the Pacification of Araucania. On the other side of the Andes, in Argentina, military actions against Mapuche groups were labeled with another euphemism, the Conquest of the Desert. Mapuche resistance, organized through local networks of alliances linking opposing factions, was initially successful in preventing the advancement of the Chilean fortified line. The pacification continued for almost twenty years, coming to an end only in 1883, with the foundation of the town of Villarica in the last area with the presence of the last insurgent groups (Richards 2013, 40). As argued by historian José Bengoa (2000), the consequences of the occupation did not differ from those of any other war of extermination (210). The dramatic death toll among the Mapuche was caused not only from military violence but also from famine and the later spread of infectious diseases unknown in the region. The near extermination of the Mapuche population has not been acknowledged until recently with the emergence of reconciliation discourses. For much of the twentieth century, official accounts, such as those present in history museums and school textbooks, understated the dramatic consequences of the invasion, replacing them with a scenario in which the Chilean and Argentinean army brought order to circumscribed conflicts between settlers and local Mapuche groups (Crow 2013, 24). Official representations of the Pacification of Araucania find little resonance in Indigenous communities, where the memory of the war is still alive thanks to place names and oral accounts transmitted across generations. As it will be illustrated in greater detail in the next chapter, specific places around the town of Traiguen, such as caves, are known as hideaways for the local population during the attacks carried out by the Chilean army in order to *arinconar* (push people in corners), a verb that people in Comunidad Contreras used frequently to describe the effects of the advancement of the military line. The Mapuche population, however, was not passive. Raids, known as *malones*, against the invaders' forts and settlements, proved effective in slowing down the Chilean military expansion. The area around today's Comunidad Contreras was the site of some of the most reported cases of confrontations between Mapuche warriors and Chilean soldiers in the national media.[6] Miguel, my host during fieldwork, recalls from oral accounts that his great-grandfather Manuel was actively involved in the insurgence: "He raided Traiguen three times. Once he even brought back tons of sheets and blankets from a shop. He just didn't know what to do with so many of them." But although the memory of violence during the military invasion is vivid in rural areas, the most compelling reminders of the consequences of war are the accounts and images of poverty that followed the postwar displacement of the Mapuche population.

## Just Peasants? Assimilation and Indigenous Difference in the Reservation Era

The invasion of Araucania set in motion the largest process of displacement in the colonial history of the Southern Cone. As the military invasion was coming to an end, the Chilean government designed a series of legal reforms aimed at introducing regulatory mechanisms for land redistribution. As prescribed by the December 4, 1866, law, land within the Mapuche region was to be distributed to beneficiaries through public auctions and colonization concessions managed by private companies. In the racial imaginaries of the time, development of the newly annexed territories could only be achieved through the labor of European settlers, ideally from Catholic areas (Klubock 2014, 46–52).[7] Soon after the end of the military campaign, land titles began to be redistributed to colonizing companies; European settlers, primarily from Germany, France, Italy, and Switzerland; and, to a lesser degree, migrants from other regions of Chile, known as national settlers (*colonos nacionales*), and Mapuche residential groups. Typically, settlers were benefited with land, domestic animals, and tools to initiate their agricultural activities (Correa, Molina, and Yánez 2005, 26–42). The lack of market regulation allowed for a gradual concentration of land in the hands of a few estate owners (*patrones de fundo*). Settler expansion led to profound changes in the southern Chilean landscape, initiating a rapid process of deforestation. Fires were intentionally set with the goal of clearing land for agriculture, an activity that, despite its prohibition, is still known today as "cleaning the fields" (*limpiar los campos*; Di Giminiani 2016, 736).[8] Settler expansion was also behind violent confrontations between European immigrants and resident Mapuche groups that lasted until the 1930s (Bengoa 1999, 172). Most confrontations resulted in the eviction of Mapuche people from the land they were occupying. Colonization was far from being

FIGURE 3 The center of Traiguen at the beginning of the nineteenth century. (Colección Museo Histórico Nacional)

the smooth process of development imagined by policy makers before the military invasion. Even to the eyes of central authorities it became clear that the state exercised a feeble administrative power over this frontier region in which land redistribution took the form of multiple conflicts involving white settlers, migrant squatters from northern regions, and Mapuche people (Klubock 2014, 31).

The resettlement of the Mapuche population was overseen by a commission named Comisión Repartidora de Terrenos Indígenas, instituted in 1883 with the objective of assigning communal land titles, known as Título de Merced (literally, "titles of mercy") to Indigenous residential groups. Households were clustered into reservations (reducciones), which were represented by local delegates known as caciques. In 35 years roughly 80,000 Mapuche were relocated in 3,078 reservations whose extension amounted to roughly 475,000 hectares (Bengoa 2000, 355), a figure corresponding to only 5 percent of the Mapuche territory before the invasion of Araucania (Marimán 2006, 121).[9] Around 40,000 individuals were left without titles, their only option for access to land being relocation to reducciones with which they had no genealogical connection. The encroachment of Mapuche land did not stop with the establishment of the reservation system. Settlers began to annex reservation land to their properties through different strategies. The most common was fence running (*corrida de cercos*), a practice consisting in the illegal extension of fences such as barbed wire over neighbors' properties. Land transactions involving caciques and settlers were also common, although reservation land was, in theory, inalienable. In most cases, settlers informally rented tracts of reservation land and then had their ownership rights recognized through the legal principle of first occupancy. It has been estimated that at least a third of the reservation land had been expropriated by non-Mapuche landowners in the first fifty years of the twentieth century (Bengoa 2000, 369). Once the reservation system was enacted, Mapuche residents had virtually no chance of purchasing land outside their *reducciones* in the absence of cash flow. The combined effects of land grabbing, population growth, and limited land access resulted in a spiraling deterioration of economic conditions in rural Mapuche areas. Rampant poverty was to become a key concern for Mapuche political leaders and policy makers, and persists to this day. While a national economic growth spurt in the 1990s and the introduction of new welfare and housing policies in Mapuche rural areas have reduced the extent of economic precariousness in the last two decades, the income gap between the Mapuche and the non-Indigenous population remains high for chronic shortcomings in access to healthcare, employment, and education (Valenzuela 2003).[10]

The most compelling effect of land shortage and increasing poverty was the forced abandonment of household farming by reservation members. Since this activity was no longer able to provide sufficient resources for an entire family, Mapuche rural residents were left with two options: to work on nearby estates or to migrate to urban areas. Working as peasants on agricultural estates was particularly harsh, as recounted by elder community members in my area of study. The working day started at sunrise and ended at sunset, an arrangement known as "from sun to sun" (*de sol a sol*). Most estate workers did not have a chance to see their families, as they often spent the night in the workers' barracks sleeping on improvised pallets. Before the labor reform introduced by Eduardo Frei Montalva's government (1964–1970), payments consisted in the assignment of a token or voucher (*ficha*) to be exchanged for food and a limited range of clothes. A small quantity of cash was given to workers only three or four times a year, such as after the harvest and at Easter. Estate workers were thus unable to buy anything but very basic goods. The most compelling memory of life in *reducciones* before the 1960s is the image of walking barefoot (*ir a patas peladas*). At the time, shoes were a luxury for many in Chile, and most people in the countryside could only afford sandals made of rubber tires. While working conditions on agricultural estates have considerably improved since the 1960s, salaries paid by large landholders are low, and in most cases employment is only temporary. For most residents of *comunidades*, working on estates is still the only option to avoid migrating away from their homes. Since the early twentieth century, generations of reservation residents have had to migrate to urban areas, mainly the capital, Santiago, but also to southern towns and mining centers in the north of Chile. Sources of employment typically followed a gendered pattern, with domestic labor in middle- and upper-class families as the main occupation for women and work in factories and mines for men. The number of rural youth migrating for educational purposes has noticeably increased since the

1990s, along with the number of Mapuche professionals working in urban centers, who find it particularly hard to return to the countryside once they have secured a job in the city. Mapuche migration to the city has adopted a dimension that matches those observed in diasporic contexts (Antileo 2010). It is not rare to find households within a comunidad where the near majority of its members have moved to urban centers. According to all national censuses since the 1990s, the majority of self-identified Mapuche people live in urban areas. Cities have become the main scenario for political activism, encouraging the emergence of new forms of indigeneity that defy racial stereotypes of Mapuche as disempowered peasants (see Ancán 2005). Yet outmigration has proved a twofold historical process for the Mapuche people. While it has elicited new processes of political consciousness, migration away from rural areas has also served as a key factor in assimilatory processes. Discrimination at schools and in the workplace has contributed to the abandonment of Indigenous practices in favor of lifestyles associated with mainstream Chilean society. While this same phenomenon has also unfolded in rural areas, detachment from kinship networks, especially those involving elder family members, caused by outmigration has contributed even more to assimilation. I return to the social consequences of migration in the next chapter. For now, let me describe some of the actions undertaken by Mapuche people against assimilation and economic exclusion.

Mapuche political organizations began surfacing as early as the beginning of the twentieth century. Despite their common interest in two themes, assimilation and economic exclusion, identified as the main public concerns of Mapuche society, organizations varied vastly in their scope throughout the twentieth century. The first of such organizations, Sociedad Caupolicán, was founded in 1910 in Temuco by a group of Mapuche entrepreneurs and politicians. Two of its primary objectives were to denounce violations committed against Mapuche people and to advocate for equal rights with the rest of Chilean society, with a particular emphasis on access to education (Foerster and Montecino 1988, 10). An openly antiassimilatory stance was adopted by the later Federación Araucana, an organization with direct links to left-wing parties. Its members were preoccupied with the advancement of legislative reforms aimed at offering economic and legal protection for reservation land (Crow 2013, 57–73). Indigenous land protection continued to be a major interest of Mapuche organizations, including those allied with conservative parties, such as the Corporación Araucana (Mariman 1999, 169). The heterogeneity of Mapuche political leaders' perspectives on assimilation, poverty, and discrimination was closely connected to differences in their political orientations. Early Mapuche organizations actively sought to establish alliances with political parties with which most of their members were affiliated. An exemplary case was Venancio Coñuepán, an entrepreneur and member of the Conservative Party, who was elected congressman in 1945 and later served as minister of land and colonization and director of the first Indigenous state agency in Chile, DASIN (Dirección de Asuntos Indígenas). For Coñuepán, Indigenous economic exclusion was a national emergency requiring an unprecedented state effort in building a development agenda in which Mapuche people could be protagonists (Crow 2013, 106). Since the early twentieth century, Mapuche people have been distributed along the entire political spectrum. Traditional preference for conservative candidates in Araucania, the region where most Mapuche settlements are concentrated, has been erroneously interpreted as evidence for a general characterization of the Mapuche as right-wing voters. Recent studies have instead shown that the Mapuche vote follows national tendencies, with the only difference being a certain inclination to vote for Mapuche candidates (Toro and Jaramillo-Brun 2014). Both Mapuche and non-Indigenous farmers in southern Chile tend to back local politicians based not only on party loyalty but also on cliental networks. More than non-Indigenous rural settlements, comunidades act as ideal sources of electoral pools, since community boards can publicly endorse candidates who previously supported the local settlement by facilitating infrastructural improvement, such as the construction of a bridge or a health facility in the area.

Political divisions within the Mapuche population intensified in the 1960s and 1970s, when the introduction of social reforms targeting economic inequality was met with defiance by the landholding elite. A first wave of moderate reforms came during the presidency of the Christian Democrat Eduardo Frei Montalva (1964–1970), who was responsible for the introduction of basic labor rights for peasants and the consequential dismantlement of the debt by peonage (bonded labor) system. Frei's government also implemented a land redistribution reform, which was intensified by the government of Unidad Popular (UP), led by the Socialist Salvador Allende, who was elected president in 1970. The general objective of the agrarian reform was to improve agricultural production, which was threatened by the vast presence of *latifundia* (private estates) throughout the national territory, and to empower small landholders through land transfer. Expropriation of unproductive properties and compensation for them was the responsibility of the Corporation of the Agrarian Reform (CORA), which also financially and logistically supported the establishment of cooperative settlement groups known as *asentamientos*, assigned with the task of developing transferred properties (Mallon 2005, 112–115). Peasants' associations and national organizations, such as the Movimiento de Izquierda Revolucionario (Movement of Revolutionary Left), carried out land takeovers (tomas) with the objective of pressuring the UP government to accelerate land redistribution. The response from the landholding elite was immediate. Landholders actively participated in smear campaigns aimed at discrediting Allende's government, the most effective of which was a national boycott of industrial and agricultural production. They also supported right-wing paramilitary groups, in particular the FNPL (Frente Nacionalista Patria y Libertad), in retaliation raids against land protesters. As political clashes intensified, the prospect of a coup became more and more likely. On September 11, 1973, the military took over the streets. The Chilean air force (Fuerza Aérea de Chile, FACh) bombed the presidential palace, La Moneda, where Allende took his own life once it became clear that government supporters could not repel the attack. The overthrow of the UP government, which was endorsed and financed by the Chilean economic elite and the U.S. Secret Service, was soon followed by a national persecution of left-wing sympathizers. For the next seventeen years, a military junta led by Augusto Pinochet—who at the time of the coup had been serving as the army commander in chief, appointed by Allende himself—was to rule the country through the systematic suppression of human rights and democratic institutions.

In the countryside, a counter land reform program was implemented soon after the military seizure of power. Most expropriated properties were returned to large landholders, while participants in land takeovers became the targets of military repression. This program had directly affected many of the Mapuche community members I met during my research. A few months before the coup, a group of residents from Reducción Contreras, as this settlement was known at that time, joined other protesters to demand the expropriation of a local agricultural estate. The toma (occupation protest) lasted a few weeks, ending with the violent intervention of FNPL paramilitaries who evicted the residents from the property by firing shotguns.[11] Soon after the coup, a large military contingent arrived in Reducción Contreras to search for participants in the land takeover. Roughly fifteen residents were taken to the detention center of Traiguen and tortured.[12] A few days later they were returned to their homes. Occasional detentions continued over the next couple of years, causing anxiety among family members at the possibility of their becoming *desaparecidos*, "disappeared" victims of the dictatorship, whose bodies were never to be found. During one of the military searches, a young resident was repeatedly hit by a soldier for not being able to reveal the whereabouts of one of his family members accused of being a left-wing supporter. A few weeks later, he died of respiratory complications. As for the rest of the country, residents of Reducción Contreras were generally divided between the UP and supporters of Pinochet's government. A feeling of mistrust among local residents continues to this day, as many believe that the names of torture and detention victims held by militaries were disclosed by at least a couple of their neighbors under the pressure of their employer, an estate owner and active supporter of the military dictatorship. During the dictatorship, military repression was particularly harsh for the Mapuche population. The reason was not simply because they were Mapuche, since the targets of the military dictatorship were left-wing supporters regardless of their ethnic affiliation. However, as argued by Joanna Crow (2013, 155), repression had a clear ethnic dimension, as the vulnerable position of Mapuche farmers within the Chilean class and racial system affected the way they were treated by the state apparatus.

The effects of the military dictatorship on Mapuche rural areas went beyond repression of left-wing supporters. With the objective of supporting private economic initiatives, in particular transnational export of primary goods, and of reducing inflation rates, the military junta introduced a series of laissez-faire economic reforms designed by a group of economists named the Chicago Boys, inspired by Milton Friedman's theory of market deregulation (Valdés 1995). While gross numbers portrayed a national scenario of economic stability, competitiveness in small-scale agriculture quickly declined with the expansion of agribusiness sectors and the curtailment of welfare policies (Kay 2002). Cyclical economic crises in the 1980s were hard on impoverished sectors of society such as the rural Indigenous population. During this decade, Mapuche rural areas were characterized by alarming figures in mortality, literacy, and salary when compared to the rest of the national territory (Bengoa and Valenzuela 1983, 133). Another significant consequence of the military rule on Mapuche rural communities was the general restriction of associative freedoms, a phenomenon constituting a destabilizing threat against the junta and an obstacle for the implementation of policies based on unmediated relations between individuals and the state. For instance, in my area of study, neighbors' associations (*juntas de vecinos*), perhaps the most important form of organization in the Chilean countryside, were headed by appointees of local authorities. In such a scenario, the only chance for Mapuche associativity was the existence of organizations acting under the banner of cultural societies, as in the case of Centros Culturales Mapuche, established in 1979 under the auspices of the Catholic Church (Mallon 2005, 252). Despite their apparently folkloric characterization, the centers were instrumental in the articulation of collaborative networks that would later converge into the most important Mapuche organization during the dictatorship, Ad Mapu, which was legally recognized in 1980 as the trade organization Asociación Gremial de Pequeños Agricultores y Artesanos Ad Mapu (Reuque Paillalef 2002).[13]

The long historical period between the beginning of the reservation system and the military dictatorship is characterized by a general continuity of governmental interest in one particular issue, that of the relation between economic marginality and assimilation. Throughout the reservation era, most Chilean policy makers, political figures, and intellectuals have advocated for a full integration of Indigenous people into Chilean society as a solution to chronic economic problems. While integration does not necessarily entail assimilation, integrationist perspectives tended to frame Mapuche marginality as part of a broader national problem, that of the disempowerment of the peasantry. The transformation from independent Mapuche farmers into poor farmers, a process brought about in part by the reservation system, was thus both material and discursive. The proletarianization of the Mapuche people is undeniable, as the historical expansion of agribusiness in Indigenous territories shows. The inclusion of Mapuche people into a peasantry conceived in a race-blind fashion, however, is not simply a self-evident representation of political economic processes, but rather part of an established assimilatory discourse of nation building. Such a discourse resonates with the narrative of *mestizaje*, a racial ideology well known throughout Latin America. *Mestizaje* refers to the historical process of miscegenation involving European and Indigenous groups in Latin America, which resulted in the emergence of a new national subject, the mestizo. By idealizing Indigenous people as embodiments of tradition and the past, *mestizaje* reinforces an image of national identity in which racial and ethnic differences are obfuscated, even while elevating white European heritage as the apex of the Latin American nation (Alonso 1994; Wade 2005). In Chile, *mestizaje* has not been the object of official celebration that it has in some other Latin American countries, and the status of mestizo is often denied in favor of identification with white heritage. Racism against Mapuche people is widespread throughout the national population, with differences in strategies to frame racial stereotypes among social classes (Pilleux and Merino 2004). While I have encountered numerous exceptions to the use of racial stereotypes in southern towns, discrimination is a defining trait of interethnic relations in southern Chile. In my area of study, for instance, townspeople share many of the social conditions of Mapuche farmers, with whom in many cases they might even be related by kinship. Yet they would often remark on their ethnic differences through offensive stereotypes, such as proneness to binge drinking, and derogatory terms such as *Mapuchito* and *Indio*. In some circumstances townspeople would assure me, a European interlocutor, that they had nothing to do with "Indians" and that their origins were purely Spanish. Activist and acclaimed journalist Pedro Cayuqueo (2014a) has defined such whitening aspirations as "the Chilean inability... to reconcile with his non-white side (*morenidad*)."

Racial hierarchies are reinforced not only through images of white superiority but also with the seemingly innocuous narrative of *mestizaje*. Such a narrative often works to blur Indigenous alterity with a national heritage discourse. This was the case with the nationalistic agenda of Pinochet's regime, where Mapuche-ness was celebrated as part of a presupposed national identity characterized by deep military values. In 1989, in the speech accepting his appointment as the *ulmen futa lonko*, the great leader, by a local Mapuche organization, Pinochet addressed a largely Mapuche audience in the town of Chol Chol with these words: "From a very early era, this pueblo tied its heroic virtues and unwavering love for our homeland to our national history. Once these values have melted with Spanish blood, they have resulted into a proud and courageous nation" (in Foerster 2002, 5). An extreme version of *mestizaje* postulates that Mapuche people no longer exist and that claims that they do are recent inventions. This view is best exemplified by 1992 National History Award winner Sergio Villalobos (2000), for whom the intentional adoption of Western beliefs and material culture by Mapuche people led to their complete assimilation into Chilean society, thus making any claims of difference a matter of political opportunism.[14] Not surprisingly, such an integrationist claim, which resonated in conservative sectors of Chilean society, was met with harsh criticism by Mapuche writers, such as political scientist José Marimán (2000), who have contextualized Villalobos's arguments as a quintessential expression of the broad phenomenon of the Chilean assimilatory nationalism.

Integrationist perspectives have not been unique to conservative nationalism in Chile. Leftist parties have also aligned themselves with Mapuche demands during the twentieth century. They have been the primary promoters of *indigenismo* in Chile, an anticolonial emancipatory discourse celebrating Indigenous culture throughout Latin America since the 1950s (Crow 2013, 84). Before the 1990s, the UP government was the only one to have introduced land redistribution mechanisms targeting specifically Mapuche groups within the context of land redistribution. However, by subsuming ethnic claims of self-governance within class politics, left-wing proponents of Indigenous reforms have often promoted an integrationist agenda (see Berdichewsky 1980). Sociologist José Saavedra (2002, 150), for instance, has recently discredited Mapuche claims of self-governance as class-based demands infused with ethno-populism (see also Marimán 2012, 19). Such an integrationist presumption gives us a hint as to why many Mapuche activists might have found in leftist parties ideal platforms to stake manifold political claims concerning intertwined experiences of ethnic and class exclusion, but have often felt unease with the little space granted to Indigenous alterity within orthodox Marxist frameworks of class divisions (Richards 2013, 194; Crow 2013, 117). The material and discursive transformation of Mapuche people into poor Chilean farmers made possible by historical processes of proletarianization and integrationist perspectives continue to inspire postdictatorship governmental actions. Despite the many continuities with the nationalist agenda of the junta military, the return to democracy represented a chance for Mapuche people to overtly challenge assimilatory governmental actions and, more generally, customary racialized arrangements of citizenship.

## Reparation Politics and Indigenous Autonomy in the Long Transition to Democracy

As prescribed by the 1980 constitution, and after a long and secretive negotiation between the military junta and moderate members of the opposition, a national referendum was held in 1988. The Chilean population was asked whether Pinochet's presidency should be extended for eight more years or democratic elections should be announced instead. By a margin of 10 percent, voters expressed their will to interrupt Pinochet's presidency, a decision that marked the beginning of the Chilean transition to democracy (Paley 2001). For grassroots organizations, return to democratic rule stood as an unprecedented opportunity to raise their claims silenced during the dictatorship. Consultation between candidates, members of civic society, and the private sector took place in the months preceding the 1990 presidential election. In a meeting held in 1989 in the southern town of Nueva Imperial, several Mapuche organizations announced their endorsement of presidential candidate Patricio Aylwin, the leader of the center-left coalition Concertación de Partidos por la Democracia, in exchange for the introduction of legislative reforms granting collective rights to Indigenous groups in the country (Haughney 2006). Concertación's success paved the way for the institution of Indigenous Law 19.253 in 1993, which, among its innovations, introduced mechanisms for the assignation of land grants to Indigenous claimants implemented under the supervision of the newly founded agency CONADI. The Indigenous Law—initially designed by a panel comprising members of different Indigenous groups known as the Comisión Especial de Pueblos Indígenas—also established new territorial units named comunidades indígenas, to act as legal representatives of local residents from one or more reducciones. However, by the time the law was ratified by the Chilean congress, there had been significant alterations reducing the extent of collective rights over natural resources and political representation for Indigenous groups (Aylwin 2002). Consequently, while the 1993 law helped improve Indigenous people's socioeconomic conditions through the unprecedented development of individualized welfare policies in housing, agriculture, and education, its mechanisms for the resolution of land disputes proved ineffective in responding to demands for self-governance. A dramatic example of the exclusion of Indigenous groups from crucial instances of decision-making came from the construction of the Ralco Dam built in 2004. This megadevelopment project entailed the controversial relocation of several hundred Mapuche Pewenche away from their properties.[15] Since this measure required CONADI approval, its first director, Mauricio Huenchulaf, an opponent of the project, was forced to resign in 1997 by President Eduardo Frei, who replaced him with a compliant governmental official (Richards 2004, 133).

Fearing that their co-option could legitimize legislative reforms curtailing Indigenous political claims, some Mapuche organizations refused to partake in the consultation agenda of postdictatorship governments (Pairicán 2014). The Aukiñ Wallmapu Ngulam or Consejo de Todas las Tierras (Council of all Lands) was one of the first organizations to take a more defiant stance toward government collaboration. Like others, it was behind land takeovers (tomas) organized with the objective of pressuring governments in the restitution of historically expropriated territories (Mallon

2005, 181). Land takeovers have primarily targeted large landholders and transnational timber companies (*forestales*), which have recently faced public criticism for the damage they have done to the environment and their expropriation of Indigenous land (see Reimán 2001). A more militant approach influenced by anticapitalist discourses has been developed by organizations such as Coordinadora Arauko-Malleko (CAM), which has been publicly condemned as the main instigator of arson attacks against agribusiness companies (Richards 2013, 175). Since 1990, land takeovers, protests, and arson attacks have been met with police repression. Confrontations between protesters and police forces have resulted in the death of numerous Mapuche activists. In 2013, the death toll extended to two non-Indigenous landowners during an arson attack. Violent episodes have come to be labeled in the public media as *conflicto Mapuche*, the "Mapuche conflict." The framing of Mapuche demands as a conflict has contributed to the forging of images of political turmoil and terrorist danger, which conservative politicians and members of the landholding elite have deployed to demand military intervention in southern Chile. In 2014, voices in favor of the repression of land takeovers converged on the organization Paz en la Araucanía (Peace in the Araucania), whose action program ranged from road blockades to lobbying in the parliament.[16]

Reactions against Mapuche mobilizations are motivated by different factors, among which we find a general defense of national cohesion, concerns over economic stability, and a will to preserve racialized privilege among white settlers. These reactions are in turn based on a diverse set of rationales serving to delegitimize Indigenous land demands. Some of them, which typically can be overheard in conversations among townspeople or read on social media, are openly racist in presupposing an inherently violent nature of Mapuche people. Most of them, however, discredit radical acts of mobilization by arguing that they are committed by small numbers of subversives who have infiltrated Mapuche rural settlements. Some of these outsiders supposedly belonged to Marxist and anarchist groups, while others were suspected to be foreign agitators, a suggestion sporadically raised by unverified news items in the media about the presence of Basque nationalists or Colombian guerrilla fighters in southern Chile. For some conservative politicians, keeping tensions high in southern Chile was viewed as a strategy designed by some Mapuche activists to maintain economic support from European NGOs (Von Baer 2003, 20). Speculative arguments on external manipulation of Indigenous rural settlements reveal a paternalistic view according to which the Mapuche are incapable of autonomous planning. Furthermore, as suggested by Patricia Richards (2013, 66), to think of Mapuche mobilization as the result of external influences means to argue that land demands are recent inventions that disrupted a long term of peaceful relations between the Mapuche people and *colonos*. Delegitimation of Mapuche mobilization has also come through the articulation of a discourse of victimhood among settlers and agribusiness entrepreneurs in the language of human rights. According to such a discourse, victimhood is a condition shared equally by the Mapuche and the non-Indigenous population, especially farmers whose human rights have been trampled on through land seizures and arson attacks. But despite casting Indigenous collective rights as a secondary concern in comparison with the individual suffering of both Mapuche people and settlers caused by land conflicts, this discourse offers Mapuche organizations a more positive nuance: at least settlers acknowledge Indigenous suffering. Furthermore, by identifying the state as the culprit in the dispossession, since it was a government-sponsored process even though it took place in the nineteenth and twentieth centuries, they demand an adequate state response to land conflicts that can hear both their perspectives and those of the Mapuche. What sort of state response is necessary clearly remains a point of disagreement.

Although it has been estimated that only a small number of communities (2.4 percent) have been involved in more extreme forms of protest (Richards 2013, 81), Chilean TV viewers and newspaper readers have learned to associate comunidades in southern Chile with images of violence and unrest. In my area of study, Mapuche rural residents find media depictions of widespread violence extremely offensive, as they reify existing stereotypes of Indigenous people.[17] As I show in the second part of this book, members of Comunidad Contreras are proud of their achievements in land restitution, especially for having creatively employed nonviolent means of mobilization. Yet many of them are sympathetic to those claimants that have been involved in violent confrontations as they know from experience that radical actions are often responses to police raids and frustrations in the claim-staking process. Voices critical of the state approach to land conflicts have spoken primarily against the idea that violence is the exclusive domain of Mapuche extremists. Physical attacks committed by self-defense groups promoted by powerful landowners against Mapuche individuals have been denounced in media and courts. Some arson attacks have been legally documented as self-inflicted attacks (*auto-atendados*) by truck owners as insurance frauds or strategies to intensify police intervention in the area (Suzuki 2015). However, it is the repressive nature of state treatment of activists that has drawn the attention of the international human rights community. Since 2000, the antiterrorist law Ley de Seguridad del Estado, a Pinochet-era piece of legislation used against political dissenters, has been applied to numerous legal cases involving Mapuche protesters. This law presupposes a series of restrictions and aggravating circumstances for anyone accused of posing a national security threat. Antiterrorist discourses have also justified military intervention in rural areas with a history of repeated land takeovers. The militarization (*militarización*) of these areas has led to an increase of police raids (*allanamientos*). International organizations such as Human Rights Watch have reported cases of torture and unlawful detention of minors (Human Rights Watch 2010, 208–10).

Prosecution of Mapuche activists has been the subject of a broad awareness campaign in which activities have ranged from denunciation of abuses on the internet to hunger strikes carried out by Mapuche activists during their detention. The campaigns have proved effective in increasingly drawing sympathies toward Mapuche demands among the Chilean population. Organizers have also reached out to the international human rights community. Concerns about police abuse have in fact led the United Nations to formally urge the Chilean government to stop applying antiterrorist measures.

Repression of militant activism was only one of the governmental strategies for pacifying land disputes in southern Chile. Among policy makers there has been a widespread opinion that Mapuche demands could be responded to through the introduction of programs designed in the language of development, a point exemplified by the characterization of CONADI, the only state agency dealing with Indigenous issues, as a development corporation. Since 1993, an unprecedented number of welfare programs have been introduced to improve standards of living among Indigenous people in the country. However, the emergence of a welfare system based on affirmative action in Chile could also be read as a threat to aspirations of self-governance among Indigenous people. This point is best exemplified by the largest and most publicly celebrated development program to this day, Programa Orígenes. Established in 2001 through state funding and a loan by the Inter-American Development Bank, Programa Orígenes was aimed at supporting local development projects concerning agricultural production, health, and community empowerment among the Mapuche (Boccara 2007). However, while its local implementation was inspired by the principles of development-with-identity, Indigenous residential groups were absent in the decision-making process. They have regularly found themselves in the passive position of accepting benefits offered by subcontracted brokers and consultants acting as intermediaries between the administrators of the program and local settlements. During a conversation with a few neighbors of mine during fieldwork, I was told about the dubious delivery of a small herd of cows to a Mapuche settlement. The animals, originally from a mountainous area, were of a different subspecies than those usually found in the central valley, the location of my study area. As soon as they were delivered, they began to attack local residents, who were left with little option but to kill them and consume their meat. The reason a breed so clearly unsuitable for local needs was delivered remains unknown. Rumors about an economic settlement between a cattle dealer and the Mapuche delegate of the "benefited" community began to spread soon after.

Governmental emphasis on development as a solution to Indigenous economic exclusion and assimilation is closely related to the idea of historical debt, with which I opened this chapter. Welfare and development interventions targeting Indigenous people in Chile reveal an understanding of reparation as a quantifiable debt whose determination nonetheless falls under governmental responsibility. The casting of the past as debt (Han 2012, 96) entails a discursive shift of Indigenous marginality from a political issue requiring reflections on justice and historical accountability to a technical question of development planning. In an interview released in 2014, the then regional authority of Araucania, Intendente Francisco Huenchumilla—a Mapuche member of the Christian Democrat party—expressed his concerns over governmental understanding of Indigenous demands: "Our region was always approached as [if] its problems were poverty and public order . . . [but] here there is a problem of [a] political nature" (in Soto 2014). The discursive shift of reparation from politics to development is thus contiguous with the very idea of *asistencialismo*, a notion that has come to define the disempowering dependency on state assistance by vulnerable sectors of the Chilean nation, including many Mapuche farmers (Richards 2013, 154).

As seen so far, the state response to Mapuche demands for collective rights has displayed a Januslike nature. On the one hand, demands that openly defy existing market arrangements have been vehemently repressed; on the other, Indigenous people have become the target of unprecedented state support targeting development with identity initiatives, educational programs, and cultural revitalization. The dichotomous nature of the state response to Mapuche mobilization reflects the well-known scenario of neoliberal multiculturalism in Latin America (see Hale 2006a; Postero 2007). The encompassment of the Mapuche population within development policies, based on the principle of individual self-realization on the one hand and the ideal of rational consumption of welfare benefits by citizen-clients on the other (see Schild 2007), responds to the objective of valuing Indigenous difference in terms congruent with the market. A similar case can be made for state intervention aimed at fostering entrepreneurial skills among Mapuche people, which is a pillar of Plan Araucanía, a governmental program introduced by the conservative president Sebastian Piñera in 2010 (Richards 2013, 211). I explore the link between Indigenous policies and neoliberalism in my analysis of land claims in the second part of this book. For now, it is important to notice that the shortcomings of governmental approaches to restorative justice have been pivotal to the articulation of a public debate on Indigenous political empowerment led by Mapuche writers and activists. Central to this debate has been the formulation of alternatives to customary paternalistic attitudes in Indigenous development reflecting the broader scenario of *asistencialismo*. Self-determination in this sense requires the opening of spaces of autonomous governance not only within both the market and the state apparatus, but also outside them. Different aspirations toward major Indigenous control over development and welfare policies have come together under the umbrella notion of autonomy (*autonomia*). While a hope for ethnic autonomy has been latent in anticolonial discourses of Mapuche politicians since the early twentieth century, it was not until the 1990s that a full-blown agenda for autonomous governance was developed. Present demands of autonomy rotate around two poles, one emphasizing the revitalization of Indigenous institutional structures as a strategy to build autonomous spaces, and the other aiming at restructuring Indigenous/state relations in ways that the Mapuche population can control governmental action affecting them (Marimán 2012, 24–25). Autonomy is thus associated with a wide diversity of actions. It can refer to the decolonization of knowledge in the intellectual field necessary to advance a contemporary Mapuche epistemology (Nahuelpan et al. 2012). It also concerns development, education, and health programs financed by nongovernmental and state agencies but run by Mapuche people (Park and Richards 2007), as in the cases of those Mapuche mayors elected as independent candidates advocating for ethnic reforms in a handful of towns in southern Chile. In the national political arena, Mapuche autonomy has been discussed mainly in reference to institutional reforms at national and regional level. This theme has been the rallying cry of Wallmapuwen, a political organization founded in 2005, which has recently been recognized as a political party after several years of campaigning and recruiting signatories. Inspired by both left-wing and ethnic politics, Wallmapuwen works to achieve a statute of autonomy for the Mapuche homeland, or Wallmapu. The idea of Mapuche autonomy sought by Wallmapuwen consists in the institution of a broader region inhabited by both Mapuche and non-Indigenous people in which Indigenous cultural rights and local instances of self-governance are promoted (Cayuqueo 2014b). For Marimán (2012, 126–30), decentralization of the Chilean state is a prerequisite for the regional autonomy of the Mapuche homeland. Mapuche demands of self-governance have mostly gone unheard in national politics. However, some recent developments invite optimism on the future advancement of Mapuche rights.

Under the pressure of Mapuche organizations and the international human rights community, in 2008 the Chilean Senate ratified the Indigenous and Tribal Peoples Convention, also known as ILO 169, an international treaty establishing consultation mechanisms with Indigenous groups for governmental and private plans. Since the ILO 169 was ratified—though with major modifications—by the senate, its impact has been limited to a few cases of Indigenous groups being enabled to halt megadevelopment plans. Bigger expectations for the advancement of Indigenous self-determination are placed upon the current plans of Michelle Bachelet's government to create a Ministry of Indigenous People, and, more importantly, to compile a new constitution that would replace the current one redacted by the military junta in 1980. Recognition of Indigenous groups in the constitution could create the environment for an extensive wave of legal reforms. But despite these auspicious prospects, doubts remain as to whether grassroots organizations will have a say on Indigenous policies or whether, as with CONADI, Indigenous politicians will be co-opted into the new governmental institution. As mentioned at the beginning of this chapter, Indigenous people in Chile are used to cyclical promises of repayment.

By projecting new forms of belonging, Mapuche theories of autonomy have challenged the traditional framework of citizenship in Chile (Richards 2013, 207). Yet even among radical groups Mapuche nationhood does not necessarily mean complete separation from the Chilean state or refusal to participate in Chilean society (Crow 2013, 183). As a matter of fact, aspirations of self-governance coexist with a fervent identification with national values and ideals. This is at least the case with numerous rural areas in Chile, where many Mapuche see themselves in a hybrid position between the two categories—Chilean and Mapuche—which are not mutually exclusive when the former is understood not as a synonym for winka, the term designating non-Indigenous people, but as a category of citizenship. During my first weeks of fieldwork, I naïvely assumed that the Chilean flag and national celebrations served as symbols of oppression that simply held no place in the Mapuche rural world. My presumption was the result of my working knowledge of autonomist movements in other countries. However, I soon realized that residents of comunidades generally did not see adherence to national values as incompatible with their own struggle for self-governance. They happily participate in the independence festivities of September, Fiestas Patrias, enthusiastically support the national football team on TV, and wave the Chilean flag during collective Mapuche rituals known as *ngillatun*. The concomitant identification with national values and aspiration toward self-governance explains why the prospect of Mapuche statehood does not resonate in rural areas. This is not only because such a political project is understood as pragmatically unviable, but also because being a Mapuche Chilean is part of how most residents of comunidades tend to frame perceptions of selfhood and belonging. As it was once explained to me by Francisca, a close friend of mine from Comunidad Contreras, "Mapuche are the real Chileans; they were here before everybody else." This widespread idea suggests that special rights for Indigenous people should not be recognized simply because Mapuche people are not Chileans, but exactly because they are "more Chilean" than anybody else. Unpacking this idea of citizenship and belonging requires a careful examination of the historical intersections between colonizer and colonized cultures. This is exactly what I set out to do in the remainder of this book, where I examine the epistemological and ontological constitution of the "ancestral territory" with particular attention to the entanglement of legal and Indigenous land ontologies.

---

This chapter has focused on the genealogy and current standing of the historical debt held by Chilean society toward Mapuche people. I have paid particular attention to how representations of key processes of debt accumulation, such as the military invasion of the Mapuche region in the nineteenth century and the establishment of the

FIGURE 4  Meeting held at the community center with local authorities and candidates during the campaign for municipal elections. (Photo by author)

reservation system, stand in today's debates of restorative justice and multicultural politics. Central to current understandings and effects of the historical debt is the contested place that Mapuche people and their land connections have held in nation building. This chapter cannot, obviously, exhaust the multiple histories of Mapuche participation and exclusion in national society. However, the overview of the contested nature of Indigenous belonging in Chilean nationhood highlights the significance of memories of dispossession in recasting current ideas about land connections and restorative justice among Mapuche people. For now, let me continue to examine the memory of colonial dispossession by looking at embodied landscape experiences and notions of place in rural Mapuche settlements. Dwelling in the landscape is an intrinsically political act once we recognize that engagement with nonhuman agencies, such as those that make up sentient lands in Mapuche rural areas, works to reassert Indigenous land ontologies vis-à-vis understandings of land as an inert and passive object of human will commonly found among winkas.

# CHAPTER 2

# BEING FROM THE LAND
*Place, Memory, and Experience*

"A MAPUCHE ALWAYS KNOWS WHERE HE [OR SHE] COMES FROM. THAT'S what makes us Mapuche." With these words, Miguel, my main host during fieldwork, explained to me why connection with ancestral land is a central element of being Mapuche. Knowing where one comes from is a reassuring feeling, and it is also a fundamental marker of difference with winkas, non-Mapuche people, who are normally unable to trace their geographical origins. This point would also explain why winkas' behavior is unpredictable and always potentially threatening. "Whenever I meet a Mapuche for the first time, I feel immediately at ease. This is not the same with the winkas; it's hard to understand what they want at first." With these words, Miguel expressed a sentiment that I have heard numerous times during fieldwork. Clearly, one can also be suspicious of Mapuche strangers. However, representations of winkas unconditionally rotate around their detachment from a place of origin and their deceitful conduct. While difference with winkas is built around ancestral land connections, the "ancestral territory" often mentioned by my interlocutors as a key articulator of Mapuche self-determination is far from being a stable geographical construct. Paradoxically, the ancestral land to which one is connected is largely the result of colonial processes of displacement and territorial rearrangements. The uncertainties and discontinuities of ancestral land connections are further problematized by a diasporic consciousness among Mapuche people. It has been estimated that roughly 60 percent of Mapuche people now live in urban areas, perhaps the major consequence of colonial encroachment over the past 150 years.[1] As in virtually all Mapuche settlements across southern Chile, life in Comunidad Contreras is profoundly shaped by outmigration. During the day residents take care of the fields left by family members who have moved to cities, while evenings are commonly spent chatting away by cell phone with distant relatives. For them, moving to the city is a necessity as well as a chance to move forward in life (*salir adelante*). Yet it is also seen as a profound threat to family bonds and the Mapuche way of being more generally.

Connection with ancestral territories is a major rhetorical feature of identity claims in societies, where ethnic difference is constructed around the opposition between autochthonous and foreign (Escobar 2008). Although ubiquitous in contemporary processes of indigeneity, claims of identity based on ancestral land connections are often subject to questioning in constructivist critiques. As seen at the beginning of this book, such critiques are often geared toward the advancement of Indigenous rights, such as those authored by Indigenous writers themselves, who emphasize the dynamic and creative forms of indigeneity in urban areas. But constructivist theses on people-land connections can also be deployed by critics of Indigenous movements to question the saliency and historical continuity of ancestral territories demanded for restitution. Central to these critiques is the question of how ancestral land can matter when the past is so distant from the present. In this chapter, I lay out the foundational argument of this book, which will allow me to argue later against the idea of the ancestral territory as either the ad hoc result of governmental action unrelated to Indigenous experiences or a rhetorical tool in the field of identity politics. In a departure from both constructivist and essentialist characterizations of ancestral land, I intend to show that the significance of ancestral land for self-determination can be framed without resorting to avowing the ability of this land to enforce unproblematic continuity with the past. To do so, I refer to the discursive, ontological, and practical manifestations of tuwün, a notion roughly translatable as "place of origin," that is frequently evoked by Mapuche people as a quintessential element of the self. Tuwün, as a form of being from the land and in the land, acts as a potentiality of the self by articulating sameness and otherness among Mapuche from different places as well as with their canonical others, the winkas. The power of ancestral land in Mapuche society is thus neither exclusively genealogical (that is, based on the cumulative influences of past dwellers) nor entirely relational (that is, based on the mutual constitution of humans and nonhumans dwelling in the environment; Ingold 2000). This chapter will elucidate the potentiality of ancestral land through a focus on the tension between local theories of place and practical engagements with place. It will be shown that the involvement of land in the process of self-making both preexists and is produced with the very act of navigating the environment. Far from being the exclusive result of human representation, land connections unfold in substantial terms.

The following pages will present some experiences and accounts, each associated with heterogeneous landscape features, that I learned about and experienced during fieldwork. Some of these features are evidently associated with Mapuche culture (*cultura Mapuche*) by members of Indigenous settlements themselves, others with national-colonial history. Some are sentient, others insentient. In southern Chile, landscapes are predicated on loose cultural boundaries as much as on different forms and sources of power embedded in the land. My intention here is not to document the diversity of human encounters with landscape features. Rather, I am interested in showing that ancestral land connections can matter in a nonrepresentational sense and without presupposing a genealogical continuity between past and present. To do so, I focus on the ambiguous status of places of memory, such as ancient burial grounds known as *eltun*, and how they exemplify the complexities of the triadic relation linking land, ancestors, and dwellers in Indigenous southern Chile. Ultimately, landscape experiences help to situate the present between two poles of alterity—namely, the ancient ones (*los antiguos*) and winkas—thus partaking in processes of self-making. Before advancing further, let us consider the main principles of the concept of tuwün in relation to anthropological notions of place and emplacement.

## Tuwün

### A "Local" Notion of Emplacement?

Place has been a contentious topic in anthropological debates since the discipline took a reflexive turn in the 1980s, when the once-naturalized ethnographic locality became the subject of intensive scrutiny. Inspired by criticisms of the conflation of space and culture in human geography (see Cresswell 2005), anthropological research has gradually dissociated from its customary understanding of place as a self-evident spatial unit that can be ethnographically observed to reach general conclusions on the workings of entire societies (Gupta and Ferguson 1992). Such distancing, mostly associated with theoretical developments on space within anthropology in the 1990s, implied that place could be approached as a highly transformative phenomenon composed of different perspectives, voices, and power relations (Rodman 1992). Taking place as an object of study means recognizing that all places are materially and discursively constructed. Central to the anthropological understanding of place is the coexistence of external forces and dwellers' actions imbricated in the ongoing process of place making. Places are the result of multiple global processes in political economy, such as capital accumulation, colonial displacement, and governmental codification of space. Yet places also materialize as a site of spatial belonging through dwellers' perceptions and emotions (Tilley 1994; Feld and Basso 1996; Lovell 1998). This is because places are relational phenomena (a place can exist only in relation to another place) that are articulated through the consolidation and dissolution of highly unstable boundaries. Experiential and political-economic dimensions of place necessarily coexist. Let us take, for instance, Mapuche reducciones, which originated in the colonial reconfiguration of space at the turn of the twentieth century and yet are objects of emotional attachment and identification by members of Indigenous communities, who nonetheless remain critically aware of the dispossession they have suffered.

Within anthropology, attention to the experiential dimension of place originated within the broader reappraisal of phenomenology in the 1990s (Desjarlais and Throop 2011). Phenomenology has offered anthropology new conceptual tools to approach the constitution of place as a process that originates in the experiential engagement with the environment. A fundamental premise to the phenomenological study of place is that both knowledge about and signification of the surroundings unfold as acts of embodiment, a point inspired by Merleau-Ponty's (1962, 134) collapsing of corporeity and subjectivity. The body is the point of connection between persons and things and, at the same time, the entity dismantling their division. As Esposito (2015) reminds us, "Just as bodies give life to things, similarly things mold bodies" (125). Knowledge about the environment, therefore, does not originate from a consensual representation of the world. Far from being a stable object of knowledge, the environment undergoes continuous formation in the very course of human movement in it (Ingold 2000, 230). Attention has been given to how bodily activities, such as walking, establish connections with the landscape and thus imbue it with particular meanings (De Certeau 1984; Tilley 1994; Ingold and Vergunst 2008). While places are individually experienced, they are also collectively significant. Inherent to phenomenological understandings of place is the tension between collective arrangements of experiences leading to shared feelings of attachment, on the one hand, and individual engagement with the world on the other (Hirsch 1995). For Edward Casey (1996), collective and individual formations of place depend largely on bodily practices: "As places gather bodies in their midst in deeply acculturated ways, so cultures conjoin bodies in concrete circumstances of emplacement" (46). A phenomenologically inspired anthropological approach to place implies a departure from semiotic and existentialist approaches, which, regardless of their differences in scope, hold a common view on space as an empty substratum to be signified by intentional human action. Semiotic approaches to space, best exemplified by the idea of cultural landscape advanced in heritage conservation (Pérez 2012, 44), are based on the nominal premise that any locality exists as a collectively signified and thus legible space. Such approaches not only reinforce nature/culture dichotomies by configuring one's surroundings as a neutral object of signification, but also relegate individual actions to mere instances of the reproduction of spatialized symbolic orders. Existentialist approaches to place are closely linked to the idea of place making, which refers to the transformation of space into place through individual experiences (Tuan 1974). In its most solipsistic form, place making is characterized by the liberal principle that place can be carved out from space as the result of socially unconstrained action. In contrast to these two approaches, a phenomenological stance focuses on the mutual constitution of people and places, since their relation necessarily "involves the recognition and cultural elaboration of perceived properties of environments in mutually constituting ways through narrative and praxis" (Low and Lawrence-Zúñiga 2003, 15).

The embodied nature of place is strictly related to the other key premise of phenomenological approaches to space: that our apprehension of the world is necessarily emplaced (Desjarlais and Throop 2011, 90). An emphasis on emplacement as the basic condition of human knowledge entails the inversion of the traditional hierarchical ordering between space and place, whereby the latter is the result of human ability to order the former (see Casey 1997). Thus, place rather than space is the a priori access to the world. The anthropological interest in emplacement owes much to Martin Heidegger's ([1927] 1996; 2001) criticism of the Cartesian and topographic principles of spatiality that have characterized dominant Western understandings of the relation between mind and the world (Weiner 2001, 10). In Heidegger's (1996) ontology, Dasein, a notion usually translated as "being-in-the-world," is the condition of possibility of any action (Dreyfus 1991, 107). As Heidegger (2001) states, "Space is in essence that for which room has been made, that which is let into its bounds. That for which room is made is always granted and hence is joined, that is, gathered, by virtue of a location" (152). Heidegger's topological stance is founded on the disclosure of the world as the unequal and indeterminate gathering of things (Malpas 2006, 221). The meaningfulness of places rotates around their ability to bring entities together and connect them. As Casey (1996) has argued, "Places gather things in their midst—where 'things' connote various animate and inanimate entities. Places also gather experiences and histories, even languages and thoughts" (24). The ontological priority of place over space implies that the world is constituted by ongoing engagement with things that are put in meaningful relations among themselves, and not necessarily as the result of human action and intentionality. In contrast with a Cartesian comprehension of isolated objects by a self-contained subject, in Heidegger's topology the world can only be disclosed to humans through their ongoing dwelling in it, an activity through which self and world are merged (Ingold 2000, 169). As eloquently phrased by Tilley (1994), "Spaces open up by virtue of the *dwelling* of humanity or the *staying with things* that cannot be separated: the earth, the sky and the constellations, the divinities, birth and death" (13; italics in original).

Phenomenological understandings of embodiment and emplacement leave us with several questions concerning the relation between place and self in Mapuche rural areas. One in particular seems crucial to the analysis of land connections. I am referring to the question of whether people make places or places make people. I am aware that this question might at first sound highly speculative, perhaps even ludicrous. Yet by bringing to light the broader issue of human agency in the making and unfolding of the world, this question allows me to problematize the validity of liberal understandings of place making in framing the significance of Indigenous land connections. Liberal understandings of place making presuppose that place is carved out of space as the result of individual experiences of signification. This scenario, as will be shown later, finds little correspondence in Indigenous southern Chile, where theories of place and self highlight the active role of place in the making of the self. Contextualizing the notions of embodiment and emplacement in Mapuche rural areas also allows me to recognize some of the potentially universal premises behind a phenomenological approach to place dissociated from the possibility that human/land connections might operate at different ontological levels. As a matter of fact, Heidegger's and Merleau-Ponty's notions of emplacement and embodiment provide us with a language with which to question mind/body dichotomies implicit to semiotic understandings of space, whereby places are the result of symbolic and topographic representations collectively applied to inert backgrounds. They also help us to realize that, by virtue of their ability to gather things and thoughts, places are imbricated in the mutual constitution of self and the world. Yet the ontological principles behind the relation between selves and the world are far from being universal.[2]

Anthropological interest in ontological pluralism has indicated that the conditions of existence and the actions of nonhumans are uneven across human societies. This point is particularly relevant to ethnographic analyses of people/land relations in contexts where the making of selves depends on specific forces in the environment itself rather than on a generalized mutual constitution of people and place. In aboriginal Australia, for instance, landscapes are punctuated by manifestations of mythological ancestors who are consubstantial with present-day dwellers (Morphy 1993). Among the Western Apache, knowledge is associated with the power of particular places to the point that, for Basso (1988, 122), people both inhabit and are inhabited by the landscape. These cases show the inconsistencies of thinking about land connections through the classic anthropological divide between representing subject and represented objects. Most importantly, while these cases reinforce the notion of emplacement as a universal condition of human existence, they indicate how places act according to ontological principles inherent to specific lived worlds. In this sense, ancestral land connections should be treated not as a localized version of a universal theory of emplacement, but rather as an opportunity to rethink, expand, and pluralize those philosophical premises that anthropology often depends upon unreflexively. In a similar vein, I resort to the discursive and experiential manifestations of tuwün to illustrate the potentialities and limitations of phenomenological thinking about place in Indigenous southern Chile.

## Belonging and Descent

In many settings, identity centers on the tension between two forms of identity—one achieved through the performance of actions in the present and one that is given as an inherited essence from the past (see Astuti 1995, 1). The questions of who is considered Mapuche and what constitutes Mapuche-ness are particularly complex, not only in broad social contexts but also within comunidades, where residents categorize people, practices, and ideas as either Mapuche or not. Self-identification in Chile is also highly unpredictable. Decades of discrimination have led many Mapuche people to consider themselves no longer Mapuche. This trend was partially inverted in the past three decades with the emergence of a large Indigenous social movement and governmental programs of cultural revitalization designed by Mapuche activists and civil servants. The context-specific nature of self-identification in southern Chile can be explained by pointing to the existence of three related ways of being Mapuche: performative, genealogical, and topological. Individual predispositions and actions, such as fluency in Mapudungun, knowledge of ritual practices, and political engagement with the Mapuche social movement, can contribute to one's identification as very Mapuche (*bien Mapuche*) as opposed to winka-like (awinkado), an attribute associated with residents who no longer identify as Mapuche or carry out activities regarded as Mapuche. Certain practices and forms of sociability, including the ritualized exchange of greetings and gifts, tend to be categorized as part of Mapuche culture. Culture in this case should be read as a category articulating reflexive awareness of the meanings associated with being Mapuche and alterity with winkas (see Carneiro da Cunha 2009). During fieldwork, some of my behaviors, considered unusual in southern Chile, such as drinking mate so slowly that it became cold, were often objects of jokes among friends at Comunidad Contreras. While there was no doubt that I was a winka, some of my behaviors, such as my fondness for *merken*—smoked chili pepper—made me a bit Mapuche in my friends' eyes.

The performative nature of self-determination in Indigenous southern Chile coexists with the genealogical and topological dimensions of being Mapuche. These two dimensions are exemplified by the prominent place that two notions hold in the definition of the Mapuche person—küpal, a term roughly translatable as "descent," and tuwün, "place of origin." In the work of Mapuche writers (Huenchulaf, Cárdenas, and Ancalaf 2004; Millalén 2006; Quilaqueo and Quintriqueo 2010), these two notions are consistently described as pivotal elements of Mapuche identity. Küpal refers to the substantive and spiritual influence of matrilineage and patrilineage on the individual.[3] Although küpal encompasses both the patrilineal and matrilineal origins of the individual (Millalén 2006, 25), a historically consistent bias toward virilocality and the customary exogamic character of the reducción has determined that members sharing the same descent are predominantly agnates. Before the military occupation of Mapuche territory at the end of the nineteenth century, Mapuche names were composite words, merging a noun inherited along the patrilineage with another provided by the grandfather to the newly born (Foerster 2010). The introduction of surnames in the nineteenth century implied that patrilineages became recognizable through paternal surnames. Küpal is a primary means to identify and situate individuals within lineages. Genealogical roots tend to be informally discussed. People sharing the same küpal are associated with distinctive behavioral features. Less frequently, descent can be formally expressed, as in the case of customary biographical oratories such as the *pentukun*, which consists of a greeting narrative whereby one presents oneself as a bundle of relations to his or her interlocutor (Course 2011, 28).

The influence of descent falls outside individual intentionality, as it is inherited and transmitted through generations. As explained by Course (2011), küpal is "understood by the Mapuche as a 'given' component of personhood fixed, immutable, and permanent from the moment of conception" (66). The centrality of descent in Mapuche personhood reveals that consubstantiality is not a condition to be reached, as in other Indigenous societies in lowland South America, where among affines' proximity, intimate living, commensality, mutual care, and the desire to become kin create the conditions for becoming consanguine (Vilaça 2002, 352).[4] During fieldwork, I was exposed to numerous anecdotes illustrating the extent of genealogical transmission. One evening, while sitting in a friends' living room sharing a—for once—light evening meal, I heard the story of a *machi* (shaman) from a settlement near Comunidad Contreras who died in the 1970s. While she was highly esteemed among local residents, her mother suffered accusations of witchcraft. In Mapuche society, the divide between a machi and a witch (*kalku*) is fine and always the result of divergent opinions among local residents. For my interlocutors that day, the witch's malevolent power was transmitted to her daughter, who was able to transform it into a benign ability to carry out ritual and healing practices. I was also told that the younger machi's brother had become a Pentecostal pastor a few years ago. When I had this conversation, he was still performing laying-on-of-hands rituals with churchgoers afflicted by diseases. These three biographies highlighted the potential of küpal to transmit physical and behavioral predispositions genealogically. Yet personal practices and choices also contributed to the transformation of potentially dangerous shamanic powers into healing abilities. A similar argument can be made about tuwün, whose influence on human behavior and practice should be understood in potential rather than deterministic terms. I will explore this point in greater detail later in this chapter. For now, let us examine some of the conceptual and practical principles behind the notion of tuwün.

The term *tuwün* can be used both as a verb and a noun, as it can be translated as "to come from" or "place of origin." As explained by poet Elicura Chihuailaf (1999, 51), it is "the basic foundation of the family, rooted in the physical space where people were born, have grown up and developed." Far from simply expressing perceptions of local belonging, the notion of tuwün constitutes an essential marker of difference with winkas, understood as people without a place of origin. Nonperformative alterity with winkas is also expressed through figurative consanguinity. For instance, the expression "people of the same blood" (*gente de la misma sangre*) is commonly employed to convey ideas of commonality among Mapuche people.[5] However, more than any other element of personhood, it is the substantial (read nonmetaphorical) influence held by tuwün on the self that constitutes otherness with winka. The very etymology of the words *Mapuche* and *winka* gives us some initial hints on the centrality of land connections in Mapuche constructions of alterity. One of the earliest references to the ethnonym *Mapuche* dates back to 1775, when the Franciscan missionary Ramón Redrado noted the use of this term among Indigenous individuals from different areas within the Mapuche region, *mapu* (Boccara 1999, 458–59). Mapuche eventually replaced *reche*, a term meaning authentic or real people, which is a common translation for most ethnonyms in Amerindian societies (Viveiros de Castro 1998; Gow 2001; Kohn 2013). The historical adoption of the category of Mapuche draws attention to the potential of colonization to prompt forms of self-identification based on the dialogical articulation of Natives and outsiders.[6]

Significantly, the term *Mapuche* can be used not only to indicate an ethnic group but also as a universal category of autochthony. During fieldwork, I often heard from my interlocutors about the presence of Mapuche people in countries other than Chile and Argentina. This is the case of TV news that showed images of Indigenous people in other Latin American countries. However, the people in question were not ethnic Mapuche immigrants, but rather local Indigenous groups for whom *Mapuche* served as a synonym. On a few occasions, I was asked about the presence of Mapuche people in Italy, my country of origin. Whenever I replied that there were no Mapuche people there, I was generally asked whether everybody was a gringo, the term generally employed in the Chilean countryside to refer to white settlers and foreigners. I explained that most Europeans are physically similar to gringo landowners in southern Chile, but unlike them, they are not settlers, *colonos*. Sometimes I even put forward the confusing idea that Italians are also Mapuche, as many of them would consider themselves Native. Just as Mapuche can be taken as a universal category of autochthony, so *winka* can be considered a synonym for settler and invader. The term *winka* is likely to be a conflation of *we* (new) and *inka*, a reference to the failed invasion of Mapuche territories in the fifteenth century by the Incan empire (Richards 2013, 229). As observed in other Amerindian contexts (Levi-Strauss 1995), the existences of Indigenous and white people are mutually intertwined. The dialogical nature of Mapuche and winka can be seen in mythological accounts as much as in everyday conversations revolving around inherent differences between Mapuche and winka. In my area of study, myths are rarely recounted. Generally, the corpus of recorded Mapuche folklore consists in some accounts published in Spanish versions during the first half of the twentieth century. One of these myths, recorded by Bertha Koessler-Ilg (2006, 163) as "Por qué el indio aborrece el color de los caras pálidas" (Why the Indian abhors the color of pale faces), tells of a common genesis for both Mapuche and winka. In this myth, a man and a woman came out of a cave (*tafü*) within the volcano (*pillan*) where living things originated. Eventually, the woman gave birth to children with pale skin and hair who resembled monsters, and thus the parents decided to kill them. Finally, one dark-skinned child was born and was spared. More white children would come, and they continued to kill them, as they knew that from "the white men, the cruel *huinca*, all catastrophes would have come in the vast kingdom of the real Indian" (Koessler-Ilg 2006, 48; my translation).

Winkas' malevolence is echoed in historical representations of non-Indigenous people. Winkas tend to be described as deceitful usurpers of land coming from remote regions. Highly individualistic, their behavior is also unpredictable. Their deceits (*engaños*) are commonly associated with the land grabbing that took place after the resettlement process, as settlers annexed large sections of reservation land by taking advantage of the low levels of financial and Spanish proficiency among the Mapuche. One of the main reasons winkas cannot be trusted is their lack of any connection with place and family. Since winkas hold no moral commitment to family members, they are thought to be destined to move restlessly across the land from place to place. This idea lies beneath accounts and expressions in Spanish, such as *torrantear como winka* (to wander around with little means as a winka does), that I have occasionally heard during fieldwork, especially from elderly residents of Comunidad Contreras.[7] Winkas' inability to settle down explains why interethnic marriages were extremely rare in the past. For much of the twentieth century, mestizo peasants were forced to wander around agricultural estates in search of seasonal employment, especially before the dismantlement of the debt peonage system in the 1960s. While Mapuche residents worked on estates under the same exploitative conditions, at least they could reside on their properties with family members. Arturo, a close friend of mine from Comunidad Contreras, explained that during his youth, roughly around the 1940s, marriages between Mapuche women and winka men were abhorred more than the ones between non-Mapuche women (*chiñura*) and Mapuche men. The opposition of parents to such marriage arrangements depended not only on the failure of winka peasants to pay the once-customary bride price (*mafun*) and thus prove that they could provide for their family in the future, but also on a serious concern over the itinerant way of life of the winkas. "If a daughter married with a winka, her family would break any relations with her. She was thought to be lost forever," Arturo told me. Today, winkas can be friends, relatives, and partners. Interethnic marriages are increasingly common, and a growing number of Mapuche rural residents label themselves as *champurreado*, a term used to designate individuals of mixed origins. Shortage of land and consequent outmigration is certainly a key reason for the high frequency of interethnic marriages. While interethnic relations have become more and more common in the southern Chilean countryside, certain relations with winkas remain distant and suspicious. In fact, not all winkas are the same, as some are more winka than others. This is the case of racist townspeople and powerful estate owners (*patrones de fundo*), with whom relations are limited to seasonal employment and, in less frequent cases, disputes about land ownership. Given the derogatory connotations of the term *winka*, the words *chileno* or *gringo*, especially for settlers of European descent, are sometimes used as alternative ways to refer to non-Mapuche people. The intersection between race and class structure in the southern Chilean countryside assigns gringo-looking individuals a high status while demoting Mapuche people to the most discriminated-against group. Therefore it is the case that while friendship and, to a lesser degree, kinship bonds are not forbidden across strict ethnic divides, close relations between white settlers and Mapuche people are rare.

As seen so far, tuwün acts as a central element of alterity in Mapuche society. Its significance, however, lies not only in engendering boundaries of otherness between Mapuche and winkas but also among Mapuche individuals from different places of origin. In order to answer the question of how the self is potentially determined by its tuwün, we first need to see who is likely to be subject to such influence. As for self-identification, geographic belonging in Mapuche society is context specific and multilayered. In some areas of southern Chile, Mapuche people identify with a comunidad indígena as well as with broader regional groups. This is the case of the Lafkenche (literally, "people of the sea") on the coast and the Pewenche located around the Andean range, where one can find *pewen*, the Mapudungun terms for the monkey-puzzle tree (*Araucaria araucana*; Le Bonniec 2002). Regional differentiations are generally deictic (e.g., people of the north, "Pikunche") and are thus characterized by shifting boundaries. In the past three decades, regional differentiations have acquired public visibility through the activities of grassroots organizations. However, it is the comunidad indígena that expresses more commonly ideas about geographic belonging, as in my area of study where residents tend to identify as Mapuche without ascribing to a regional affiliation. As I will show in part 2 of this book, land claims express first and foremost loyalty toward one's Indigenous community, which is nonetheless compatible with narratives of pan-Mapuche identity and demands for autonomy (see Caniuqueo 2011).

The malleability of geographic belonging is largely given by the porosity of tuwün as a social group. The question of who is associated and who is not with a particular tuwün is by no means evident. Group formation is an extensively discussed issue in the anthropological literature on Mapuche society (Course 2011; Faron 1961; Stuchlik 1976). Attention has been paid primarily to the composition of two groups, lof and *rewe*, built around kinship networks and ritual practices, and their relations with the colonial institutions of the reducción. Lof are kinship units that are formed for special occasions, such as funerals. The term *rewe* corresponds to both a sacred site and a congregation gathered for the celebration of ngillatun rituals, a point I discuss in greater detail in chapter 6. Lof and rewe do not necessarily correspond. The same can be said about comunidades indígenas, administrative units that formally replaced the reducción in the 1990s and whose membership is based primarily on residence. Identification with a tuwün implies belonging to one of the patrilineages associated with a comunidad, and is usually recognized through paternal surnames. Therefore, a comunidad can encompass more than one lof or vice versa. In my area of study, given the relative separation between Mapuche settlements often several kilometers away from each other, the comunidad, lof, and rewe tend to match up to the point that any collective ritual is defined as community activity even when not all residents participate in it. With the exception of those few Mapuche individuals who have bought land and moved to a comunidad indígena with no genealogical ties, all the residents of a reducción share the same place of origin. Accordingly, identification with tuwün involves all those individuals who belong to one of the patrilineages rooted within the reducción.

The patrilineal bias of tuwün can be explained by pointing to the once strictly enforced virilocality. Virilocal residential arrangements, however, have decreased steadily as a consequence of the legal introduction of cognatic inheritance in the second half of the twentieth century and land shortage. Married couples are thus offered the choice of moving to a property owned by the wife's family, a phenomenon that during fieldwork was translated to me as *aneucon* (literally, "to follow one's wife"). While uxorilocality bears a negative social connotation, it has led to the historical appearance of new patrilineages, whose membership to the tuwün is not questioned. Similarly, patrilineages that have appeared as a consequence of displacement in the aftermath of the Araucanian invasion by the Chilean army in the nineteenth century are unconditionally regarded as part of the place of origin. In Comunidad Contreras, there are several patrilineages. Some of them correspond to the surnames that first appeared in the Título de Merced, the official document that established the foundation of any reducción. Others were originally from different areas and were allowed to settle in this reducción by the ruling cacique at Contreras at the end of the nineteenth century.[8] These patrilineages adopted the cacique's surname to justify their presence to the Chilean authorities. Yet sharing a surname does not mean that local residents do not recognize different patrilineages, and in most cases they employ different epithets to patrilineages associated with the same surname. In Comunidad Contreras, for instance, one lineage is known as Contreras gringo, since according to local accounts one of the oldest traceable antecessors was a child adopted from a poor non-Indigenous family, a common practice during the first half of the twentieth century in my area of study. Patrilineages established through uxorilocality are also considered part of the same tuwün. In Comunidad Contreras, at least two patrilineages associated with Spanish surnames appeared as a consequence of non-Indigenous men marrying women from the settlement decades earlier.

The porosity of tuwün as a social group stems largely from the fact that geographic belonging not only is structured around descent principles but also is processual. For instance, as I show in part 2, residents who have recently moved to an Indigenous community might be regarded as legitimately entitled to land assignation in the event of a successful land claim only if they have been particularly involved in community activities. In comparative terms, the descent-based and processual nature of tuwün situates geographic belonging among the Mapuche in a middle ground between that of Andean societies—where stricter principles of patrilineal descent are at work in structuring group conformation, as in the case of *ayllu*, or "rural communities" (Harris 2000, 170)—and Amazonian groups, where the ready availability of communal land and flexibility in the articulation of consanguinity and affinity (Viveiros de Castro 2001; Vilaça 2002) make possible the constant inclusion of outsiders (Gow 1991, 55). Significantly, the coexistence of performative and genealogical principles in Mapuche notions of selfhood and place is strictly related to my definition of tuwün as a potentiality of the self.

## Selfhood and Potentiality

In introducing the notion of tuwün, I have proposed that it concerns the physical and behavioral predispositions shared by a group of people residentially and genealogically linked to a particular place. During my stay in southern Chile, I heard numerous anecdotes about behavioral traits shared among members of the same comunidad. For instance, all members of an entire reducción are thought to be more inclined to a specific habit, such as excessive or limited wine drinking. The attribution of shared traits for the members of the same tuwün rests on the particular ecological condition of this geographical space. Topographic features, such as the presence of hills and proximity to the sea, are reflected in shared abilities concerning agricultural production. On one occasion, my host Miguel criticized a recent project of the Chilean government supporting agricultural microenterprises: "The state treats all the Mapuche people as the same, but we are very different. Those at the coast have little to do with us who live off farming."

Congruent with the centrality of küpal in Mapuche personhood, the influence of tuwün is mediated by descent. Each individual is affected by his or her tuwün in two ways: through the direct influence of the physical surroundings, and through the cumulative transmission of the influence of past dwellers of the area (Pichinao, Huenchulaf, and Mellico 2003, 609). This is the reason that a place of origin continues to hold an influence over those community members who have migrated to urban areas. This explains why tuwün is better translated as place of origin rather than birth. The influence of tuwün, however, is not simply transmitted genealogically within patrilineages sharing the same place of origin. Physical surroundings play an active role in shaping commonalities among dwellers from the same place of origin. The premise of this idea is that the landscape is populated by forces that exist outside of human control, usually known as newen, also referred to as *fuerza* in Spanish. Newen consists of a "volitional multiplicity of forces inherent within and constitutive of the world" (Course 2012, 10). Invisible to the human eye, newen can only be placed temporarily under human control through exchanges in ritual contexts. This force is irregularly distributed in the landscape, and some places are thought to be more powerful than others. Water sources and forests in particular are likely locations for a concentration of newen. This topological principle indicates that places of origin are inherently different, as the forces that constitute them are irreducible to a singular cause or explanation. This point can be elucidated by looking at ideas about knowledge transmission and acquisition exemplified by the notion of *kimün*. This term refers to the understanding of cosmological relations among humans and nonhumans, including ngen spirit masters. During fieldwork, I was offered working definitions of kimün as "knowledge from nature" rather than "of nature." Kimün is inherited from previous generations, the "ancient ones," as well as acquired through the direct observation of natural phenomena (Ñanculef 2003). It is also derived from forces outside the sphere of human control and intentionality. Shamanic knowledge makes a perfect case for the noncumulative nature of kimün. Machi and other healers with knowledge of herbal medicine (*lawentuchefe*) acquire their knowledge from experienced engagement with their local surroundings as much as they receive it from previous generations. Yet the power of machi is given mainly by the *machi püllü*, the specific spirit that guides a machi's actions, and the *filew*, the generic ancestral spirit of all machi (Bacigalupo 2007, 24). Neophytes become machi after a painful process associated with possession (27). Knowledge about the environment is thus not only generally emplaced but also coproduced by people and their tuwün. Specific beings and newen forces within a tuwün partake in the formation of knowledge itself, a point I explore in greater detail in the next chapter.

The active role of the physical surroundings in shaping commonalities among dwellers from the same tuwün is closely associated with the sentient nature of the landscape. In Indigenous southern Chile some topographic features, such as rivers and forests, are endowed with sentient features and are thus able to respond to human actions and interact with local dwellers. In some rural areas, hills are endowed with the potential for movement, a phenomenon closely related to the Tren Tren myth. This account is widely known throughout Chile, and it is often recounted in school textbooks and other educational sources. The myth tells of the fight between the Tren Tren hill and the malevolent snake Kai Kai that once caused the sea to rise in order to kill all humans. As the sea was rising, the entire population began to climb up toward the Tren Tren hill to find refuge. Then, this hill elevated so that humans could be saved (Faron 1964; Millalén 2006, 21). A few hills are identified as Tren Tren in the coastal area of Southern Chile. Significantly, they are associated with the most dramatic natural disaster in the recent history of southern Chile, the 1960 Valdivia earthquake. This earthquake, the strongest ever recorded, caused enormous tsunami waves, and in coastal areas many Mapuche people found refuge in hills identified as Tren Tren, where ngillatun rituals were carried out. Among sentient landscape elements, we can also find sacred rocks. Once extremely common across southern Chile (Guevara 1910, 551), today only a few rocks are considered as *ngenkura*, sacred rocks. Not only are they able to move, but they can also respond to human petitions by acting as an intermediary between humans and the divinity Chao Dios. The most famous of these rocks is Piedra Santa, which has become an important shrine visited by Mapuche people and winkas alike, who leave ex-votos (offerings in fulfillment of vows) around in the feast day of Saint Sebastian, January 20 (Schindler 2006). Finally, rivers and other sources of water are also sentient, as they can be associated with ngen spirit masters, a point I examine in greater detail in the next chapter. The existence of sentient beings in the Mapuche landscape is evidently not a consensual matter. During fieldwork, I was exposed to often contradictory opinions about the ability of topographic features to engage in intersubjective relations with humans that are pivotal to understandings of the self in Indigenous southern Chile. Some Mapuche rural people are skeptical about the sentient abilities of topographic features, while others openly label them as superstitions (*supersticiones*). Yet the possibility for sentient action among landscape features indicates that self-making in Mapuche society depends partly on a relational network involving both humans and nonhumans.

The combined influence of landscape features and transmission from past generations on knowledge and self-making in Mapuche society suggests that the power of tuwün is best understood in both relational and genealogical terms. As proposed by Ingold (2000), a relational model presupposes that "both cultural knowledge and bodily substance ... undergo continuous generation in the context of an ongoing engagement with the land and with the beings—human and non-human—that dwell therein" (133). In contrast, a genealogical model of Indigenous societies presupposes that social reproduction is ensured by undisturbed cultural transmission from past to present (134). My use of the term *genealogical* differs from Ingold's, as it suggests that types of transmission understood as substantial rather than cultural, such as those of küpal and tuwün, can coexist with relational processes of self-making, which, as seen earlier, depends on engagement with sentient elements of the landscape. The fact that the influence of tuwün is neither exclusively relational nor genealogical is reflected in the theoretical possibility of winkas being affected by sentient landscape features. As the following chapter will show, it is not ethnic identity per se that determines openness to sentient landscapes but rather an education of attention (Ingold 2001) acquired through environmental engagement as much as genealogical transmission. Yet by itself, the interaction with sentient landscape features does not lead to being subject to the influence of tuwün. Ultimately, it is the combined effect of all topographic features within one's tuwün that is transmitted to those individuals with genealogical links to a particular place of origin.

As we have seen so far, tuwün is an essential feature of self-determination in Mapuche society. However, this point should be read neither as an essentializing demarcation of Indigenous identity within rural lifestyles (Ancán 2005) nor as an indication of a lack of panethnic belonging. Clearly, it would be absurd to argue that life in the city necessarily leads to one's complete assimilation into winka society. Indeed, cultural revitalization and political activism are spearheaded by urban migrants (Briones 2007). Yet in my area of study, any rupture in the relation with one's tuwün, which is generally produced by outmigration, tends to be understood as a potential loss and threat to cultural resilience. Urban life is associated with ethnic discrimination, individualism, and insecurity, given that rural Mapuche residents are likely to attain low-paid technical jobs and live in marginal sections of the city. Friends at Comunidad Contreras often explained to me that living in the city means losing one's freedom and experiencing a general feeling of being trapped inside buildings (see Webb 2014, 233). While non-Indigenous farmers in the area express similar concerns about moving to the city, for Mapuche residents, migration toward urban areas entails a loss of the cooperative kinship networks that people can rely on in times of necessity, such as building a new house or the upcoming harvest. As I show in chapter 4, kinship and property relations are activated and shaped by work exchange and cooperation. Most importantly, migrating to the city means a potential loss of those predispositions shared by people from the same place, since any place of origin acts upon the individual both through genealogical transmission and through engagement with the environment. Ultimately, the disruption of one's link with his or her place of origin means that the influence of tuwün on future generations might vanish, thus contributing to a gradual transformation into a winka.

In order to acknowledge the centrality of tuwün in selfhood without resorting to reductionist perspectives on place and indigeneity, I propose that this notion is best understood once defined as a potentiality of selfhood rather than its determination. By potentiality, I refer to the tension between what might happen and what actually happens. In a departure from the classic dichotomization of potentiality and actuality, Giorgio Agamben (2005) sees the former not as actuality waiting to happen but rather as an indeterminate force (*dynamis*) leading to nonbeing as much as being. Following Agamben's definition of potentiality, I see tuwün not as life waiting to happen but as a force in itself with an indeterminate end. Therefore, while tuwün acts as a compelling influence on each person, the individual is not bound to actualize those predispositions associated with his or her place of origin. Let me briefly refer to an anecdote from my fieldwork to illustrate this point. Liscán, Miguel's father, once told me the story of a man living in a nearby community. At some point in his life, he decided to sell his land to a nearby estate owner and move to the town without consulting his sons, who lost their inheritance as a result of their father's decision. A few years later, the man died alone in poverty. In explaining the reason for this man's behavior, Liscán attributed it as much to the man's individual agency as to certain tendencies observed in the settlement he was originally from. Residents of this man's community, I was told, were prone to heavy drinking, tended to be right-wing voters, and were all employed by the same landowner—three factors that might make one susceptible to being tricked into selling one's land cheaply. According to numerous rumors I heard, this was precisely what happened in this man's case. Yet for Liscán, the primary author of this tragedy remained the man himself.

The active influence of ancestral land on selfhood points to marked differences between Mapuche notions of personhood and the liberal principles of self-making, according to which the self is a project consisting exclusively of individual intentions and actions (Battaglia 1995). Furthermore, by emphasizing the ability of land to directly influence selfhood, the notion of tuwün establishes an ontological inversion inherent to the notion of place making between land as object and people as subjects. As proposed by José Quidel (2016, 718), according to Mapuche thinking (*rakizuam*), all lands or spaces are living beings (*kom mapu ta mogeley* in Mapudungun), and thanks to them human life is possible. Rather than an object to which meanings are attached, land is thus a plenary and sentient entity. Yet to reduce Mapuche personhood to the influence of land and descent is to reinforce a romantic inversion of the liberal ideal of self-making and place making that is sometimes projected onto Indigenous subjectivities. Significantly, it also denies the valorization of autonomy and individualization observed, for instance, in Mapuche society (Murray et al. 2015). As shown by Course (2011), Mapuche personhood is predicated upon the individual's intentional and autonomous participation in social relations centered on exchange and reciprocity. Sociability is indeed a necessary condition for one's existence as a person (*che*), since the individual is ultimately the result of a bundle of relations that one has encountered autonomously during one's lifetime (36–43). The nondeterministic relation between land and people inherent to the notion of tuwün dissolves the object/subject division in favor of an emphasis on the mutual affect between these two entities. Phenomenological understandings of emplacement as the primary access to the world thus need to be reconsidered in those contexts, where place itself acts as a generative power. On the one hand, the signification of the landscape unfolds as an immanent and situated engagement with the world that can be paraphrased as "being in the land." On the other, tuwün presents a theory of selfhood in which the self is the result of a force transcending individual experiences and positionality—in other words, a "being from the land." This tension can be ethnographically made sense of when we explore some of the things landscapes can do and say in Indigenous southern Chile.

## Landscape Beyond "Culture": Traiguen and Comunidad Contreras

A visitor's impression of the landscape of rural southern Chile is likely to be colored by the profound inequalities between estate owners, mainly white settlers, and smallholders, mainly mestizo farmers and residents of Mapuche communities. At least this was so in my case. During my first weeks of research, I traveled frequently between the countryside around Comunidad Contreras and nearby towns, in particular Traiguen, an activity that residents of comunidades also do on a regular basis. Comunidad Contreras is located eighteen kilometers from the center of Traiguen, a toponym deriving from the Mapudungun term *trayenko* (waterfall). The Mapuche etymology that this town shares with other locations in the region should not be interpreted as recognition of Indigenous identity. A stroll around the center is enough to reveal a barely visible presence of Mapuche heritage. Wide cobblestone *avenidas* and large wooden houses with high ceilings, roofs made out of adobe bricks, and austere façades with pastel colors stand as reminders of the golden age of this town. The "granary of Chile" was the most common epithet for Traiguen, once the wealthiest agricultural center in the region. Monuments and street names celebrate icons of colonization and industrial expansion, those who transformed Traiguen from a military outpost during the Invasion of Araucania (1863–1884) into a major commercial hub in the region. Among the few reminders of Mapuche presence for the visitor is the presence

FIGURE 5  Street in Traiguen. The monument commemorates the first electric train in Chile, whose operation started in 1901. The local rail system was owned by José Bunster, one of the wealthiest entrepreneurs and landowners in the country of that time. (Photo by Cristian Urrutia Salgado)

of elderly women dressed in ceremonial clothes, usually referred to as *papay* in Mapudungun, selling agricultural produce at the local market.

The trip from Traiguen to Comunidad Contreras lasts approximately forty-five minutes by bus on a dirt road. The imposing shape of the snow-capped volcano Llaima accompanies the visitor along the entire journey. The view of vast fields, the clearest indicator of the nearby presence of an agricultural estate (fundo), is occasionally interrupted by barns and groups of small houses clustered together, which, during fieldwork, I learned to identify as Indigenous communities. Plaques are rare sights on this trip, with the exception of a few signs pointing to agricultural manufacturing plants, rural hamlets, and schools. A Swiss flag indicates the presence of an agricultural school founded by a settler at the beginning of the twentieth century. Once at Comunidad Contreras, the open grassy fields can be seen from a distance. Intricate yet orderly lines of barbed wire enclose private plots, which are used for crops or animal husbandry. Small patches of forest can be found only around the main river, the Quino, which separates the settlement from two large estates. Most homesteads are concentrated along the three unpaved roads crossing the settlements, though a few of them are connected through smaller paths. Homesteads typically encompass a wooden house with a metal roof, an orchard, a barn, and at least one animal enclosure. Indistinguishable from common houses, four evangelical temples are scattered around Comunidad Contreras. The center of the settlement is usually associated with the crossing of the two main roads, from where the two buses connecting Comunidad Contreras with nearby towns start their trip. In its proximity one can find the local school, a large one-story building painted yellow with a soccer pitch annexed to it, and a wooden building used as a community center. Five minutes' walk away lies a *ngillatuwe*, the ceremonial field where large collective rituals, ngillatun, are celebrated once a year. This ceremonial field can be recognized by the presence of a sculptured tree trunk, the rewe, surrounded by wooden shelters, or *ramadas*.

As suggested by Hirsch (1995), "There is . . . the landscape that we initially see and a landscape which is produced through local practice and which we come to recognize and understand through fieldwork and through ethnographic description and interpretation" (2). During fieldwork in southern Chile, my impressions about the local landscape were constantly confirmed, contradicted, and reframed by new encounters with sites that were meaningful to local residents in ways I did not expect. Among the many things I learned about the local landscape was that rivers and forests are valued not only pragmatically but also aesthetically among local residents, who praise their beauty and the peace around them as well as the resources they provide for domestic activities. The same holds true for a completely different component of the local landscape. Agricultural fields that are well taken care of are also subject to positive judgments. A "beautiful field" (*un campo bonito*) is one where sheaves are high and uniform, an image that reveals the hard work the landowner invested in the sowing. A beautiful field can thus be admired even when it is owned by estate owners (*dueños de fundo*), who can be described with praise or reprobation according to the political orientation of the person judging them.

Another significant lesson about the local landscape was the importance of certain sites that, albeit belonging to and administered by the state, are seen as part of the community (*de la comunidad*). The status of roads and bridges, mainly built out of wood, is a recurrent topic of conversation among local residents. Anytime a road or a bridge is repaired or constructed, residents discuss how local administrators have heard their requests or simply have begun their electoral campaigns. In contrast, neglect of countryside roads and bridges reinforces existing perceptions about being discriminated against by local administrators who disregard the conditions of farmers and Mapuche. Sites that one could associate with the colonial culture are among the localities to which Mapuche residents attach a sense of belonging and emotional connection. Cemeteries are perhaps the clearest example of these sites. In Comunidad Contreras, the local cemetery is located on a property of less than half a hectare donated by one resident in the 1950s. While its administration is officially dependent on the municipality of Traiguen, in practice the maintenance of this site depends on the Indigenous community. A resident whose property borders with the cemetery has been chosen by the community board as the person in charge of keeping records. All tasks necessary to maintaining these sites are agreed upon during board meetings and distributed among the members. Some residents consider it a Mapuche cemetery, although in most cases funerals are no longer conducted according to Mapuche norms. In Comunidad Contreras, the last *eluwün* (Mapuche mortuary ritual) adhering to customary etiquette dates back to the 1980s.[9] In the cemetery itself, Christian religious elements like crucifixes coexist with Mapuche features like the orientation of all tombstones to the east, the cardinal point to which all ritual practices are oriented. The reason that people in Comunidad Contreras see their cemetery as Mapuche thus has less to do with customary practices than with the fact that funerals and the administration of the cemetery itself help materialize kinship connections within the settlement, thus reinforcing the boundaries of community membership.

So far we have seen only a few examples of the complexities of landscape experiences and meanings in rural southern Chile. While many more examples could be

FIGURE 6  Fields within an Indigenous community. Fences are used to divide individually owned plots and prevent domestic animals from leaving pasturelands. (Photo by author)

added, taken together they highlight the limitations of thinking about landscape in culturalist terms in our case. The idea of a "Mapuche landscape," which resonates in scholarly and public debates concerning heritage conservation in Chile, originates within the global emergence of cultural landscapes in the 1980s (Pérez 2012). The political gains of the cultural landscape movement have been noteworthy in the area of heritage protection. However, in overestimating the role of specific landscape elements in indexing local customs and traditions, there is an evident risk in purifying local landscapes by excluding those sites that might be locally relevant but do not index self-evident cultural formations. Landscape experiences of Mapuche rural residents encompass encounters with sentient beings and nonsentient elements of the landscape that may not necessarily be labeled as culturally Mapuche and yet are pivotal to local understandings and senses of belonging. Significantly, certain sites that are most likely to be categorized as Mapuche do not necessarily express unproblematic continuity between past and present. This is the case with places of memory, namely those sites that are most clearly associated with the presence and influence of past dwellers. They highlight the contemporary significance of ancestral land connections inherent to the notion of tuwün without forcing us to think about Mapuche society as genealogically continuous.

## Places of Memory: Past and Present Selves in the Landscape

One of the main things landscapes can do is articulate representations of the past in dynamic ways (Bender 1993 and 2002; Ingold 2000; Stewart and Strathern 2003). The articulation of continuity and disruption with the past originates in the relation between the personal biographies and collective narratives that characterize any landscape. As proposed by Tilley (1994), "Daily passages through the landscape become biographic encounters for individuals, recalling traces of past activities and previous events and the reading of signs" (27). The mnemonic abilities of landscape are not uniformly distributed but tend to converge on particular sites, which I have previously defined as places of memory. These sites can be artificial or topographic. In many cases, they are visible only to local dwellers. The landscape across rural southern Chile is dotted with places of memory. While some act as reminders of Indigenous land occupancy, others commemorate agrarian transformation triggered by settlers. Commemoration of settler expansion materializes not only in official monumentality but also in more intimate settings, as settlers with both small and large holdings have strong emotional feelings of attachment to land. Place making among settlers typically rotates around family efforts in converting inhospitable places into home

(Dominy 2001; Di Giminiani and Fonck 2015). Far from being a mere lack of land connections, place making in this case rotates around the eventfulness of settlement as the moment through which history erupts in a previously empty space. A different understanding of history is embodied in Mapuche places of memory. Most of them correspond to place names, which generally consist in the association of a topographic feature with episodes from the past or mythological accounts (see Santos-Granero 1998). In my area of study, place names, known as *üy mapu* in Mapudungun (Catriquir and Durán 2007, 67), are typically associated with past events in which both humans and nonhumans, such as ngen spirit masters or animals, were involved. For instance, the river Tricauco—literally, "the water of *chufka*," the austral parakeet (*Enicognathus ferrugineus*)—takes its name from a tale about a bird that used to linger around this river and, by moving his head, signal to the Mapuche warriors if their path toward the Chilean military lines was clear.

Among places of memory, eltun, ancient burial grounds, are certainly the most ubiquitous.[10] These sites, once widespread throughout southern Chile, were abandoned as a consequence of the institution of community cemeteries in the second half of the twentieth century. Prior to this, burial grounds could be found virtually everywhere, according to many community members. The spatial organization of the eltun in Comunidad Contreras followed three principles. Firstly, they were built on higher ground so that they would not be flooded following heavy rain; secondly, they were located near clusters of homesteads belonging to the same lineage; and thirdly, they were oriented eastward in accordance with the spatial organization of Mapuche rituals. The high death toll from the war with the Chilean army (1861–1883) and the concomitant outbreak of epidemics (*viruela*) led to an increase in the numbers of burial grounds, while funerary rituals, known as *eluwün*, were often shortened. In Comunidad Contreras, after the institution of a community cemetery in the 1950s, names of the residents laid to rest in ancient eltun gradually became harder to identify as generations advanced. In the memories of elder residents, eltun were once characterized by the presence of wooden crucifixes, which stood alongside features more directly connected to Mapuche iconography such as the *chemamüll* (literally, "wooden people"), which are anthropomorphic wooden statues representing the deceased.[11] Now, most eltun appear as barren stretches of land around which no activities, either agricultural or religious, are carried out. Only residents living in their proximity know of their existence. Miguel once showed me an eltun located not far from his house on an estate bordering Comunidas Contreras. A few months earlier, an archaeologist from a local NGO had visited this burial ground to ascertain whether it constituted strong evidence for ancestral land occupation and should thus be mentioned in the community land claim. Miguel had known about the site since his childhood, when he and his friends used to go there to look for ceramics. For many years it stood at the side of a large barley field. During the 1960s, one of the estate supervisors (*capataz*) ordered a few workers to till the area of the eltun in order to expand the amount of land available for agriculture. For people in Comunidad Contreras, this action was seen as disrespectful to Mapuche culture.

This account is just one of many associated with ancient eltun that I heard during fieldwork. They were extremely diverse, ranging from reports of mysterious apparitions, which some residents treated with skepticism, to more mundane accounts of the lives of the people buried in them. Some residents of Comunidad Contreras recognize the possibility that ancestors buried at these sites can engage with the living in unpredictable ways. This is the reason that eltun should be treated with respect—in order to avoid vengeful retributions from the people buried therein. However, this attitude should not be read as evidence of ancestor worship, especially since in my area of study no rituals unfold around eltun. My observation does not necessarily apply to the whole region. As archaeologist Tom Dillehay (2007) has argued, a few ancient sites, such as *kuel* (manmade mounds where renowned public figures were buried), still serve as the settings for ancestor worship. While one cannot exclude the possibility for eltun to be the setting of religious practices, there are several reasons to question interpretations of the significance of these sites centered exclusively on their association with ancestor worship. Ancestor worship is associated with notions of fertility and regeneration (Bloch and Parry 1982), as in the Andean region (Orlove 1998; Harris 2000). However, this is not the case in southern Chile. Ancient burial grounds tend to be unproductive stretches of land. Francisca, a community member, once explained this point with a Spanish saying: "Where there are dead, nothing grows" (*Donde hay muertos, no crece nada*). Furthermore, mortuary rituals in Mapuche society do not seem to follow the logic of Hertz's model ([1907] 2013), according to which rituals serve to depersonalize the dead into benevolent spiritual forces. Rather, they serve to ensure the separation of the deceased from the world of the living that is necessary to reach the "upper world," *wenumapu* (Alonqueo 1979). An example of this point comes from the ritualized oratory discourse *amulpüllün* (literally, "making the spirit/soul leave"; Course 2011, 96). As argued by Course, in the *amulpüllün*, a key moment of the mortuary ritual *eluwün*, the life of the deceased is recapped in great detail before the burial in order to free him or her from existing social relations (106). This would be an exact inversion of the traditional Hertzian model of ancestor veneration.

Mapuche religiosity customarily has been interpreted according to the prominence of ancestor worship. This interpretation is largely built upon the observation that mythical ancestors, *antupainko*, act as intermediaries between humans and spirits in certain situations (Foerster 1993, 94). However, in contrast with Faron's (1964) influential definition of Mapuche religiosity as ancestor worship, in the area around Comunidad Contreras mythological ancestors are not the recipients of ritual actions and offerings. Offerings and incantations such as those performed during the propitiatory ngillatun ritual are directed toward the main deity, *ngenchen*, also referred to as Chao Dios in my area of study. This is not to say that ancestors hold no significance in Mapuche religious practices. For any ritual to be successful, it is necessary not only that all participants have complete faith in it but also that they reproduce its constituent practices in precise accordance with norms transmitted from previous generations. There is little space for improvisation, since failing to adhere to the ancient ones' teachings can limit the efficacy of petitions made by the ritual congregations. I explore this point thoroughly in part 2 of this book. For now, it is important to realize that, rather than on their ability to fulfill ritualized petitions, the importance of the "ancient ones" centers on knowledge transmission. Mapuche mortuary rituals hardly fit into the analytical category of ancestor worship, whose application in the description of rituals generally run the risk of translating heterogeneous and ambivalent relations between the living and the dead into a hierarchical model. Thus, reducing Mapuche ritual practices to the category of ancestor worship is an oversimplification of the indeterminate nature of ancestral spirits in this society (Course 2011, 102).

The role of burial grounds in rural Mapuche communities poses a direct challenge to any functional interpretation of ancient sites as symbolic reiterations of the ancestral past in the present. Their significance, I claim, lies in their ability to dynamically articulate change and continuity between present-day dwellers and their predecessors. As with other Indigenous societies in Latin America (Rappaport 1998, 155), among the Mapuche, ancestors are regarded as holders of great riches, which were eventually raided by colonialists. For example, accounts about eltun commonly emphasize the large amount of silver buried therein, the most potent signifier of wealth along with livestock. Older residents of Comunidad Contreras remember that it used to be very common for women to wear *trapelakucha*, large silver necklaces, in their daily routines. Today, silver jewelry tends to be very modest and is worn only for special occasions, such as collective rituals. Ancient sites not only inform present-day dwellers about past riches but also highlight the superstitious and illiterate nature of previous generations. In my area of study, specific locations are associated with accounts of the war with the Chilean army (1861–1883), when raids by Chilean soldiers forced Mapuche people to retreat to hideouts. In Comunidad Contreras, one cave in particular is acknowledged as the main hideout during the war and is supposedly also the burial ground of many ancestors. This cave is known by some community members as *curaruca* (literally, "house of stone"), while others simply use the general term *reni*, which indicates an area with high concentration of *colihue* (*Chusquea culeos*), a Gramineae bush similar to a bamboo. One day, Liscán took me to see this site. On that occasion my hosts explained to me that "the ancient ones" believed that the cave stretched all the way to the hills of Quicha Mahuida, roughly ten kilometers away, where they were able to seek refuge. Today, such rumors are treated with skepticism by most people in Comunidad Contreras. As Liscán reflected, "People used to believe whatever they were told because they were not educated."

Residents' experiences with places of memory reveal perceptions of relatedness between the living and their predecessors in seemingly contradictory terms. On the one hand, the ancient ones are celebrated for their wealth, knowledge, and values, such as respect (*respeto* in Spanish, *yewen* in Mapudungun) toward natural phenomena and people, which exemplify Mapuche lifestyles and are today threatened by increasing adoption of winka practices; on the other, ancestors are censured for their superstition and lack of education, which made them soft targets for winkas. As we will see in greater detail in the following chapters, the inclusion of colonial culture in Mapuche society has been characterized by a contradictory mediation between continuity and disruption with the past, since the incorporation of winka practices and lifestyles has been a historical necessity for Mapuche people to resist assimilation. By articulating ambivalent memories about the past, places of memory in and around Indigenous communities in southern Chile make visible the dilemma of having to be winka-like in order to remain Mapuche. Landscape thus situates being Mapuche as a shifting position between two poles of alterity—one temporal, the other social—corresponding to the ancient ones on the one hand, and the winkas on the other. Places of memory help members of Indigenous communities to make sense of the present by articulating continuity and necessary disruptions with the past. In doing so, they also point to a profound difference between the Mapuche and winkas. One fundamental expression of ancestral land connections is the ability of places of memory to reveal who one is. While some residents are remarkably more knowledgeable about their tuwün than others, the ability to relate one's present condition to that of those who once occupied the same area is thought of as a fundamental element of Mapuche-ness, as opposed to being like winkas, who are defined by their lack of connection with any place of origin.

Having seen the abilities of landscape experiences to frame dwellers' relationships with past generations, we can now go back to the question with which I began this chapter: How can ancestral land matter when the past is so distant from the present? At first, this question seems to be animated by an analytical interest removed from the sociopolitical concerns that directly affect Mapuche people. However, it can still be a politically effective question, as we saw in the debates on Indigenous rights in the previous chapter. Discourses and truth claims in the public arena are built around the apparent incongruence between the spatially mobile and transformative nature of indigeneity in the present and the cultural significance of the ancestral territory. Generally, in settler ideologies Indigenous status is imagined as necessarily genealogical (Povinelli 2016, 172). Critiques of ancestral land claims impose a choice between two incompatible conditions for ancestral land connections: either Indigenous people are unmistakably the same as those people who once dwelled in the ancestral land—an idea that expresses a view of non-Western time as inherently reiterative (Fabian 1983)—or they are no longer Indigenous and therefore claims based on the cultural significance of ancestral land are mere rhetorical strategies to attain resources. The two conditions belong to two interpretative frameworks, which I have previously defined as essentialist and constructivist. While essentialist interpretations of Indigenous land connections assign to Indigenous claimants the unachievable objective of complying with historical continuity, constructivist interpretations run the risk of underestimating the power of ancestral land as a motivation for political action, seeing it instead as a strategic symbol for redistributive claims.

My answer to the question of the contemporary significance of ancestral land draws upon the observation that in Mapuche society, place and landscape are actively involved in processes of self-making. The notion of tuwün, as we have seen, implies a theory of space in which selfhood is the result of relational and genealogical articulations of land connections. Selfhood is predicated not only on emplacement as the primary access to the world, a point inherent to phenomenological approaches to place, but also on genealogical connections with an unbounded locality (tuwün) that act as a given element of the person and a potentiality of the self for each Mapuche individual. Being from the land is ultimately revealed through landscape experiences (being in the land) that help dwellers make sense of the cumulative effect that the past might have on them. The significance of ancestral land in Mapuche society can thus be acknowledged without resorting to overarching notions of ancestor worship and historical continuity as necessary conditions of Indigenous identity. My argument suggests that the strength of indigeneity does not stem only from public and discursive articulations of identity but also from those emplaced experiences informing different ways of being Indigenous. As a corollary to this point, any explanation of the significance of ancestral land connections based on metaphor theory fails to acknowledge the agential and sentient character of ancestral land, which can be abstracted respectively from the theoretical principles of tuwün and landscape experiences therein. Metaphor theory disregards language use in relationship to land use in its everyday form (Povinelli 1993, 698) while framing the active role of land in self-making processes as a consensually agreed upon performative utterance. In southern Chile, land connections appear to unfold more as a meaning-making relation between two subjects than as the signification of an object by human subjects. As I argued at the very beginning of this book, land connections are best understood as an affective relation. Gilles Deleuze (1990) has provided a theory of affect according to which the terms of any relation are defined by their mutual influence. Affect is produced by the interaction between two powers, that of acting and that of suffering action. Rather than a psychological connection, affect for Deleuze is a bodily ability in which one undergoes somatic changes in the encounter with another being (Protevi 2009, 49). Lands are sentient not only because they are present in the self substantially but also because they respond to human actions. The type of land connections unfolding in Indigenous southern Chile presupposes that land and its dwellers have bodies that are continuously constituted. Therefore, dwelling on sentient land means attempting to recognize the ways in which land acts upon human life as a responsive subject.

In this chapter, I have shown some of the ideas and practices that contribute to the mutual constitution of people and land in Indigenous southern Chile—the process that mostly concerns this book. The incongruity of the ontological divide between subject and object in the explanation of land connections is further shown by the ability of landscape features to act in response to human actions. So far we have seen some of the sentient actions performed by landscape elements. The next chapter will be devoted to the uncertainties surrounding the existence of sentient beings and spiritual forces in the landscape. Uncertainties, I will claim, cannot be explained only by pointing to a decline in cultural understandings of the environment. Rather, they are best understood once contextualized within a perceived crisis in environmental relations and values that was generated by the historical adoption of invasive agricultural practices associated with settler expansion and seen as antithetic to Mapuche socio-ecological practices. Paradoxically, most Mapuche farmers I have met during fieldwork recognize these same practices as beneficial since they have helped them to endure in their agricultural practices and, consequently, to put a partial halt to migration away from their place of origin, a phenomenon identified as one of the main threats to the continuity of being Mapuche.

# CHAPTER 3

# WORKING THE LAND

*Environmental Anxieties, Care, and the Quest for Endurance*

**IT WAS A SUNNY AFTERNOON WHEN MY HOST MIGUEL AND I DECIDED** to pay a short visit to a family living nearby his house. We took a shortcut and started walking down a gentle hill. A few moments later we reached a flat terrain—an area with no houses that I had not seen before. A few cows were grazing. My attention was immediately drawn to a spot roughly five meters in diameter in the middle of this small flat area. What stood out was the lush, vivid green grass. By that time, my knowledge of the local area was good enough to realize that that the particular spot was rich in subterranean water. Then Miguel pointed to the spot and said, "This is a *menoko*. It means 'eye of the water' in Mapudungun, and there's water trapped underneath it." We reached the *menoko* and stepped onto its center. To my surprise, my feet did not start to sink as they would have on a muddy surface or a pond. Rather, as I started making small jumps, it felt as if the soil was moving sideways with a wave motion. Miguel explained to me that animals are attracted to these sources of water and often remain trapped thereby. Only a few weeks earlier a resident had to drag his cow out of this *menoko* with the help of a large ox. Miguel added that back in the day, the ancient ones treated these places with great reverence, while today one would simply avoid them in order not to get stuck in them. Soon after, we continued on our way to meet Miguel's neighbors.

This was my first encounter with a *menoko* during fieldwork. In the previous months, I had heard on numerous occasions about the life power associated with water sources, such as rivers and caves. Water sources are crucial for all farmers; as smallholders in Chile, the Mapuche also face infrastructural limitations and recurrent droughts. For many of them, water sources are populated by vital forces known as newen, and by ngen spirit masters who are endowed with sentient abilities that allow them to act upon human actions. Water sources can also cause inexplicable visions, known as *perimontun*. To me these ideas and experiences about water sources seem to corroborate one of the commonplace representations of Mapuche people in Chile: that Mapuche people are unconditionally committed to conservation since they are guided by a sense of stewardship toward nature, which contrasts with Western predatory approaches. Such an essentialist representation, however, is at odds with some basic observations of ordinary life in Mapuche farming settlements. Furthermore, accounts about life forces in the environment are not short of contradictory interpretations among the same members of Indigenous communities. While some discredit them as legends (*leyendas*), others value them as part of the Mapuche culture (*cultura Mapuche*) and thus something to be preserved for future generations. Well into fieldwork, I realized that, generally, residents of comunidades are skeptical of any claim that unquestioningly supports the existence of spirits and life forces in the landscape as well as of any categorical attempt to deny their existence.

The problem of ambivalence concerning environmental notions in Mapuche society has produced two mutually exclusive explications, which mimic the false binary associated with land connections seen earlier in this book. For many observers, the existence of life forces in the environment and ideas about sentient landscapes prove that Indigenous societies are committed to conservation thanks to historically continuous ecological values. This is the case with some environmentalist groups and NGOs in Chile, which, as elsewhere, have resorted to Indigenous symbolism as a mode of critique against capitalist conceptualizations of natural resource use (Dove 2006). The embroilment of Indigenous symbolism in environmental action has come to be known as the ecologically noble savage myth (see Nadasdy 2005), an idea that openly criticizes environmentalist tendencies to project a romanticized non-Western lifestyle as a reverse image of industrial predation of nature. Antiessentialist critiques such as the "ecological Indian" help us to avoid reducing indigeneity to adherence to customary environmental values. However, by debunking claims of diversity by Indigenous people concerning ecological relations, antiessentialist critiques can also work to delegitimize demands over natural resources that are articulated around ideas of stewardship. Since the beginning of my research of Mapuche land politics, I have met several social scientists, NGO workers, and state officers working for environmental agencies who openly questioned the validity of Indigenous valorization of environmental values. Usually, my interlocutors would point to the fact that Mapuche farmers in southern Chile are not at all different from their non-Indigenous neighbors, inasmuch as both use invasive fertilizers, hunt wild species that could prey on their livestock, and cut trees indiscriminately to the point that they constitute a threat rather than a solution to environmental sustainability. It is hard to disagree with the fact that there are blatant contradictions between practices and ideas of environmental engagement. Yet I cannot help but perceive a condescending tone in those voices that in the name of antiessentialism question the genuineness of claims by Indigenous people based on environmental concerns. In most cases, these critiques reveal an implicit understanding of Indigenous perspectives of human/environmental relations as either beliefs—that is, constructs that culturally represent a scientifically indisputable reality out there (Povinelli 2016; Viveiros de Castro 2011)—or rhetorical devices designed to attain political benefits in line with the general objective of strategic essentialism.

My hesitation toward both interpretations of Indigenous environmental values concerns mainly their either/or structure. In this chapter, I argue that it is possible to think about Indigenous contemporary experiences through the idea of sentient ecologies without abstracting them from the colonial process of assimilation, which is behind the decline of environmental values in the first place. As proposed by David Anderson (2000), sentient ecologies are characterized by the inherent principle that human actions are understood and acted upon by other sentient beings, actions that in turn shape human intentionality. In Mapuche rural areas, the principle of sentience in the network connecting different beings is not exempt from uncertainties and actions that contradict the idea of their very existence. Social and ecological historical predicaments threatening life forces in the landscape are mutually produced. On the one hand, becoming winka-like (*awinkarse*) makes one less inclined toward the recognition of sentience in natural phenomena like water; on the other, that same incorporeal vitality is threatened by deforestation and soil impoverishment caused by modes of environmental engagement associated with colonial culture. For this reason, ambivalences in environmental values and knowledge cannot be explained simply by evoking fractures and erasures in the all-too-human realms of culture and society. Rather, I claim, they are best understood as inherent features of a lived world. For Peter Gow (1991, 26) the concept of the lived world reveals an ethnographic project of elucidation of a found situation, as opposed to any preconceived ideas of what form that lived world must necessarily take. Here, I am interested in the ontological and epistemological context in which Mapuche farmers reassess and reframe environmental values in practice. Drawing on Ingold's (2000, 9) suggestion that ways of acting in the environment are also ways of perceiving it, in this chapter I look at farming, movement through the landscape, and other instances of environmental engagement to contextualize Mapuche environmental values, knowledge, and notions about sentient ecologies within existing concerns over land degradation and conservation. For the Mapuche farmers I met during fieldwork, farming implies a practical and unstable mediation between care for the land and its degradation, the former being associated with customary values and the latter with the winka world. Invasive agricultural practices, such as timber plantation expansions and use of fertilizers, have offered the

Mapuche a means to survive on their smallholdings and thus avoid migration toward urban areas. Yet these very practices, which are historically associated with settlers' expansion and colonial culture, are understood as antithetic to Mapuche environmental values, upon which self-determination is predicated. The problematic incorporation of ways of knowing and acting toward the environment associated with the winka leaves Mapuche farmers with an open dilemma: in order to be Mapuche, a category of existence that among many things implies preservation of and survival on the land, one needs to adopt winka practices and values. Let me now introduce some of the main principles of Mapuche cosmology in order to explain some of the so-called ambivalences between environmental practices and ideas.

## Ecological Relatedness and Cosmological Indeterminacy

Typically associated with historically dominant trends in Western thought such as Cartesianism, naturalism consists in belief in the self-evidence of nature as an ontological field separated from the human realm of culture of society. In naturalist models, nature shares none of the inherent traits of humanity since, as Descola (2013) reminds us, "What differentiates humans from nonhumans [in naturalism] is a reflective consciousness, subjectivity, an ability to signify, and mastery over symbols and the language by means of which we express those faculties" (173). Naturalism has never been uniformly accepted in Western thought. The great narrative of the human transcendence of nature concerns specific historical imaginations, such as those that emerged alongside the notions of production and civilization that accompanied the industrial expansion of eighteenth-century Europe (Ingold 2000, 77–88). In Western thought, naturalism has coexisted with occasional openings, contradictions, and overt criticisms, as phenomenological revisions of mind-body dualism and ecologically oriented deconstruction of human exceptionalism in the twentieth century illustrate. While the manifold character of the Western understanding of nature and culture is evident, naturalism has historically constituted the central denominator of difference between industrial and nonindustrial societies. As a matter of fact, ecological critiques of the limitations of naturalism in Western thought have been produced largely by encounters with philosophical systems emphasizing the relational nature of human and nonhuman entanglement. These encounters emerged in the historical context of colonial violence. In the ideological project of European expansion, mastery over nature has served to legitimize direct control over Native people and the imposition of colonial notions of nature on colonized groups (Argyrou 2005, 5). In the socio-evolutionary thought of the late eighteenth century, lower levels of humanity were typically assigned to nonindustrial societies whose religious notions, animism in particular, supposedly revealed an inability to draw categorical distinctions between humans and other beings (Praet 2014, 3). Later attempts to acknowledge the logical consistency of non-Western ontologies converged in a comparative study of environmental notions. Anthropology in particular has highlighted the universalistic predicament of attempts to explain environmental notions in terms of a nature/culture divide, although the very idea of nature as a field ontologically separated from the human world is absent (Strathern 1980; Descola 2013).

The notion of nature presupposes a space of separation between the nonhuman as an object of observation and the human as a subject who observes nature from an external position, a point echoed by Tim Ingold (2000), for whom "the world can exist as nature only for a being that does not belong there" (20). In semiotic and cognitive understandings of social communication, the world-out-there is formed by inert matter and objects to be signified by human cognition. Such an ontological premise makes little sense in nondualist ontologies, as in Western deconstructions of naturalism, represented by phenomenology for instance, or in non-Western societies characterized by relational ontologies. In contrast with dualist ontologies, relational ontologies are those characterized by an understanding of being that is centered on the interconnectedness of different types of entities (see Escobar 2010). In relational ontologies, beings are not differentiated according to preestablished boundaries between ontic categories. Rather, difference among singularities is context specific, as it depends on the particular relations through which these singularities are entangled. The underlying principles of relational ontologies can be found in the Mapuche understanding of nature/culture. While the term *nature* lacks any corresponding word in Mapudungun, Mapuche writers have articulated alternative translations for this term in order to highlight the pivotal difference between Mapuche relational thought and Western dualistic understandings of the nature/culture divide. Ramon Maureira and Javier Quidel (2003), for instance, have proposed the term *ixo fill mogen*, roughly translatable as "the totality of the diversity of life," to express the idea of "biodiversity." In a similar vein, Elicura Chihuailaf (2008, 10–11) has translated *fill mogen* as "nature."

The relational character of Mapuche environmental thought is reflected in ideas about knowledge accumulation and transmission. Customary knowledge, kimün, focuses on the understanding of ecological and social connections. In the previous chapter, I argued that this type of knowledge is at once experiential, relational, and genealogical; it is based on careful observations of the interactions among species and landscape features; it is also instilled by nonhumans, as in the case of *pewma* (dreams) and *perimontun* (daydreaming visions), which are usually caused by life forces in specific localities and places and can inform one about future events (Maureira and

Quidel 2003); and finally, it can be transmitted by older people (*fütakeche*) to the youth (*wekeche*) through suggestions and recommendations known as *gülam* (Millalén 2006, 25). Kimün is not uniformly distributed, as only a few individuals are acknowledged as *kimche* (literally, "wise people"), a category usually extended to older people who have acquired knowledge through experience. Ultimately, environmental knowledge is acquired as a consequence of emplaced experiences and as the influence of the physical surroundings on the individual mediated through descent. This is a reason the residents of comunidades I met during fieldwork tended to define kimün as knowledge "of nature" as well as "from nature." Kimün can be cultivated through careful observation of the affective relations established between different beings. Attention to the ability to affect and be affected by different beings originates mainly in human needs. During fieldwork I was offered several examples of the importance that any being can have for agricultural work. While traveling in an oxcart with my host Miguel, a cricket landed on one of the oxen. Miguel pointed at the cricket and told me that the legs of these insects can be ground to a paste and fed to animals that do not urinate properly to prevent more serious diseases in the future.[1] He then added that the ancient ones knew about the importance that any being could have on human practices and lamented the current decline of kimün, as veterinary drugs had almost entirely replaced customary remedies. The type of relational knowledge exemplified by past uses of crickets can be defined as paradigmatic, since in this model singularities are described and analyzed according to the relations that connect them rather than according to a logic of predicates preexisting each singularity as in taxonomic classifications (Descola 1996, 92).[2]

In the model of Mapuche environmental knowledge sketched so far, affect constitutes a central mode of relation between different beings. However, capacity for affective action does not encompass the entire universe of beings, since some beings are recognized as having more sentience than others. This is the case of key species, such as domestic animals, a point that I will explain in ethnographic detail later in this chapter. The same holds true for nonhuman entities inhabiting the local landscape, like the ngen spirit masters introduced in the previous chapter. Ngen, a term also referring to the verb "to own," are singular entities controlling a specific landscape feature, such as a tree or a river. While animals can be sentient without the necessary presence of a correspondent ngen, topographic features are sentient only inasmuch as they are controlled by a particular spirit master. Spirit masters are also the hypostasis of general categories and elements, such as water or wind. As for newen forces, ngen are not uniformly distributed across the landscape. It is not only certain areas that are known for the presence of numerous ngen, but also certain elements that are more likely to be associated with ngen in comparison with others, as in the case of water (*ko*). The behavior of ngen spirit masters is highly unpredictable, and they can act mischievously against humans. This is why humans are supposed to show respectful conduct toward ngen, such as not lighting campfires in forests thought to be populated by spirit masters. Spirit masters can be found in numerous Amerindian groups, especially in lowland South America (see Fausto 1999; Kohn 2013; Viveiros de Castro 1998). These spirits are generally classified as nonhuman persons in animistic societies, where personhood is extended to all nonhumans with social attributes, such as having a hierarchy of positions and kinship practices (Descola 1996, 86). The term *animism* is not short of controversial interpretations (see Bird-David 1999; Brightman, Grotti, and Ulturgasheva 2014; Willerslev 2007; Viveiros de Castro 2004). My intention here is not to delineate a comprehensive scenario for this phenomenon but rather to contextualize Mapuche notions of nonhuman agency and highlight the ways they reflect and contradict the general principles of animism. For Descola (2013), animism does not refer to a religious orientation but rather to an ontological configuration in which "difference in physicalities [serve] to introduce discontinuity into a universe peopled by persons with such disparate outward appearances yet at the same time so human in their motivations, feelings and behavior" (131). In animism, differentiation among beings depends on the possibilities inherent in the body for interentity communication. As suggested by Viveiros de Castro (1998), far from being the form of an inner essence as in Cartesian dualism, the body in animism is the site of subjectivity, since the body consists of "an assemblage of affects or ways of being that constitute a habitus" (478).[3] However, despite their potential for social action, ngen can hardly be assumed to be nonhuman persons, a category typically employed as an intrinsic indicator of animist ontologies. As argued by Course (2011), to be a person (*che*) in Mapuche society entails two necessary conditions—a human body and proper sociality—since "only when the physicality of the human body (form) exists alongside the capacity for human sociality (action) are 'real' people recognized as such" (32).

The hybrid status of ngen as neither fully a person nor an asocial being prompts us to abandon any overarching definition of Mapuche ontology and recognize the historical intersections of apparently animistic notions with principles suggesting a more rigid boundary between humans and nonhuman entities. These intersections are historical, as they depend on colonial trajectories of assimilation as well as other processes concerning change and continuity in subsistence practices. The most emblematic case of entanglement of animist and other ontological principles is that of the Mapuches' historical adoption of pastoralism and sedentary agriculture. A gradual shift from hunting-gathering to agriculture had begun before colonial contact, although it accelerated as a consequence of the introduction of new species during the Spanish crown regime and the republican period that followed it in the nineteenth century (Bengoa 2000, 23; Dillehay 2007, 82). Pastoral societies are typically characterized by notions of control and domination over animals, an explicit point of divergence with the terms of engagement found in animist societies, in particular those relying on hunting-gathering as the main mode of subsistence (Ingold 2000, 61). Pastoralism implies an ontological differentiation of entities related through hierarchies of dependence rather than the bonds of reciprocity found in hunter-gatherer societies (Descola 2013, 371). Hierarchies between humans and nonhumans in pastoralism are also evident in the objectification of animals as differentiators of wealth and status. The term *kullin* can be translated as both "money" and "livestock." Even before monetization in the twentieth century, the Mapuche were among the very few Amerindian groups in South America who used animals as objects of exchange in the once-customary payment of bridewealth (*mafün*). Another major difference between animist and dualist societies practicing agriculture is the role of transcendental divinities acting as intermediaries between humans and nonhumans. Such a hierarchical arrangement of the human, the natural, and the supernatural is also present in Mapuche society. Ngen associated with specific singularities coexist with a transcendental entity understood as an omnipotent being, the ngenchen (literally, "the owner of people"). In mythological accounts, ngen were fabricated by hand by two entities, Füta-Chachai (old man) and Ñuke-Papai (old mother, or woman; Grebe 1986, 140), which are generally considered as manifestations of ngenchen. In fact, as indicated by Martin Alonqueo (1979, 223), *ngenechen* (a variant of ngenchen) manifests itself through four divine personae: Füta Chachai, Ñuke Papai, Weche Wentru (young man), and Ülcha Domo (young woman).[4] The role of ngenchen in relation to other ngen has generated diverse interpretations. One of them has been advanced by anthropologist Louis Faron (1964, 50), who has defined ngenchen as the Supreme Being and Lord of the Mapuche for occupying a privileged position in the pantheon. Regardless of their heterogeneity, all interpretations of ngenchen point to a hierarchical relation between this particular ngen and others.

As for animism, any attempt to define Mapuche religion as polytheistic or monotheistic adds little value to our understanding of Mapuche religious thought (Course 2011, 154). We have seen that hierarchical differentiations separating transcendent beings from others coexist with animistic principles exemplified by the actions of ngen spirit masters and relations among beings unfolding immanently. The inadequacy of my discussion of transcendence and immanence in Mapuche cosmological relations should be read as a warning against the risks of trying to abstract environmental notions into a stable cosmological model. On a broad level, cosmology refers to the variable understanding of the relations between humans and nonhumans that hold the cosmos together and differentiate it internally. With its emphasis on relatedness, cosmology structures our being in the world by providing principles that "refer less to the content of cosmos than to the logic or logics of connectedness and separation that organize cosmos" (Handelman 2008, 182). In anthropology, traditional understandings of cosmology reinforced a hierarchical separation between "modern" and "primitive" knowledge by framing the latter in a discourse about the world as a self-contained and ordered whole (Abramson and Holbraad 2014, 8). The essentializing effect of cosmology consists of the imposition of cosmological knowledge as a necessary condition for an individual to be considered a member of an Indigenous group. In Chile, as elsewhere in Latin America, Indigenous knowledge has been typically mapped through a particular type of cosmological representation known as *cosmovisión* (literally, "the view of the cosmos"). First popularized by anthropologists, *cosmovisión* provides an image of the Mapuche cosmos organized along different planes of existence and populated by hierarchically distributed categories of beings (see Bacigalupo 1996). A *cosmovisión* is typically assembled from shamanic knowledge, which is ignored by many Mapuche people with no expertise in ritual, and purified through the exclusion of Western cosmological elements, especially those associated with Catholicism, which have historically been included within Mapuche religious practices. To think of human/environmental interactions through the pictorial idea of *cosmovisión* means to impose a space between the observer and the world reminiscent of naturalism. Today, cosmology is no longer thought of in terms of tradition. Modern circumstances, such as those emerging from the field of politics and economics, also have a cosmological capacity, as they are able to generate multiple imaginings of worlds and their horizons (see Abramson and Holbraad 2014). This is the case of Indigenous southern Chile, where cosmological relations illustrate the coexistence of often contradictory ontological principles. The entanglement between these principles, as seen earlier, is produced historically as a consequence of the asymmetrical encounters between colonial and colonized cultures.

A more ecologically sound approach to environmental notions implies not only a recognition of the unbounded and entangled nature of Mapuche cosmology but also a recognition of the indeterminate character of cosmological relations, which take form only through concrete experiences and the discourses that flow from them. In Indigenous southern Chile, the actions of life forces, tutelary beings, and sentient elements of the landscape are subject to uncertainties and doubts of all sorts. No cases show this point more clearly than the often divisive opinions about the actions of ngen spirits. On numerous occasions, I have discussed with friends at Comunidad Contreras the presence of ngen in certain places. Reactions from my interlocutors were mixed. Some quickly discredited any rumors about encounters with ngen by labeling them superstitions (*supersticiones*). These types of reactions came mainly from those residents, such as more fervent members of evangelical churches, who feel uncomfortable with Mapuche heritage and hope for their definitive assimilation into Chilean culture. Others treat encounters with ngen as extremely frightening moments, since the sight of a spirit master is interpreted as a premonition of a future tragedy hitting the witness directly or their loved ones. It is often the case that one person can have ambivalent opinions toward ngen, questioning their presence without discarding the possibility of their existence. One can joke and laugh about events involving ngen on one occasion and describe them with apprehension in another. These ambivalent attitudes toward spirit masters suggest to me that cosmological indeterminacy is not a phenomenon to be ascribed to the realm of a culture in which uncertainties about the world would depend on inconsistencies in its representation. Rather, I would like to suggest that doubts and uncertainties are produced by two related factors, one concerning the varying conditions of perception through which one perceives sentient beings and life forces in the landscape, and the other concerning the material conditions that allow these beings and forces to thrive.

In his critique of cognitivist interpretations of religion, Tim Ingold (2001) has suggested that experiences that are typically labeled as beliefs are part of a broader process of educating attention, through which the perceivers learn to attend to the world. Inexplicable experiences do not simply originate as a direct perception of a ready-made world. Rather, they lie "in the perception of a world that is itself continually coming into being both around and along with the perceiver him- or herself. It is because such perception is intrinsic to the process of the world's coming-into-being that it is also imaginative" (Ingold 2014, 157). Encounters with ngen are neither the exclusive result of a direct perception of a ready-made world nor the mechanical implementation of cognitive schemes. In Indigenous southern Chile, doubts about encounters with ngen and other sentient beings in the landscape can be explained by evoking the primacy of individual experiences in asserting truth claims, a point resonating with the more general valorization of personal autonomy in Mapuche society discussed in the previous chapter (see Course 2011). As suggested by González (2015, 157), the veracity of what is experienced does not depend on the context of events but rather on the way the phenomena are presented to the experiencer. In rural Mapuche areas, personal truth claims are thus not based on consensual and stable representations of the world (i.e., the idea that spirit masters do not exist) but rather on the linguistic conditions through which a personal experience is conveyed, since one can always lie about encountering a ngen. Uncertainties and doubts in the perception of life forces and sentient beings in the landscape are individually differentiated not only because abilities to articulate truth claims are different but also because proclivity toward the perception of such beings is individually formed through learning life processes (see Luhrmann 2010). I was told by my interlocutors that ngen and newen forces are more likely to be perceived by those who are less winka-like. This does not mean winka-like Mapuche or winkas themselves are unable to perceive them. However, encounters between sentient beings and winkas are less likely since an ability to perceive them is linked to lifelong processes of learning through both shared experiences and communication. During my stay in rural southern Chile, for instance, I did not encounter a ngen spirit. However, my experience is not enough to lead me to discredit their presence, as I was also unable to recognize and discern the behavior of many other beings in the landscape, such as wild and domestic animals, with the same perspicacity as my hosts and friends. The other source of uncertainty about the presence of life forces and sentient beings in the landscape refers to those processes affecting the material conditions that allow these beings and forces to thrive. Specific places, such as watercourses and forests, are thought to be powerful as they are populated by ngen spirits and newen forces. These entities are highly mobile and their presence is chronologically unstable, as their permanence depends largely on environmental conditions. Degradation, including soil depletion and deforestation, constitutes a material threat to their very existence. It is possible, then, that one would fail to perceive these forces in the environment simply because they are no longer there. Let me tackle this possibility by examining some of the anxieties about water loss and soil degradation that inform the widespread perception of a current socioecological crisis among Mapuche farmers.

## Worrying About Water and Land

The climate of southern Chile is typically oceanic, with a rainy and cold winter and, especially in areas farther away from the coast, a dry and hot summer with temperatures reaching over 30 degrees Celsius.[5] Droughts are common in the summer. During my first months of fieldwork, Comunidad Contreras was severely affected by a two-month drought. The communal well could only dispense a small amount of water to individual households for a few hours a day.[6] Grass was short and showed buff tones. Smaller watercourses and mires were so dry that cows and oxen had to be taken to the nearby Quino River to drink. Residents were worried about the status of their animals, evidently too thin to be any good for sale. Anxieties generated by summer droughts are common among small and large landholders alike. However, their consequences are far more drastic for the former, whose land properties generally lack irrigation systems and other technologies designed to help them cope better with water scarcity. Mapuche and non-Indigenous smallholders are also concerned about the increasing demand for water by agribusiness companies, mostly located near their own fields. The Chilean juridical framework regulating water use, the Water Code of 1981 in particular, is shaped by laissez-faire principles permitting the acquisition of water rights with little state interference (Prieto and Bauer 2012). It is often the case that Mapuche farmers are unable to divert water through canals, not only because of the economic unfeasibility of such infrastructural effort but also because water rights (*derechos de agua*) on sections of a river located in the surrounding areas of a *comunidad* are likely to have been previously acquired by a nearby estate owner.

That water levels and soil fertility are decreasing is common knowledge among the Mapuche farmers I met during fieldwork. Our conversations tended to include accounts juxtaposing the remarkable fertility of the land in the past with the soil poverty of today. During one such dialogue, my host Liscán remarked this difference: "Back in the days you would simply sow seeds and plants would grow in abundance." One could be tempted to treat this past/present divide as yet another example of nostalgic representations of the past that help the narration of present anxieties. However, water loss and soil fertility are more than mere topoi of the present. In many studies, water loss has been linked to two related historical processes: deforestation for field clearing at the turn of the twentieth century and expansion of monocrop timber plantations, which began in the 1940s. Ecological data indicates deforestation and plantation expansion are direct causes of biodiversity loss (Nahuelhual et al. 2012) and reduction in water yield (Little et al. 2009). Deforestation in southern Chile coincided with the arrival of white settlers and the institution of large agricultural estates in the late twentieth century. Clearing of native forestation by settlers was achieved through intentional fires, an activity commonly known as "cleaning the fields" (*limpiar los campos*). In southern Chile, deforestation refers primarily to the loss of the Valdivian temperate rain forest, more commonly known as native wood (*bosque nativo*), a term articulated in opposition with that of exotic plantations (*plantaciones de especies exoticas*) comprising mainly imported species of eucalyptus and pine trees. Along with deforestation, the expansion of timber plantations stood as the major change in the southern Chilean landscape. The image of barren hills covered by scattered trunks is the most dramatic example of the impact of timber plantations in this area. The spread of timber plantations in Chile dates back to the 1940s with the introduction of the earliest laws aimed at promoting the modernization of the forestry industry. Only with Augusto Pinochet's regime, however, did the forestry industry boom through the allotment of subsidies and tax incentives established in the forestry law of 1974, Decree 701 (Klubock 2014; Clapp 1995). Measures introduced by Decree 701 were capitalized upon by a handful of timber companies (*forestales*), which thrived on the export of timber from nonnative species.[7] State support, ideal environmental conditions for commercial exotic species such as the *Pinus radiata* and the *Eucalyptus globulus*, and increase in timber demand from Asia have favored the expansion of the timber industry. Legislation favoring the spread of commercial plantations is subject to criticism by both environmental and Indigenous rights organizations, which accuse *forestales* of causing soil erosion, the reduction and casualization of rural employment in comparison with other primary activities, and the expropriation of Mapuche land (see Reimán 2001). Properties owned by *forestales* remain the main target of land

FIGURE 7  Plantation of young eucalyptus trees near Traiguen. (Photo by author)

takeovers (tomas) by Mapuche activists, which are met with violent repression by police, a proof for many observers in Chile of the vast influence of timber companies in national politics.

In Mapuche rural areas, native forest loss was caused primarily by gradual timber extraction and the expansion of farming activities toward forested areas caused by land shortage. With the exception of the comunidades located in mountainous areas around the Andean range, in most settlements only small sections of native vegetation have been left. In Comunidad Contreras, patches of native woodland are found only around the steep banks of the Quino River, which are clearly of little use for crop growth. I remember vividly my first experience of walking toward the native forest around this river from the flat agricultural fields that comprise most of Comunidad Contreras. Walking around these two types of terrain produces two completely different sensory experiences. Upon entering a native forest during the dry summer months, temperatures drop quickly and humidity can immediately be felt on the skin. One also needs to adjust the sight to the intricacies of the vegetation. In contrast with the wide horizon of the rest of the countryside, visibility is restricted here. Sounds also change. Birds flock to the native forests, making it an almost impossible task to recognize exactly where the uninterrupted twittering comes from. One's sense of smell also becomes activated. Different flowers and plants, such as ferns, populate the undergrowth, so that scents intermingle and potentiate each other. These sensory experiences are best made sense of in contrast to the perceptions unfolding in other ecological niches in the southern Chilean countryside, agricultural fields and timber plantations in particular. The sensory contrast between these two emplaced experiences is reflected in descriptions of landscape by Mapuche farmers highlighting the presence of life forces and, more broadly, nonhuman vitality in native forests. Representations of *mawida*, a Mapudungun term referring to both forest and mountains, insist on the presence of different forms of life forces, mainly associated with newen, and specific entities such as ngen spirit masters. Given the concentration of spirit masters, native forests are the places that most need to be approached with attitudes of respect (*respeto* in Spanish, *yewen* in Mapudungun). This mode of relation encompasses avoiding campfires, unnecessary felling of trees, and loud screams. Ngen can be upset by these attitudes and react mischievously against humans. In some rural areas of southern Chile, especially around the Andean range, some hills are labeled "resentful" (*celosos*) and will purposely act to disorient those humans who do not conduct themselves properly. Disorientation is usually caused by the sudden appearance of thick fog. This phenomenon, known as *kolüm*, is usually caused by a misbehaving ngen (Course 2010a, 251–52) or, less frequently, by a witch (*kalku*). "Native forests" also tend to be mentioned as essential elements of Mapuche environmental knowledge, since herbal remedies, known as *lawen*, abound there. While medicinal plants, such as the canelo tree, can be planted near the house and used to heal physical discomforts through infusions and the application of leaves on the skin, the majority of *lawen* are extracted from the native forests. Farmers also value native forests for their ability to retain underground and surface water. A field without the presence of a nearby native forest is destined to have a low yield.[8]

In line with their positive role in retaining water sources, the cosmological significance of "native forests" cannot be thought of without water. Transculturally, the idea of water tends to be associated with the regeneration and wellbeing of individuals and collectivities (Strang 2004, 83–91). This also holds true for Mapuche notions of body and healing displayed in medicinal practices and ritual actions. In rituals such as the ngillatun, water is appealed for by the congregation. For this reason, water can be splashed around attendees through the waving of canelo branches previously immersed in clay jars full of water. This element is also key in the celebration of the *wiñol tripantu* (return of the sunrise) or *wetripantu* (literally, "the new sunrise"), as commonly known in my area of study. The *wetripantu* takes place during the winter solstice between June 21 and 24, coinciding with the patron day of San Juan and the more general renewal of the agricultural cycle. It consists of a night-long festive celebration that is customarily concluded at sunrise by a bath in the cold river.[9] This act is intended as a cleansing of disease (*kutran*), a point consistent with the potential of running water (*witrunko*) in healing practices and ideas about human health. Among the causes of diseases, lack of balance and irregular movement of bodily fluids are two of the most commonly evoked by machi healers in their diagnosis. For instance, *la*

FIGURE 8  Crossing the Quino River by log bridge. (Photo by author)

*sangre que sube* (literally, "the rising blood"), usually develops after giving birth and menstruation, and causes tumors, cysts, and hematomas (Bacigalupo 2007, 30). The cosmological centrality of water is further reflected in the concentration of newen forces and ngen spirit masters around water sources. This is the case of *menoko* and *reniko*, a mire whose presence is signaled by groups of *reni* (*Chusquea culeou*), also known as *colihue*, which are bamboos native to the Valdivian temperate rain forest. Life forces and spirit masters located around the *renikos* and *menoko* produce visions known as *perimontun*, during which the experiencer can perceive the presence of a spirit master (Course 2011, 31) or of humans delivering messages about future events. The particular power of water sources explains why machi (shamans) can visit waterfalls (*trayenko*) to ask for rain and good luck (Bacigalupo 2007, 53).

The cosmological significance of water is further illustrated by the centrality that *ngenko*, the spirit master of water, holds among all spirit masters. Generally, the presence of spirit masters is variable, as some of them are rarely mentioned or simply absent in some rural settlements. In my area of study, the *ngenko* is actually the only ngen that consistently appears in accounts. Throughout fieldwork, I heard about mysterious sightings taking place in the proximity of one river in particular, the Quino. These sights generally involve a mermaid or undine (*sumpall* in Mapudungun, or *sirena* in Spanish) and the floating skin of a black bull (*kürü kullin* or *kürü toro*).[10] Encounters with these entities are very brief, and in those cases where witnesses bring friends and relatives to the scene immediately after the encounter, these creatures are nowhere to be seen. These sights are frightening, not only for the uncanny moment of the encounter itself but also, as mentioned above, because they are thought to augur future tragedies for the witness or close family members. As suggested earlier, encounters with ngen are not short of controversial interpretations by local residents, who in some cases might discredit them as superstitions. Regardless of the ambivalence of local interpretations, accounts about the *ngenko* reveal the coexisting vitality and danger of water.[11]

The vital yet dangerous nature of native forests makes a stark contrast with timber plantations, which lack all of the life energies that characterize the former. Native forests are not completely immune to human control, as exotic species, such as the grey poplar (*Populus alba*), are common therein. Yet timber plantations are the result of a type of agricultural action based on an ideal of production and instrumental to the loss of life forces, including water. Monocrop timber plantations look and feel completely different than native forests. Plantations are characterized by lines of ordered trees, usually one of two species, eucalyptus or pine. Even to the unexperienced visitor, they seem and feel dry. The absence of undergrowth and birds, and the ochre color of the soil, are clear indicators of this particular condition. The absence of water sources in and around plantations makes these places a drain on soil fertility rather than a resource that maintains and increases it. Local residents were skeptical about the presence of newen and spirit masters in these spaces whenever we discussed the differences between native forests and plantations. Among non-Indigenous and Mapuche smallholders, the extension of timber plantations varies greatly across southern Chile, since in rural areas with low agricultural productivity, farmers rely more heavily on timber commercialization. In Comunidad Contreras, plantations are located mainly on steep hills where cereal growth is unfeasible and, if in the proximity of houses, they serve primarily as windbreaks. For most households, plantations are essential sources of wood for construction and heating.[12] Plantations also serve as investments in the future. In order to maximize profits, timber from exotic species is typically sold between ten and fifteen years after planting. Therefore, it is often the case that eucalyptus and pine trees are planted by a young couple in the hope that in twenty years' time their children will be able to use this timber for building their houses. While there is a general consensus about their detrimental effects among farmers, plantations abound in Indigenous settlements thanks to government subsidies (*bonos*) financing plants, seeds, and machines used for commercial forestry, as well as the economic viability of timber as a cash crop. In the mid-1990s, smallholders were included in the subsidy scheme introduced by Decree 701, a policy that intended to incorporate small-scale farmers within the timber market. In contrast with native forests, timber extraction in plantations is highly deregulated. Although in Indigenous communities, monitoring by the National Forest Corporation (CONAF, Corporación Nacional Forestal) is infrequent, the risks of running into an expensive penalty for cutting native species without a permit are too high for farmers.

So far, we have covered how deforestation, soil erosion, and water loss are embedded in the landscape experiences and discourses that inform a widespread sense of environmental crisis. Present images and feelings about landscape experiences are contrasted with representations of the past centered on the vitality of the land. Through such contrast, embodied perceptions of environmental crises also inform the fragility of Mapuche environmental values, respect in particular, threatened as it is by the historical spread and adoption of invasive agricultural practices, exemplified by the reliance on water-intensive timber plantations by Indigenous farmers themselves. Mapuche farmers, however, have not simply turned their backs on the environmental values that they recognize as quintessential to Mapuche-ness. The balance between the desire to act respectfully toward one's surroundings on the one hand, and adopting the agricultural practices associated with the white settlers' mode of relating to the environment on the other hand—which has become necessary to survive as a household farmer and avoid outmigration—is fragile. The unstable mediation between a desired adherence to Mapuche values and a genuine interest in adopting environmental practices and technologies from the winka is not simply part of a narrative about the predicament of acculturation. This conundrum is enacted in practice in the very act of attending to the land to ensure its productivity. This is why it is worth looking at farming as a self-reflexive act imbued with moral meanings about the place of humans within a relational world.

## Farming and the Morality of Care

Most of the things I have learned about farming in southern Chile came from the experience of working side by side with my hosts at Comunidad Contreras—Liscán, Miguel, and Francisca. As for the rest of the central valley located between the coastal and Andean mountain ranges, the main agricultural activities in and around

Comunidad Contreras are cereal production and livestock, mainly cattle. The ratio of land allocated to each activity is determined largely by the minimum requirement of space for cereal production to be profitable. Therefore, families who own fewer than five hectares of arable land are unlikely to dedicate themselves to cereal production and thus would typically complement other farming activities with employment in nearby estates. Oats are mainly given to animals or sold at the local market. Wheat is stored for domestic consumption and sold to local retailers. Cows and oxen can either be sold at livestock auctions or butchered and commercialized among neighbors and acquaintances in town. This choice depends on price fluctuations in the auction market and the costs associated with the transport of the animals, for which trucks need to be hired. In rural southern Chile, among Mapuche and non-Indigenous farmers alike, women and men tend to concentrate in different types of agricultural activities. Wood chopping, for instance, tends to be treated as a male practice. One could draw a similar conclusion for work in gardens (*huerta*), an activity mostly carried out by women. However, there is no strict labor division, and supposedly gendered activities can be carried out by either men or women without them suffering disapproval from neighbors and family members. Especially in households comprising older couples whose sons and daughters have moved elsewhere, wives and husbands work together in the completion of farming activities.

For residents of Comunidad Contreras, the day starts early. One of the first things to do is feed the cattle with oats and guide them from enclosures near the household to larger fields where they can graze freely. Cattle need to be routinely examined, mainly by looking at their conduct, if one wants to ensure a well-fed and healthy herd. Similarly, property fences must constantly be inspected to repair any breaks and prevent animals from wandering away and grazing on sowed fields. Most of the daily activities are carried out according to the needs of the season. Summer is a time of intense activity. The most important event of the entire year, the harvest of oats and wheat (*cosecha*), takes place in January, the middle of the austral summer. In the preceding weeks, local residents prepare their fields for this activity or are employed as temporary workers (*temporeros*) on nearby estates for this task. Farmers' own harvests usually go by the name of *trilla*. Albeit common among both Indigenous and non-Indigenous farmers, *trilla* shares many of the features of *mingakos*, the customary Mapuche collective works event. In many rural areas, *trilla* is the only type of festive work party. Typically, a tractor driver from a nearby town will arrive in a rural settlement to offer his or her service to cereal owners. Family members who own the fields to be harvested are assisted by their neighbors with sealing, loading, and storing polypropylene bags filled with cereal grains. As a token of gratitude, a large meal is offered to both machine owners, who are also compensated with cash, and the neighbors who helped. They are also expected to reciprocate when it is the neighbors' turn to harvest, which is likely to

FIGURE 9  Cereal harvest, or trilla. (Photo by author)

take place in the same week. Activities in the winter tend to be less intense, with the exception of cereal sowing (*siembra*) at the very beginning of this season.

During my first weeks of fieldwork, I often asked friends at Comunidad Contreras whether there were discernible differences in the ways winkas and Mapuche people carry out their agricultural tasks. My question seemed odd to my Mapuche and non-Indigenous interlocutors alike. For them, there was no such thing as Mapuche or winka agriculture conceptualized as two self-contained sets of practices, notions, and technologies. The only differences that truly mattered to them were those concerning the astounding inequality gap concerning access to land, technology, and financing schemes between small landholders and estate owners. Yet in some conversations with friends at Comunidad Contreras, the differences between Mapuche and winka perspectives toward farming were emphasized. Such differences were explained to me by pointing to the significance that land connections hold for Mapuche people in contrast with winkas. Hortensia, a resident from Comunidad Contreras, once raised the point that concern over the fertility and health of land among Mapuche farmers might depend on their rootedness to specific localities: "The Mapuche have their own place, while winkas can leave their towns or fields whenever they want. We would like to live off our land, but we have to work for a patrón [the estate owner] or ask for the help of the state." The reader is by now familiar with the significance that tuwün holds for Mapuche ideas and practices of self-making. Connection to a place of origin is simultaneously emotional and structural, since property configurations and restricted purchasing power among Mapuche farmers hinder the acquisition of land outside of one's comunidad. The centrality of connection to the land in Mapuche notions of self is generally juxtaposed with the erratic nature of winkas. In my area of study, a common opinion posits that estate owners have no attachment to their land, which they see as a purely economic resource. Such a perception is generally reinforced by recent accounts of settlers who quickly sell their properties and move to swanky neighborhoods in the capital, Santiago, when offered a good price. Representations of winkas as unable to articulate emotional attachment to their land clearly underestimate the power of the sense of place in settler societies, where geographic belonging is built around a moral appraisal of the heroic act of domesticating wild spaces and converting it into agricultural land (Di Giminiani 2016; Dominy 2001). Yet by overemphasizing differences concerning attachment to the land, representations of placeless winkas serve to highlight how some inherently Mapuche notions of land connections pervade ideas about farming and environmental care.

Among Mapuche farmers, anxieties over detachment from one's tuwün ultimately converge into the question of how to ensure enduring fertility for the land, both for oneself and for future generations. The vitality of land, largely dependent on water circulation, has become feeble so that farmers need to act in ways that allow flora and fauna to thrive while being under human tutelage. My interlocutors during fieldwork typically phrased this idea with references to care (*cuidado*) toward land. The category of respect, we have seen, is understood as an ideal mode of relation with nonhumans, independent from ideas of human control over the environment. Care, in contrast, comprises a whole range of actions intended to improve both the economic benefits of farming and the well-being of the land. For people at Comunidad Contreras, the enormous difficulties associated with subsistence farming were worth it if residents were able to sustain their families and thus avoid migration to the cities. Care and preservation of one's property could provide children and grandchildren with a chance to live in the comunidad along with their kin instead of moving to the city. The premise behind the idea of care is the reciprocal nature of human/land interactions.

My host Liscán once explained this point to me with the following words: "We have to care for the land and protect it. The land will give you back only what you gave it." Giving to the land comprises a heterogeneous set of practices that materialize through both ritual actions and ordinary practices of farming. For instance, in rituals and formal meetings run by Mapuche organizations, one is expected to spill a few drops of the beverage on the ground upon receiving a drink of *muday* (corn beer) or wine, typically from a mug shared by the attendees. As I was told by friends in Comunidad Contreras, the meaning behind this gesture is to partly give back to the land goods that were initially given by the land itself. An idea of land as giver is also present in the expression *ñuke mapu*, "mother earth," a term frequently evoked in the work of Mapuche writers (Cuminao 2007, 158).[13] Ideas of reciprocity with the land are common in the Andean highlands, where the Pachamama cult presupposes the presence of a tutelary deity mediating between land and humans (Harris 2000). Although Mapuche society has historically shared some social features, such as work parties, with Andean groups, human/land reciprocity in Indigenous southern Chile cannot be explained exclusively in terms of ritual exchanges, as is the case in Andean societies farther north. As seen earlier, reciprocity in the ritual contexts is directed toward the main deity (ngenchen). Accordingly, the idea of human/land reciprocity can be more adequately approached once contextualized within a broader field of intersubjective daily relations involving the many beings with which farmers interact as part of their daily labor.

Closely related to human/land reciprocity is the idea of growth and protection of animal and plant species inherent to local explanations of farmers' ecological role. Crop rotation to minimize soil impoverishment is just one of the many ways in which a farmer can care about the land. Another way is by attending to crops and helping them to reach a healthy maturation. On one occasion, while tilling the soil around potatoes soon to be harvested, Liscán pointed at a group of potatoes that were remarkably smaller than the rest. "See, those are *papa wuncha*. It means that they are orphans, just like those children who have been neglected and grew up by themselves." Liscán explained to me that these potatoes (*papas*) were orphans (*wuncha*) because they had not been sown properly and thus were forced to grow up too close to others and compete for nutrients. He added that they were unlikely to endure through the winter. Images of farming centered on education and growth, such as the "orphan potatoes," can be found in numerous societies. As suggested by Tim Ingold (2000), "The work that people do in such activities as field clearance, fencing, planting, weeding and so on, or in tending their livestock does not literally make plants and animals, but rather establishes the environmental conditions for their growth and development" (87). Therefore farmers do not produce crops, an idea associated with the industrial cosmology, in which resources can be created *ex novo*. Rather, they direct life processes over which they do not have full control (200). Among Mapuche farmers, care for the land is thought to contribute not only to plant growth, and thus to the increase of land productivity, but also to the development of healthy crops beneficial to human well-being. While food purchased from towns is highly valued when used in gift exchanges between neighbors and friends, homegrown food (*iyael mapu*; literally, "food from the land") provides a defense from diseases and boosts the health of its consumers (Bonelli 2015).

Ideas about growth and control can be found also in relations involving domestic animals. Once again it was my mentor Liscán who taught me about the responsibility of cattle owners toward their animals. In rural southern Chile, oxen are the most important working animals, as they can transport all sort of goods by cart, as well as drag tree trunks during logging. Training an ox is a long and difficult process. Typically, young oxen are paired with older ones, who can show them how to pull a cart properly. For several months, I joined Liscán while he trained a young ox he had recently bought. At first he pointed out the mistakes of the trainee as it struggled to move in unison with its more experienced partner. In those cases he would yell at the animal and, if necessary, direct it with a light bamboo stick. As time passed, Liscán would point out the improvement of the young ox, which would soon be able to work on its own. Similarly to the description of the "orphan potato," the relationship between domesticated animals and humans is articulated along a continuum that encompasses human and animal sociality. Older oxen and cattle owners are related to younger ones in hierarchical terms, with humans in the role of owner and educator. Human/animal relations in pastoral societies are characterized by a bond of dependency, which is often "reciprocal and somewhat utilitarian, as the protection of non-humans usually ensures beneficial effects" (Descola 1996, 91). While my joint experience with cattle training unmistakably points to a hierarchical ordering between humans and nonhumans, the relation between an ox and his owner can still be defined as one of coshaping. For Donna Haraway (2008, 42), "coshaping" consists in a type of interspecies exchange unfolding in knots of mutual communication. The training of the oxen unfolds as an intersubjective relation in which, albeit from asymmetrical positions, two subjects respond to one another's actions and thus shape their subjectivities as that of the trainer and the trainee. Care, again, is the defining trait of such a relationship.

The observations I have just shared point to a subjacent idea of care. Far from being a rhetorical construction of indigeneity, the idea of care pervades the practices through which Mapuche farmers attempt at striking a balance between care and exploitation of land (*explotación*). In contrast with the practical act of caring for the land typically associated with Mapuche environmental knowledge and values, for residents of comunidades, exploitation refers to a predatory attitude toward the environment commonly associated with settlers' practices. While care and exploitation are conceptualized as two socially distinguished sets of attitudes toward the environment, Mapuche farmers' engagement with farming necessarily entails both modes of engagement. As critiques of the dichotomy between scientific and Indigenous knowledge in development studies have shown (see Agrawal 1995; Sillitoe 2007), local knowledge is neither static nor closed to external influences and their adaptations. Agriculture requires attention to both genealogically accumulated knowledge and those practices introduced by settlers in the local area.

## The Ways of the Ancient Ones, the Ways of the Winka

Notions and practices associated with "Mapuche culture" are not necessarily those that constitute daily life in comunidades. This is certainly the case of environmental values, such as respect and knowledge (kimün). Both of them are thought to be held by the ancient ones. In some cases, values and knowledge have been successfully transferred to present generations; in others, they have not. Among Mapuche farmers, it is a common opinion that the ancient ones had a much more comprehensive understanding of environmental relatedness. This idea is not at all new. At the beginning of the twentieth century, the cacique Pascual Coña ([1930] 2010) stated in his memoirs that the *kuyfi ta che* (the people of the past) "could name the stars that shine in the firmament, the birds that fly in the sky, the animals that go around the earth and the different types of insects, even the fishes that swim in the rivers and the sea" (94). While the question of why the ancient ones' knowledge has weakened is complex, the colonial process of forced assimilation into Chilean national society is certainly a paramount cause for such a decline. The ancient ones, I have heard numerous times, were protective of their own knowledge to the point that they occasionally refused to pass on linguistic, symbolic, and practical elements of Mapuche society to younger generations. As I will show in the next chapter, parents were compelled to teach their sons and daughters to act as chilenos and chilenas as a means of self-defense against discrimination and other types of abuse in schools and the workplace, mostly due to widespread illiteracy among rural smallholders in the past.

There is another reason that customary environmental knowledge may have declined. Local residents might treasure practices informed by the value of respect, but they are also aware that, given the land shortage, they may not be able to make ends meet if they apply these practices. The institution of the reservation system forced Mapuche residents to abandon flexible strategies of land use characterized by usufructuary rights over large tracts of land and adopt more invasive approaches to farming and livestock in restricted spaces. Deforestation, we have seen, came as more and more tracts of the reducción were converted into agricultural land and cultivated intensively. Today soil depletion is a direct consequence of overexploitation of land. In explaining some of the main changes between the past and the present in Indigenous settlements, friends in Comunidad Contreras provided concrete examples of how the ancient ones showed respect to both humans and nonhumans. One frequently mentioned example was the ritualized permission directed to the corresponding ngen before chopping down a tree. This permission is generally sought to avoid negative repercussions from the associated ngen. Liscán, when making this point, drew a comparison between past and present generations: "People back in the days used to ask permission before cutting trees. Now, they see a forest and just want to cut it down." Today, in my area of study at least, ritualized requests for permission to cut down a tree are extremely rare. When it is done, it is performed at a special occasion during which one can extract leaves and branches to be used for ritual or healing practices.

Along with other images, the picture of respectful ancestors using ritual to ask spirit beings for logging permission reinforces the past/present divide of environmental attitudes examined throughout this chapter. The ancient ones might be praised for their environmental values, but they are simultaneously criticized for their inability to cope with the land shortage, as present residents do. In this sense, respect toward land is an idealistic goal that belongs to a past where resources were abundant. As explained by Francisca, the mentality of the ancient ones was characterized by a lack of interest in saving and accumulating goods for the future benefit of younger generations: "Ancient Mapuche were not accustomed to think about their future, they were living for the day. Nobody was thinking about saving crops for winter." Francisca went on to describe harvests in the first decades of the nineteenth century. At one time Juan Contreras, one of her ancestors and the wealthiest community member during his lifetime, used to strike numerous half-share agreements with other local residents, as he was the only one owning machinery: "A few days after the harvest, many residents who were working for him during the harvest used to come to his house and ask for more bags of wheat. In the meantime, they had sold all the cereals assigned to them and used it all [the money] for the celebrations that followed the harvest." In describing this scene, Francisca remarked that this mentality was the reason their ancestors had been unable to adapt to the spiraling effects of land shortage. Generations of Mapuche residents had to learn to invest their energy and economic resources extremely carefully as a result of the economic restraints imposed by the land shortage. In the past forty years, the detrimental effects of land shortages have been augmented by a dramatic decrease in competitiveness among smallholders.

In the struggle for survival in household farming, then, respect appears more of an ideal value than a guiding principle for agricultural activities. For people at Comunidad Contreras, success in farming depends on factors other than customary values. A successful farmer would typically be described as someone with planning skills, an eye for detail, and perseverance in the face of constant threats to crops and animals, such as diseases and wildfires. These skills apply equally among Mapuche and non-Indigenous landowners. Successful farmers are generally those who are able to sustain their families without having to rely on year-round employment on nearby estates. Their efforts are rewarded with approval by some of their neighbors and family members but also with envy (*envidia*) from others. In rural southern Chile, envy is a common theme in conversations among both Mapuche and chilenos, who often identify this feeling as the main cause of conflict among neighbors. Conversely, local residents who leave their fields unattended or even barren (*pelados*) are often criticized for being lazy or simply for complying with the need to work for nearby estate owners, patrones. But despite their growing irrelevance in ensuring a successful enterprise in independent farming, it clearly would be a mistake to treat customary knowledge and values as mere elements of tradition. As seen earlier, they are linked to ideas about land fertility and its well-being. Farming in Mapuche rural areas entails an ongoing mediation between the values and knowledge associated with the ancient ones and the more invasive practices of the winkas. This circumstance was eloquently explained to me by Liscán, while discussing how risks are taken in agricultural production: "On the one hand, we know everything from our ancestors, but on the other, we also imitate the rich people [*los ricos*]." The "rich people" refers to the nearby estate owners, who are responsible for the introduction to the Chilean countryside of many technologies and machineries developed in industrial countries. In many cases, residents of comunidades own old machines, such as wooden threshing machines and harrows, which were sold or simply given to them by estate foremen (*capataz*). Similarly, the type of grain they choose to sow depends on fluctuations in the market, and only when a crop does well on the nearby fundo will Mapuche farmers be keen to experiment with the new types.

The "rich ones" are not the only source of inspiration in the adoption of new agricultural strategies. There are state agencies that channel fertilizers, vaccines, seeds, and machineries. INDAP (Instituto de Desarrollo Agropecuario, or the Institute for Agricultural Development) oversees most subsidies (*bonos*) to smallholders, through either general programs or ethnically designed ones. Agricultural functionaries typically travel from town offices to the countryside to offer different types of benefits to smallholders following a self-established agenda of work indicators, such as the number of farmers participating in an extension program (*cursos de capacitación*), for which they are audited on a yearly basis. Mapuche farmers I have met during fieldwork generally concur that wealthy settlers enjoy greater state benefits as they are able to attain advantageous credit schemes run by INDAP itself. This is because they have more social capital, which allows them to acquire better knowledge of the inner workings of state subsidy programs. They also have more economic capital, which gives them access to benefits and credit schemes aimed at funding larger projects requiring large initial investments. Typically, Indigenous farmers and smallholders alike are given no choice about the benefits they are endowed with by state functionaries. In most cases, they have to accept low-quality fertilizers even though they are aware of the risks they pose to the soil and crops. The allotment of agricultural benefits follows the pattern of *asistencialismo*, a notion that I have described in chapter 1 as a welfare strategy based on dependency by citizens defined as vulnerable. For friends at Comunidad Contreras, the state is ultimately responsible for offering environmentally unfriendly solutions for their farming strategies, which they nonetheless need. Relations with agricultural agencies reinforce a perception of the state as a ubiquitous yet unempathetic presence in the life of Mapuche farmers.

The asymmetrical relation between the knowledge and values associated with the ancient ones and those drawn from the winka examined in this chapter suggests that farming cannot be reduced to either an unproblematic reproduction of customary knowledge or the eradication of Indigenous values in favor of an indiscriminate adoption of settlers' modes of agricultural work. Rather, it consists of a reflexive act through which transmitted knowledge is constantly reexamined and adapted to the stimuli and perceptions of a changing environment. In most contexts, agricultural knowledge thus appears as a set of context-specific improvisational capacities (Richards 1993). More broadly, far from being an inventory of transmitted items stored in memory and reproduced through precise replicas of past performances, knowledge in general is remembered and put to practice as a skilled response to changes and modifications in the environment (Ingold 2000, 147). Analytical attempts to systematize local knowledge into a coherent Indigenous system are destined to fail. Respect, we have seen, is a value that on a practical level is manifested through acts of care and reciprocity toward the land and at the same time constantly contradicted through actions comprehended as invasive and detrimental toward land. Care and exploitation, Mapuche and winka environmental values, become inseparable in the attempt to ensure the continuing fertility of land and the endurance of any household threatened by the prospect of its members becoming estate workers or having to migrate to the city.

I began this chapter by systematizing Mapuche environmental knowledge and values into a general cosmological model in order to identify some of the key ontological principles guiding relations between sentient and insentient beings. I then questioned the systematic nature of this model by drawing attention to the indeterminate nature of human/environmental relations in the Mapuche lived world, where spirit masters—and nonhuman sentience more broadly—are open to contestation, uncertainties, and outright denial. My explanation for the indeterminacy of the Mapuche environment is drawn from local perceptions of environmental crisis. In fact, such a crisis refers on the one hand to the perceptual conditions through which nonhuman sentience is perceived as threatened by a loss of key values such as respect, and on the other hand to the material degradation of the local environment responsible for the loss of life forces in the local landscape. Customary knowledge and values thus express an ideal mode of environmental engagement upon which self-determination is predicated. Yet in a context characterized by land shortage and decreasing soil fertility, farming only becomes sustainable when agricultural practices and techniques associated with settlers are fully adopted. Among members of comunidades, farming constitutes an unstable mediation between Mapuche and settler modes of environmental engagement. This activity articulates in practice the dilemma of wanting to protect land while simultaneously having to exploit it. Ultimately, in order to be Mapuche (a condition that implies rootedness to the place of origin) winka practices such as reliance on disruptive agricultural practices need to be adopted even though they contradict the values of the ancient ones. The paradoxical adoption of winka practices in order to ensure the continuity of being Mapuche is further explored in the next chapter, where I analyze the predicament of adopting colonial culture as a means to remain Mapuche in the historical context of land tenure and property formalization.

## CHAPTER 4

# OWNING THE LAND

*Entitlement, Assimilation, and Other Dilemmas of Property*

TO BE A LANDOWNER IS A GREAT SOURCE OF PRIDE AMONG MAPUCHE communities. Most residents identify themselves in equal terms as small farmers (*pequeños campesinos*) in contrast with settlers, who are usually referred to as the "big ones." Yet the amount of land owned by a family within a comunidad is the most important sign of its relative success in farming in comparison with neighbors. Who owns what, how properties were passed on through generations, and the current status of family disputes over inheritance rights is common knowledge. During one of my early visits to Comunidad Contreras, my host Miguel explained to me that good relations among family members and neighbors depend largely on property relations: "Here, private property is always respected." Land ownership is not only one of the most frequent topics in conversations among family members and neighbors but also a distinctive element of the local landscape. With the very few exceptions of properties that are recently transferred to Mapuche farmers through the land subsidy program or are almost inaccessible forested areas, all community land is distributed among residents through individual title deeds. More than the presence of sacred sites or places commonly taken as representative of Indigenous culture, it is the geometrical mosaic formed by barbed wire fences that indicates that one has just entered a Mapuche area. The large plantations within agricultural estates, or fundos, are in sharp contrast with the smaller properties within an Indigenous community, which rarely exceed five hectares each in the central valley.

The respect for private property demonstrated by Miguel as he introduced me to the social life of his comunidad was at odds with the mainstream images through which Mapuche society is represented in Chile. As is the case with the colonial imagination in general (Rosaldo 1989), Indigenous societies are conceptualized through images of unity, cohesion, and communitarian life. In popular stereotypes, "tribal" people are "whole human populations whose main social experience consists of undifferentiated unity of consciousness, following from their enduring intimate copresence in the same living spaces" (Stasch 2009, 1). A corollary to this misconception is that in nonstate societies, land ownership can only be collective. Representations of communalism originate in a long history of thinking about the non-Western world through reverse images of industrial society. Within colonial narratives of modernization, communalism has been presented as both an obstacle to be overcome for economic development to thrive and a nostalgic image that is longed for. The misconception of communalism in colonial representations overlooks the possibility that Indigenous societies might be internally differentiated and that intersubjective relations could be dynamically articulated by individuals with agency, rather than mere implementers of mechanical bonds of solidarity, to paraphrase Durkhemian language. It also presupposes that the introduction of property law led to an eradication of those local forms of sociality and environmental engagement that inform a sense of belonging in these societies. The pervasiveness of private property in Mapuche settlements is evident. In this regard, there is no apparent difference between Mapuche and winka farmers. Their social relations and landscape experiences are equally shaped around property relations. Yet the significance of land ownership in Indigenous communities is more than the result of colonial assimilation. Friends at Comunidad Contreras often reminded me that, unlike winkas, they own the land to which they belong. During fieldwork, I have learned that the ways land is preserved, transferred, sold, and inherited follows the established pattern of property law. However, these processes also unfold through practices shaped around apprehensions over the fragile bond between the individual and her or his tuwün, the place of origin, the connection upon which Mapuche personhood is built. Entitlement to land reasserts property theory while also reaching beyond the documentary regime to incorporate other ways of establishing and articulating land connections.

In this chapter, I examine the ways in which property theory is simultaneously fully embraced and contested by Mapuche farmers. To do so, I focus on the dilemmas of property, at once a mechanism of assimilation and a historical defense against colonial encroachment. The dual nature of property lies partly in its enablement of colonial encroachment and partly in its potential for strengthening Indigenous land connections beyond existing legal frameworks. My focus on the twofold nature of property in Mapuche engagements with land stems largely from recent anthropological attempts to problematize the notions of ownership and proprietorship (see Hann 1998; Verdery and Humphrey 2004; Strathern and Hirsch 2004; von Benda-Beckmann, von Benda-Beckmann, and Wiber 2006; Strathern 1999). Historically, anthropological research on property shifted from a descriptive task of framing and translating normative and legal codes of ownership to an examination of the institutional and cultural contexts within which such codes operate (Hann 1998, 7). Rather than a structural framework for action, property is today understood as an ideological apparatus, as a contested field of governance, and as a set of social relations. As suggested by Verdery and Humphrey (2004), the problematization of property implies a set of interrelated questions:

> How property comes to be the label under which certain kinds of phenomena are arrayed; how the concept enters into political argument, such as in native land claims cases; how the "persons" and "things" of a property relation come to be understood as persons and things; how its real world effects emerge from the ways in which property itself is constituted as real; what it entails as a native concept or category, replete with its own native "theories"; and what consequences those property theories have. (2)

An empirical approach to the relations linking persons and things of property pushes us to direct our attention to the broader context of sociality, on which property relations are partly dependent and of which they are partly constitutive. It also requires a focus on the epistemological and ontological qualities of the thing owned inherent to the particular scenarios in which land connections unfold. As posited by Hann (1998), "At any one time within each culture concepts of ownership and possession are likely to vary greatly for different categories of object" (2). Among all objects of property relations, land is clearly a special one. In many settings, land is both object and subject of belonging. The practices and discourses on property that I discuss in this chapter illustrate an unresolved tension between two historically linked modes of relating to land. In Mapuche rural areas, practices and ideas of land ownership emerge from the asymmetrical encounter between Indigenous and legal land ontologies, the former establishing a relation of mutual constitution between people and land, the latter reinforcing an object/subject divide built around an idea of ownership independent of the agential possibilities of the object owned—land, in this case. In the experiences of Mapuche rural residents, these two analytical types of land connections are inseparable, coexisting in contradiction and mutual definition.

In order to illustrate the asymmetrical and yet productive relation between Indigenous and legal land ontologies, I examine past and present Mapuche farmers' engagements with property regimes. I pay particular attention to the consequences of land formalization, mostly known as division (*hijuelación*), which lasted several decades and formally ended in the 1980s with the endowment of individual titles of property to occupants of reservation land. In modernist narratives, land formalization based on private property features frequently as a solution to underdevelopment (Li Murray

2014a, 3). Such a perspective on land formalization reveals a moral discourse on land ownership observed in many colonial contexts, whereby entitlement to land is conditional to the improvement of its productivity, a condition to be achieved only through private property (Li Murray 2014b, 590). Loosely inspired by John Locke's theory of property, discourses legitimizing the dismantlement of customary land tenure put forward an idea of land as "the passive object of human activity and ignores all forms of value that are not easily priced on the market" (Kolers 2009, 64). By reducing the value of land to labor invested in the improvement of its productivity, such an understanding of land excludes other potential values and affordances of land, such as those upon which belonging is predicated in Mapuche society.

We have seen earlier in this book how present-day critiques against Indigenous land claims reproduce modernist narratives of progress that have traditionally sustained the ideology of settler nationalism. In this chapter, I challenge the modernist celebration of land formalization by illustrating some of the negative consequences perceived by Mapuche farmers concerning labor arrangements and the restructuring of social life within Indigenous communities as a bundle of property rights. I also challenge the teleological premises of critiques of land formalization that argue that the introduction of property is an all-or-nothing effect leading to forced assimilation of Indigenous people. To do so, I show how Mapuche rural residents have used property technologies to resist colonial action while simultaneously molding them according to their concerns over land connections, sociality, and assimilation. Ultimately, the historical impact of property in Indigenous southern Chile is best understood once contextualized within the broader historical inclusion of colonial culture in Mapuche society. In this chapter, then, I continue to explore the conundrum generated by the significance of land connections in self-determination that I began in the previous chapter: in order to preserve the land connections upon which Mapucheness depends, one has to adopt elements of winka culture. I illustrate this conundrum as it is articulated by Mapuche farmers in their own reflections and anxieties about the fragile continuity between past and present, increasingly characterized by anxieties about becoming winka (*awinkarse*). The dual nature of property is perhaps the most obvious case of colonial otherness being both necessary and treacherous.

## Property Law and Tenure in the Colonization of Mapuche Land

As in the rest of the Andean region, historical sources on land ownership are mainly drawn from chronicles written by members of the Spanish army and missionaries. The leitmotif of colonial historiography in Latin America was the categorization of

Indigenous land ownership as a simple system lacking any durable norm or pattern (see Cohn 1996; Pels 1997). A partial recognition of the complexity of Mapuche land tenure came only in the nineteenth century thanks to the earliest autobiographies of Mapuche war leaders (see Coña [1930] 2010) and records of oral history (see Latcham 1924). These sources portray a scenario for land tenure characterized by simultaneity of ownership and usufructuary land use. Territorial rights by kin groups were likely to be publicly acknowledged through the presence of ceremonial grounds, as research in landscape archaeology has suggested (Dillehay 1990). Within kin groups, large tracts of land were unclaimed or held collectively as pasture land. Smaller sections were subject to ownership claims by households based on occupancy and effective use. Topographic features such as stands of trees served as geographic markers of land ownership among households (Latcham 1924, 323). Farmed land was also associated with a specific person, identified as *gen te*, a Mapudungun term that the seventeenth-century Jesuit missionary Luis de Valdivia translated as "owner" (Inostroza 2011, 108).[1] Ownership was inalienable, and although land transactions were extremely rare among Mapuche people, they were explicitly forbidden. This prohibition was directed primarily at settlers, who were buying land from Mapuche people even before the violent annexation of Indigenous land into Chilean territories in the nineteenth century. Halfway through the nineteenth century, the cacique Mañil Bueno asserted, "Our law is definitive, as it forbids any sale of land to Spanish people under death penalty notwithstanding the later restitution of this land. These same laws only allow the Mapuche to live in their properties during their life and to leave them to their descendants along the male descent line" (in Pavez 2008, 313).[2]

Land redistribution and use among members of a local unit, lof, and ownership claims were regulated under the mediation of the local leader, or lonko (Faron 1961, 51; Pinto 2003, 85). As seen in chapter 2, lonko are the headmen of the dominant lineage, whose role is attributed according to the principle of primogeniture. Lonko were likely to interfere with ownership rights only in specific cases, such as migration of lof members and open disputes. For instance, Lorenzo Kolimán, at the turn of the twentieth century, recounted that the permission of the lonko was necessary for those residents who intended to relocate elsewhere or occupy unclaimed land (in Guevara 1913, 27). Similarly, newcomers could thus settle in a new lof if they could count on the lonko's approval. The flexibility of land occupation was certainly a factor facilitating the resolution of disputes mediated by lonkos, as residents had the option of leaving their settlement to end a conflict. Dispute settlement mechanisms were part of a broader normative framework, known as *ad mapu*, which anthropologist Louis Faron (1964, 11) defined as a type of customary law sanctioned by both supernatural and human forces. Their success depended largely on the lonko's oratory skills. Customarily, a lonko's firstborn son was educated according to a strict etiquette aimed at forming them as orators (*hueipife*) and mediators (Bengoa 2000, 68). The effectiveness of a lonko's mediation depended not only on pragmatic use of language but also on those oratory skills that Pierre Clastres has identified as inherent features of Amerindian chieftainship. In Clastres's (1987) model, Amerindian internal resistance against concentration of authority implies that the chief's words expressed the collective immanent power enjoyed by a local group rather than serving as coercive messages (153). Situations needing mediation could not be resolved with coercive language.

The enactment of the reservation system at the end of the nineteenth century implied the eradication of the mediation and decision-making procedures designed to regulate land access. Through the allotment of collective land titles (Títulos de Merced), the decimated Mapuche population was confined within small plots of land known as reducciones under the authority of a cacique acting as a local delegate. The legal origins of the resettlement process (*radicación*) date back to 1866, when a few years into the invasion of Araucania, the Chilean government passed a law (Ley del 4 Diciembre 1866) declaring Mapuche land *terra nullius* and converting it into state-owned land (*terrenos fiscales*). Resettlement began as early as the end of the invasion in 1884 and lasted for over forty years, with the last reducción allotted in 1929. A special commission, Comisión Radicadora de Indígenas, was in charge of the allotment of land grants, which were assigned only to those groups of Mapuche who petitioned for land access and could prove their occupancy of a delimited area for more than five years. The numerous restrictions on land-grant petitions led to many caciques being denied property titles, and as a consequence, numerous landless Mapuche were forced to relocate to other reducciones or to seek work on the newly founded settlers' estates.

The case of Comunidad Contreras exemplifies the profound consequences for the Mapuche economy and political life brought about by the resettlement process. Reducción Contreras was founded on November 24, 1884, when the cacique Manuel Contreras was endowed with a Título de Merced categorized as 18-B in the state cadastre. Cases of reducciones represented by caciques with Spanish surnames are common in southern Chile. For local residents, the reason is that the resettlement commission assigned Spanish surnames to caciques whose names they found too difficult.[3] Títulos de Merced consist of a map indicating the extent of a reducción and a title of property providing names of households entitled to land access within the settlement. As reported in the Contreras title, sixty-three heads of households lived in this reservation, which extended for 770 hectares, corresponding to an average of 12.22 hectares per household. A few years later, displaced families were accepted in this settlement. This phenomenon was not at all rare in southern Chile, as the recruitment of newcomers was a source of status and a potential expansion of alliance networks for local caciques. Relocated residents typically adopted one of the surnames common in the settlement in order to avoid disputes over land access rights.[4] A key concern for a cacique was collective land protection. Relations with white landowners were tense, as reducciones became subject to land grabbing by settlers soon after their establishment. Land grabs were carried out mainly through transactions involving unintelligible contracts and unfair exchanges between goods and land. Expropriation could also occur through the extension of property boundaries made of excavated canals, parasitic plants known in Spanish as *maleza* or *carumba*, or barbed wire. This strategy, known as "fence running" (*corrida de cerco*), was facilitated by the illiteracy of Mapuche caciques, who were often unaware of the legal boundaries of their reducción indicated in the collective titles of property (see Richards 2013, 52). In some cases, caciques were at the forefront of a defense against land grabbing. In others, they were silent accomplices who accepted deals unfair to their settlement members in exchange for personal gain. Segundo, a man from Reducción Contreras, once described to me a typical scenario of land expropriation:

> The patrones used to know all the caciques in the area quite well. At that time there were no signed contracts, they simply agreed on things. The patrón would call the lonko and promised wine and horses in exchange for land. Later, while the Mapuche were celebrating with the wine they were given, the patrón would tell his workers to run the fence around a large space.

Land grabbing continued to be a major source of worry for residents of Mapuche settlements for the rest of the century. Another key concern was the growing number of property disputes among residents themselves. As a consequence of competition over decreasing land access, property disputes among neighbors increased dramatically. Such an increase can also be associated with the decline of the role of caciques in mediating property quarrels. This decline was caused by the introduction of legal mechanisms facilitating the recognition of individual land ownership within a reservation. This legal change meant that caciques were no longer necessary in mediating between Mapuche landowners and the state. Law 4.169 of 1927, and subsequent legislation in 1930 (Ley No. 4.802) and 1931 (Decreto ley No. 4.111), instituted a special Indians' court (Juzgado de Indios) to solve property disputes and oversee the assignation of individualized titles of property.[5] These courts, as I show in more detail later in this chapter, reviewed property disputes both among reducción members and between caciques and settlers. As a consequence of these early land formalization reforms, between 1930 and 1972, 832 of roughly 3,000 reducciones were divided into individual properties (Correa, Molina, and Yánez 2005, 61–62). Albeit not divided, the rest of the reservations were also affected by land formalization, as they were generally characterized by the co-presence of unclaimed commonage, individualized land properties, and land lacking titles of property but subject to individual ownership claims. The introduction of individual title deeds and the consequent eradication of intermediaries, such as caciques, between Mapuche people and the Chilean state enabled the governmental function of legibility, which for James Scott (1998) constitutes a basic principle of modern statecraft. In the past century, governmental agencies in general have become increasingly concerned with improving their knowledge of national populations. In order to standardize disparate sources of information, "officials took exceptionally complex, illegible, and local social practices, such as land tenure customs or naming customs and created a standard grid whereby it could be centrally recorded and monitored" (2).[6] To this day, land is a privileged object of standardization, since its economic value depends largely on inscription devices, such as surveys and tax assessment, which aim at quantifying affordances of land—namely, what land enables—for different actors (Li Murray 2014b, 590). This was also the case in southern Chile, where land formalization facilitated the incorporation of updated and increasingly precise information about Mapuche land use.

A deceleration of land division appeared plausible during the Unidad Popular (UP) government (1970–1973), when strategies of collective land use for peasants benefited by land redistribution were designed within the broader process of agrarian reform. Although ethnicity held virtually no relevance in the redistributive agenda of the UP government, in 1972 an unprecedented legal reform (Law No. 17.729) introduced mechanisms for the restitution of reservation land expropriated by non-Indigenous landowners (Correa, Molina, and Yáñez 2005, 159–200). Yet the prospects of this legislative reform never materialized. Soon after the 1973 coup, Pinochet's military dictatorship carried out a nationwide project of counterreform. As part of a broader process of natural resource privatization, land division accelerated abruptly. In 1979, Decree 2.568 prescribed the division of all reducciones through the allotment of individualized titles of property (Mallon 2005, 8). Another of its effects was the lessening of many of the existing restrictions on Indigenous land transactions, thus paving the way to a revival of Mapuche land loss at the hand of non-Indigenous speculators and estate owners. Not surprisingly, Decree 2.568 was met by an outcry from Mapuche organizations and international human rights groups. In fact, the most prominent Mapuche organization of the 1980s, Ad Mapu, was initially formed as a reaction against this law (Richards 2013, 62). Given the political repression of that time, the reaction of Mapuche organizations to the decree consisted mainly in coordination of workshops and meetings to warn reservation members against the dangers of the law to their land access. Private land ownership continues to be a defining trait of Mapuche social life in rural areas, despite the restrictions on land transactions introduced in 1993, which were designed partly as a response to Indigenous rights organizations' concern to protect Mapuche land.

Before I explore the complex impact of land division, I want to stress the significance of land formalization within national discourses of development and assimilation. As seen in chapter 1, for much of the twentieth century, the Chilean political elite saw full inclusion into Chilean society as the only viable solution for surmounting poverty in Mapuche rural areas. Indigenous land tenure was seen as an obstacle to the inclusion of Mapuche people within the projects of modernization and nation making. For most designers and supporters of land formalization policies, modernization could only occur through the replacement of nonjural forms of land ownership with private property. For much of the century, this opinion gathered consensus, with the exception of left-wing commentaries that advocated collectivization and thus shared a disapproval of Indigenous land ownership with their political adversaries. As in the case of Decree 2.568, land formalization was also justified as a measure against discrimination, a claim that presupposes that discrimination could be overcome only through assimilation.[7] Indigenous reactions against land formalization focused on the threat posed by this process on both land grabbing and Indigenous political representation through the individualization of Mapuche-state relations. While political fragmentation and land loss can be clearly associated with land formalization, perspectives on this phenomenon among Mapuche people are divisive. Significantly, divergent opinions reflect political divisions among right and left sympathizers only in part. In narrating the history of land formalization, most residents of comunidades I met during fieldwork identified its negative consequences while simultaneously welcoming it as an opportunity that provided Mapuche people with a legal defense against land grabbing by settlers. The rationale was that reservation members would be more vigilant against land grabbing if this affected their private properties. One of the early voices in favor of land formalization was Manuel Manquilef, a prolific writer and member of the parliament elected from the ranks of the center-right Liberal Democratic Party in 1926. Manquilef identified the lack of property rights as a condition of vulnerability of Mapuche people and campaigned for a land reform program aimed at privatizing reservation land. His assimilatory views were opposed by contemporary Mapuche political figures, to the point that he was expelled from the most important Indigenous organization of the early twentieth century, Sociedad Caupolicán (Crow 2013, 67–69). Manquilef's position represents a time in Mapuche political history that shares little with later Mapuche political stances. Yet his understanding of property as a potential means of preventing abuses by settlers resonates with a number of the accounts about land formalization that I have heard in my area of study.

In order to make sense of the contradictory perceptions of land formalization in Mapuche rural areas, I draw on Hann's (1998, 3) invitation to look analytically at both macro and micro levels of property relations. In my analysis, the macro level of property relations refers to power relations with winkas, settlers in particular, while daily interactions among residents of the same comunidad belong to the micro level. I am aware that such an analytical distinction oversimplifies the complexities of land transactions, as well as the numerous intersections between winkas and the Mapuche world that I have paid particular attention to throughout this book. Nonetheless, while we should remain conscious that the map is not the territory, such a division allows me to illustrate ethnographically the different limitations and possibilities offered by property technologies in framing relations that are seen as asymmetrical, such as those involving settlers and state actors, and relations that are understood as symmetrical, as with the interactions among members of Indigenous communities. Let me begin by exploring some of the ways in which land formalization impacted relations with settlers.

## Acting Like and Against Winkas: Documents and Education

Among residents of reducciones, access to documents was a major aspiration as it could provide caciques, and Mapuche farmers in general, with the means to protect themselves against settlers' abuses. Cautionary tales about the power held in documents circulate across the southern Chilean countryside. Most of these tales relate how documents, more than any other means, served to strip the ancient ones of their land, as their illiteracy made them easy prey for the winkas. Some of the accounts of land grabs that I heard were accompanied—either from the individual telling the tale or the audience—by a reference to a maxim well-known in rural southern Chile: "Like the king who will be beheaded" (*Como el rey que le van a cortar la cabeza*). This maxim is a synecdoche for a longer story about an illiterate farmer. One day, the protagonist was approached by a messenger who handed him a mysterious letter. Since the farmer could not read the message, he asked the messenger to explain what the letter was about. The messenger told the farmer that whoever received the letter was going to be proclaimed king. Joyful about the unexpected lucky turn of events, the farmer traveled to the main city to be named king. However, only on his arrival was he told the real meaning of the letter: its bearer was to be beheaded immediately. Around Comunidad Contreras, this account about the dangers hidden in contracts is well-known by Mapuche and chilenos alike. However, it is imbued with a particular significance among residents of Indigenous communities, as it is often mentioned in conversations about the history of land loss, whose consequences they suffer today.

Accounts about the past reinforce not only the inherent dangers of contracts but also the need for Mapuche farmers to master the use of documents as a strategy of self-defense against winkas. The potential of documents in the defense against colonial encroachment is closely linked to the centrality that formal schooling holds in the historical consciousness of many of the Mapuche residents I met during fieldwork. As with documents, formal schooling was a desired means of defense and political action, even though it simultaneously served as a strategy of assimilation. In Comunidad Contreras, the consolidation of formal education within the settlement was regarded by older residents as the most memorable political success before the land claim. For much of the twentieth century, formal education was limited to a few hours of teaching a week by a couple of residents who had been educated in primary schools and had children in their houses. The only option to access formal schooling was to leave the settlement and move to a boarding school in town. For most parents at that time, this was certainly not a viable alternative as children were actively involved in household activities. This situation culminated in a campaign by a handful of reservation members for the construction of a school within the settlement in the 1960s. Residents had witnessed the edification of a school in a nearby rural settlement made possible by a donation from the Rockefeller Foundation, which at that time was financing educational programs across the country. The Rockfeller family was in fact a prominent actor in the Chilean mining industry. A group from the reducción traveled to meet delegates from the Rockefeller Foundation in a nearby town, where one of the schools financed by this foundation was just being inaugurated. There, they staged a short parade with traditional paraphernalia and music, followed by a speech from a community representative appealing for the construction of a school in their community. The petition proved successful, and a few months later the school was built. The construction of the school in Comunidad Contreras is today celebrated as part of the historical transformation of Mapuche people from helpless victims to political actors able to function efficiently in the winka world. Even before the occupation of their territory, Mapuche political leaders were keen to have their sons educated in Spanish precisely to prevent them becoming "servants of the Chileans," an expression used by the Mapuche resistance leader Quilapán in reference to the strategic value of formal education (Crow 2013, 49). Today, residents in Comunidad Contreras are extremely proud of those young family members who access higher education. As my host Miguel once stated during a lunch with some non-Mapuche friends of his, "Now it is different. The Mapuche, we have our own lawyers, our own anthropologists, our own doctors. Winkas can no longer fool us the way they used to do."

The benefits of formal education, however, are only one side of the story. Formal education has also been understood as a means to dominate Indigenous people since the construction of the first schools in the Mapuche region. For most Mapuche, the classroom stands as the first space where race- and class-inflected hierarchies of inequality are experienced, as in most cases teachers are not Indigenous townspeople.

FIGURE 10  School in Comunidad Contreras. (Photo by author)

Even when they are Mapuche, teachers are not necessarily loyal to their Mapuche roots or its politics. Whiteness pervades not only teacher-pupil interactions but also ideas about national belonging and knowledge about official history, which often reinforce assimilatory narratives based on the idiom of *mestizaje* (see Radcliffe and Webb 2015). Memories of school are thus unconditionally shaped by the experience of discrimination. As recounted by Nelly, the ritual organizer of Comunidad Contreras, children felt embarrassed to show that they were Mapuche to their teachers: "I only spoke Mapudungun in my house, but it was prohibited at school. Children were made fun of for mispronouncing Spanish words." The experience of discrimination can also contribute to the awareness of one's status as a colonized subaltern. Such a recognition is pivotal to the formation of a political consciousness of the urgency of Mapuche projects that foster political autonomy and prevent assimilation. In relating their biographies, many Mapuche writers and leaders talk about *mapuchización* as the process through which a forced desire for whitening induced through education was replaced by a desire to reestablish links with Mapuche culture and political activism. In a recent interview, historian Fernando Pairicán (2014) draws attention to countering the effects of discrimination: "In my *mapuchización*, racism was important. During all my childhood and later in my teenage years, I was told in the Chilean schools that I was an *indio*, an inferior category . . . Later there was a time of frustration, questioning, and a will to become white (*blanquearse*)."

Traditionally, state approaches to Indigenous participation in education have centered on the development of positive discrimination politics, such as the endowment of grants, known as *beca indígena* (Indigenous scholarships), which provide economic assistance to Indigenous pupils and university students. While this policy responded to the demand for access to education as a strategy to improve socioeconomic conditions by Indigenous organizations, it did not address the assimilatory consequences of formal schooling. In the last thirty years, Mapuche activists have demanded educational reform under the banner of "intercultural education," a system that would be able to integrate Indigenous knowledge and language in school and university curricula. In response, a few governmental plans were designed. In many schools with high percentages of Indigenous populations, traditional educators (*educadores tradicionales*) are employed to teach Mapudungun and other aspects of Mapuche culture to pupils. The limitations of intercultural education, however, remain evident as these educators enjoy far lower rank than certified teachers. Furthermore, discrimination against rural Mapuche children continues as schools in the countryside deliver lower quality education in many aspects, including being understaffed (see Webb 2015).

Mixed feelings about formal schooling in Indigenous rural areas are best approached once situated in the broader historical canvas of the incorporation of colonial culture into Mapuche social life. The quandary of the necessary inclusion of colonial culture verges on one question in particular: Is the pragmatic incorporation of elements of the winka world, such as documents, possible without simultaneously bringing about assimilation? Not only is such a question central to my analysis, but it also resonates in the numerous dialogues I have had with Mapuche rural residents. Exposure to winka culture, associated mainly with educational experiences and migration from Mapuche settlements to urban centers, is seen as the main cause of the widespread condition of being awinkado, or winka-like. Being awinkado is lamented as a feeling of loss related to practices such as linguistic fluency, knowledge of rituals, and social etiquette linked to the value of respect that make a person Mapuche. It is a matter of concern for most Mapuche people exactly because it is not restricted to specific individuals; it is a generalized social condition characterizing the Mapuche population in both urban and rural contexts. In my area of study, many residents assert their status as awinkado. In chapter 2, I suggested that being Mapuche is a genealogical, topological, and performative category. Individuals can be more or less Mapuche in relation to their adherence to behavioral etiquettes, linguistic skills, and modes of conduct seen as inherently Mapuche. Accordingly, being winka-like does not depend exclusively on genealogical connections. As the result of a gradual historical increase in interethnic partnerships in Chile, many residents of comunidades are *champurreado*, or children of interethnic parents. But by no means are *champurreados* congenitally more winka-like, as they can embrace Mapuche practices as much or even more than neighbors and family members with no genealogical connection to winkas (González 2016, 92).

Although being winka-like is directly correlated with Mapuche presence in non-Indigenous social spheres characterized by institutional and everyday forms of racism, active participation in Chilean institutions does not necessarily entail the abandonment of Mapuche practices. In theory, reaching a balance between participation in the winka world and adherence to Mapuche lifestyles is possible. However, such a balance depends exclusively on deliberate attempts to persistently acquire knowledge about the Mapuche world throughout one's life, since mastery in Mapuche practices and ideas requires an ongoing cultivation, as seen early in this book. The difficulty of striking a balance between incorporation in the winka world and resistance to assimilation is exemplified by the role that Mapuche political representatives play in rural areas. In most comunidades, delegates tend to be elected among community members on the basis of their educational background and knowledge of Chilean politics and bureaucracy. Most delegates have acquired enough expertise in Chilean politics through education and work experience in nearby towns to secure community benefits from state agencies. But in other cases, someone who would not normally qualify as an ideal delegate because of their inexperience with Chilean politics and administrative matters is designated by older community members because of their expertise in ritual.

Involvement in politics often generates suspicions and resentful feelings among community members based on the potential benefits brought to a delegate. The legitimacy of political leaders thus rests on the ongoing mediations that they engage in with Chilean institutions and community members. Legitimacy from community members is acquired through continuous acts that reaffirm the delegate's commitment to community matters. A display of such commitment also clears any doubt that involvement in political affairs, generally recognized by Mapuche rural residents as lacking in moral integrity, has not caused the delegate to become a winka—in other words, an individual acting mischievously and dishonestly. To clarify this point, we can refer to the story of Nicolás Contreras, the last cacique of Comunidad Contreras, who died in the 1930s. His family history is blurry—an unusual occurrence in Mapuche society, where knowledge of lineages and kin relations is highly valorized. His descendants believe that Nicolás was a Chilean child of European descent, adopted within the cacique's family. His nickname, El Rusio, a Chilean expression referring to people with pale skin and light hair, seems to support this assumption.[8] Thanks to his fluency in Spanish and his wealth, Nicolás was able to create a vast network of sharecropping agreements for both Mapuche and Chilean farmers of the area. Caciques were often the richest individuals in the reducción, since they were informally assigned with more land during the resettlement and in the later processes of land division. The high status that Nicolás enjoyed in the community was amplified by the friendly relations he built with estate owners in the area. However, numerous also were the property disputes with settlers that put his political skills to the test. As recounted by his son Liscán, during the 1930s Nicolás was involved in a dispute with a landowner who had ordered his workers to dig a canal outside his property borders and well within those of the reducción. Nicolás confronted the estate owner and the two engaged physically, although there were no serious injuries. The dispute went to court. In contrast with the majority of land disputes between estate owners and Mapuche people, Nicolás Contreras was successful. A judge in Traiguen compelled the estate owner to fill up the canal and refrain from similar acts in the future.

Nicolás Contreras is remembered by his descendants for his commitment to community members as much as his ability to function in the winka world. His case stands as a paradigmatic example that a balance can be struck between the incorporation of colonial culture and adherence to Mapuche practices through political acts of mediation with community members and Chilean authorities. This balance, however, remains hard to achieve. This is even more evident outside the sphere of political leadership, where the adoption of winka knowledge and practices leads more often to self-inflicted assimilation than the pragmatic harnessing of colonial culture. Formal education and involvement in Chilean politics, we have seen, often augur an intrinsic failure to incorporate winka culture without turning winka. However, it is the rise of evangelism in the past five decades that, more than any other phenomenon, has contributed to the intentional conversion into winka by many Mapuche. In my area of study, residents of comunidades tend to categorize themselves as either Catholics (*católicos*) or Evangelicals (*evangelicos*). While the Catholic Church was one of the main contributors to colonial processes of assimilation through forced conversion of Mapuche people in missions and religious institutions, since the beginning of the twentieth century it has become increasingly more tolerant of syncretic religious expression as part of a broader attempt to bring Indigenous people closer to the Catholic doctrine. One of the most visible consequences of Catholic tolerance toward syncretism is the ubiquitous presence of Christian iconography in Mapuche rituals. *Católicos*, a category with which even machi shamans typically self-identify, do not see the simultaneous observance of Mapuche and Christian religious practices in contradictory terms and actively participate in both sets of rituals. In contrast, *evangelicos* generally do not participate in Mapuche rituals, as they consider them "pagan" beliefs that pose an insurmountable obstacle for a full conversion into born-again Christianity.

Throughout Chile, evangelical churches have been on the rise for the last three decades. In Comunidad Contreras, the oldest evangelical church—belonging to the Christian and Missionary Alliance founded in 1887 in the United States—was built by a group of residents with the help of church members from town in the 1970s. At the time of my fieldwork in 2008, there were at least three more evangelical churches belonging to different congregations and more have been built since.[9] One factor contributing to the historical spread of Evangelicalism has been the scarcity of the Catholic Church in the countryside, as clergy activities concentrate in towns. Evangelical churches, typically referred to as temples (*templos*), consist of small houses built by groups of local residents with the support of pastors from nearby towns. Another significant factor is the prospect of becoming a "new man" (*un hombre nuevo*) or a "new woman" (*una mujer nueva*) as promised by Evangelicalism. In my area of study, Evangelicals are known for following strict codes of behavior, in which drinking alcohol and cursing are prohibited. Among Mapuche and chilenos in rural southern Chile, there is a widespread perception of the positive contribution that conversion to Evangelicalism has brought in reducing alcoholism, a phenomenon that raises deep concern because of its impact on individuals' health as well as the local and wider economy. Abandoning Mapuche practices is necessary in order to embrace a faith purified of any interference on the way to becoming a "new person." The analysis of the complex impact of Evangelicalism on the continuity of Mapuche practices certainly deserves a more adequate discussion. However, my intention is to draw a connection between the spread of evangelical churches in southern Chile and the phenomenon of becoming winka. Certainly, it would be a mistake to think that participation in evangelical churches leads to the unconditional abandonment of Mapuche practices. In Comunidad Contreras, for instance, many residents who self-identify as Evangelicals participate only intermittently in church activities and, more importantly, do not refrain from participating in Mapuche rituals. Yet among many Evangelicals, being winka-like remains a desired condition and a first step toward a desired regeneration process in which one can no longer be Mapuche. This point explains the apprehension of Mapuche ritual experts and political leaders over the spread of Evangelicalism.

The historical adoption of winka practices, notions, and goods, including documents, thought to be necessary to remain Mapuche requires a domestication of difference that is always on the verge of failure. Being awinkado stands in the middle ground of an unbalanced relation between continuity and assimilation. Rather than an exclusive process of syncretic integration, Mapuche inclusion of colonial culture is characterized by a "transformative capacity to become white" (Course 2013, 774).[10] In comparative terms, other-becoming in Mapuche society appears less of an open-ended process than in other Indigenous societies of the region. Other-becoming is a central theme in Amerindian studies. In a departure from acculturation narratives in which attraction toward colonial culture leads to assimilation, anthropological research in the past four decades has paid particular attention to those processes allowing for the incorporation of Western goods and notions into Indigenous cosmologies (see

Gow 1991; Hugh-Jones 1992; Kelly 2005). In his analysis of Amerindian mythology, Levi-Strauss (1995) has suggested that the "opening to the other" observed in Amerindian thought reflects a broader cosmological principle according to which the reproduction of the world depends on the opposition of forces, such as social groups, embedded in a "dualism in perpetual disequilibrium" (239). Like other Amerindian groups, white people were understood as necessary others, for which conceptual space was made even before colonization (220). Rather than transforming into others, incorporating otherness produces a continuous process of transformation, over which Amerindian people can have partial control (Gow 2001). Other-becoming is not restricted to the ethnic sphere. It concerns a broader ontological principle whereby boundaries between sameness and otherness are not preestablished. Other-becoming thus encompasses all transformative processes involving interspecies relations, including alterations in the afterlife, shamanic practices, and kin memberships, as in the case of consubstantiation among affines (Gow 1991; Viveiros de Castro 2001).[11] This point is crucial in explaining why other-becoming in Mapuche society is less of an open-ended process than in other Indigenous groups in the region. Mapuche ontological differences between categories of being are more stable than in other Amerindian cosmologies. The significance of the idiom of descent, for instance, makes consubstantiation an unfamiliar prospect in Mapuche ideas of selfhood. Furthermore, interspecies transformations in ideas about an afterlife and shamanic practices are not acknowledged in substantial terms.[12]

The cosmological openness of Amerindian societies has been similarly highlighted in historical and ethnographic works on Mapuche society. At the height of the invasion of Araucania, powerful caciques used to wear Argentinean and Chilean military uniforms during ceremonies, including burials, partly as an act of imitation, revealing a fascination with winka power, and partly as a demonstration of the ability to capture that power (Foerster and Menard 2009). The inclusion of colonial culture extends also to shamanic and ritualistic practices, in which Chilean flags and elements of Christian religion, such as Bibles, feature as one of the many means to attain divine intercession (Bacigalupo 2007, 159). The inclusion of nationalistic emblems cannot be entirely abstracted from the pervasiveness of nation making in Indigenous life, as seen in chapter 1. However, there is a broader recognition of the positive value of otherness in Mapuche society. Winkas, we have seen, are necessary not only for the pragmatic incorporation of tokens of power, such as documents, which they have historically produced, but also for the general significance of otherness in self-making. Mapuche ideas of personhood presuppose the self as a lifelong project dependent on relations established with different types of others, including nonconsanguineous Mapuche and winkas (see Course 2011, 2013). Despite the undeniable opening to the other in Mapuche society, other-becoming can and often does result in assimilation. This point is shown clearly in the adoption of property notions and technologies. While documents and titles of property have better equipped Mapuche residents against abuses perpetuated by winkas, their adoption has reconfigured relations among kin and Mapuche neighbors, since property relations are guided by principles that are at odds with Mapuche values and practices of sociability. A look at the impact of land formalization on the process of winka-becoming can help us unfold this point.

## Life Divided: The Sociability of Property

The introduction of private property in Mapuche settlements cannot be reduced to a single governmental plan. Rather, it was a long, discontinuous process supported by different ideological claims on the benefits of land formalization. As seen earlier, the first instances of land division (*hijuelación*) took place in the 1930s. The dismantlement of collective ownership concluded in the 1980s with the implementation of Decree 2.568. Comunidad Contreras belongs to a minority of reducciones, roughly a quarter of the total, that had been divided before the implementation of the decree. Land division was officially carried out in 1952, many years earlier than most reducciones in the area.[13] A plausible explanation for the early division of Reducción Contreras is that state functionaries in charge of land formalization tended to prioritize more populous settlements. Another explanation raised by some older community members is that a few local residents had formally petitioned for land division as a consequence of increasing land disputes and individual requests for property deeds. Older residents remember the allotment of individual plots as taking place over a few days. One morning in 1951 a surveyor from Santiago arrived at Reducción Contreras with a couple of assistants. They built a tent in the middle of the settlement and for the following three days visited each household in the settlement to complete a survey concerning household composition and land use. At the end of the survey, the boundaries of each property were demarcated by drawing lines in the soil. The functionaries were treated with both reverence and suspicion by local residents, as they were the first representatives of the state to ever reside in the community. Residents who collaborated with the state functionaries as informants and translators were compensated with cash. During and after the land division, complaints about the amount of land assigned were numerous. Residents complained that land distribution was unequal and that relations who had migrated away from the settlement were not endowed with property titles. All legal mechanisms facilitating land division were based on a land-to-the-occupant law, so that many community members living in urban centers lost their land rights to their tenants (Crow 2013, 156). Complaints by residents of Reducción Contreras remained unheard by the state functionaries.

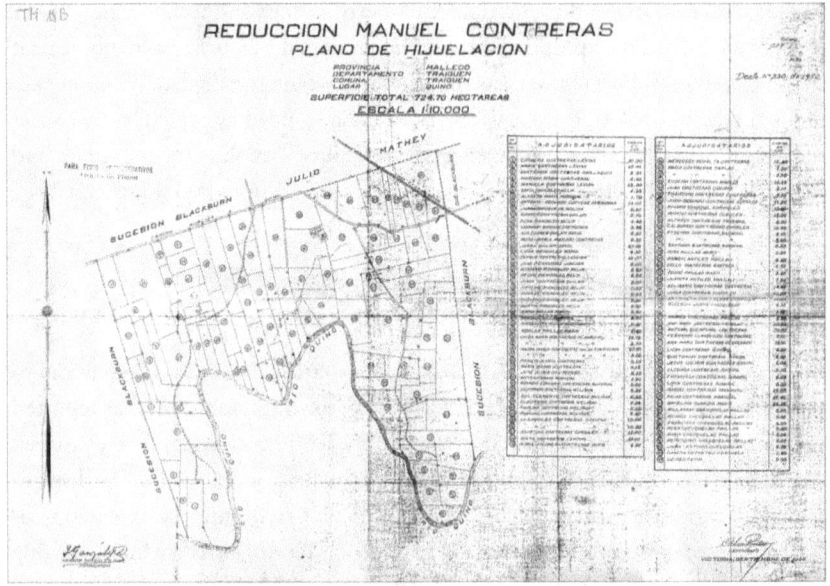

FIGURE 11  Map of land division. (Archivo AGAI CONADI)

The consequences of Indigenous land division are hard to pinpoint. Opinions by local residents are heterogeneous, some highlighting the benefits brought by the introduction of individual titles as protection against land grabbing, others making the opposite case. In examining the impact of land formalization, we should begin by rejecting the idea that this process was a mere imposition of a privatized system of land tenure over a communitarian form of land ownership. We have seen that even in precolonial times, land tenure was characterized by a flexible system of redistribution among and within kin groups. Contemporary understandings of individual ownership as a basic right may be explained not as the result of assimilation but as part of a broader valorization of personal autonomy observed in Mapuche ideas of selfhood and sociality. While certain agricultural products, seeds in particular, are equally distributed among household members, goods, animals, and, to a lesser extent, crops are unconditionally objects of individual ownership. The preponderance of individual ownership can be further observed in the difficulties in enforcing cooperative work in Mapuche settlements, which many residents of comunidades report as a debilitating factor in community politics. Such difficulties can certainly be linked to the process of depoliticization of rural populations during the military dictatorship (1973–1990), when neighborhood committees and unions were curtailed, and that of assimilation, as residents with little ethnic identification tend to show equally little loyalty to community causes. However, even the more politically engaged residents find it perfectly logical to resist the cooperative schemes typically implemented by NGOs and state agencies, since cooperative labor arrangements often prove to be unjust toward those residents who put more efforts into these initiatives.

Although land division did not cause any abrupt change on ownership practices, its impact on practices of sociality proved to be far-reaching. Land division is strictly related to increasing inequality of access to land among reducción members. Land, we have seen, had never been equally distributed since the institution of the reducción. Caciques often owned more land than anyone else within a settlement. Yet the formalization of land ownership implied a further differentiation among reducción members. Those households with fewer heirs were less affected by the fragmentation and dispersal of family owned land. Residents who were able to keep more hectares were also more likely to increase their purchasing power and expand their properties by buying up their neighbors' land. While inequality within Mapuche settlements should not be overstated, as residents consider themselves to be in an equally marginal position in relation to non-Indigenous landholders, land formalization certainly played a central role in increasing competition over land. This phenomenon also explains why land formalization failed to deliver on the promise of eradicating ownership disputes, which had historically served as its main political justification and acceptance by Mapuche farmers. While border disputes among neighbors decreased as a consequence of plot demarcation, tensions within households quickly mounted, especially between siblings who were excluded and those who were included in the category of legitimate heirs. For local residents, property and inheritance disputes remain very constant features of social life in comunidades.

In residents' perceptions, the most pervasive effect of land division was the gradual proliferation of individualistic lifestyles. In my area of study, to be individualistic (*individualista*) encompasses a wide variety of behaviors. A common example is that of spending time at home without engaging in relations of mutual help and visits with kin and neighbors. This type of conduct is subject to disapproval, not only because by withdrawing from social networks one loses the opportunities given by mutual relations of help, but also because the enactment of one's social predispositions is morally praised. We have seen that in Mapuche social thought, selfhood is built around relations with others established through exchanges of help, food, and visits. For most Mapuche residents in my area of study, individualism is a defining trait of current social life as opposed to that of the ancient ones. Among the many factors favoring the rise of more individualistic lifestyles, land formalization was certainly a significant one. One of the most direct consequences of land division in Comunidad Contreras was the dispersal of households throughout the settlement. Customarily, households belonging to the same patrilineage were clustered together. Since most heirs were assigned land distant from their parents' house, newly formed couples moved to their new property in order to farm it and prevent occupation by their neighbors, as was often the case. As recounted by Ramón, who had lived through the land formalization, the proliferation of new houses dispersed throughout the settlement coincided with a decline in the once customary practice of daily visits: "People began to pay more and more attention to their houses. Nowadays, people do not visit each other as they used to." A similar point was raised by the early twentieth-century historian Tomás Guevara, who associated the increasingly individualistic ways of life in reducciones with the individual necessity to protect land owned by each household against dispossession (in Correa, Molina, and Yánez 2005, 48).

For most members of Comunidad Contreras, the decline in mutual visits epitomizes the loss of certain values, such as hospitality and respect, thought of as essential features of a Mapuche person. Respect is a mode of conduct crossing the ontological barrier between the social and the natural. Previously, we have explored the significance that the value of respect holds in environmental notions and practices. Respect also concerns relations with strangers and kin. Among different instances of respect, deferential attitude toward one's elders is commonly mentioned as a marker of difference between past and present lifestyles. My host Miguel explained to me that his grandfather could never be approached directly by one of his in-laws (*chedküy*), but rather all questions and requests had to be mediated by older family members. Hierarchical differences between age groups were part of a more general moral dedication toward family duties. The term *kimpeñpewün*, for instance, designates unconditional mutual help among family members (Millalén 2006, 38). Another instantiation of the value of respect, which I learned during fieldwork, concerns formalized practices of exchange. *Trafkin* in particular sanctions a lifelong alliance and friendship between two individuals, generally belonging to different local patrilineages, who have exchanged goods of different types, including domestic animals. Individuals bonded through a *trafkin* will be expected to address each other as *tañi* (my) *trafkin* for the rest of their life. The objective of this practice is the establishment of long-term relationships between people not related through existing networks of kin commitment. For this reason, difference in economic value of work or goods exchanged is underestimated. The significance of *trafkin* in the establishment of friendship bonds has decreased in the last decades. The same can be said about other practices of mutual exchange, such as the work parties known as *mingakos* discussed in the previous chapter, whose continuity is threatened by increasing reliance on remunerated services offered for the construction of a house or for agricultural tasks. For many in my area of study, decline in these practices is lamented as yet another evidence of the growing prevalence of becoming winka.

The logic behind sociability based on the value of respect contrasts sharply with principles of property relations structured around the use of contracts and documents.

While documents and contracts formalize relations among residents in terms of limitations and rules, Mapuche ideas of sociality presuppose the establishment of relations of mutual exchange of affection and goods, which need to be constantly reasserted in practice and always depend on the autonomous choice of the individual (see Course 2011). Contracts are generally understood as features of winka sociality as they raise suspicions about the possibly mischievous character of the parties involved. In contrast, reliance on oral agreements is praised as an instance of the value of respect. As Jesús, a man in his sixties, once explained to me, the infringement of oral agreements was unthinkable to previous generations: "Back in the days, you would simply shake hands and that would sanction an agreement forever." While residents of comunidades tend to morally condemn the breach of oral agreements and associate it with winka behavior, documents and contracts are by now ubiquitous features of Mapuche social life. They can be deployed in arranging land leases, sharecropping agreements, and usufructuary concessions. While the frequency of contracts increases in relations with winkas, they are also understood as a necessary means to sanction transactions with members of the same comunidad and family. Frequent family tensions over inheritance and land use rights are mostly solved through legal action, as would be the case for neighboring settlers.

The consequences of Mapuche land division, which I have briefly examined, bring into question the optimistic prospect of the modernization narratives behind property formalization. Economic self-realization, empowerment in the agrarian market, and settlement of property disputes within Indigenous communities remain unaccomplished promises decades after land division. The future envisioned in modernization narratives also encompasses a much more controversial scenario, one presupposing the eradication of Mapuche ideas about land ownership and belonging. We have seen that the impact of land formalization has been profound in reasserting the historical dilemma generated by the incorporation of colonial culture. Reliance on documents, which was experienced as an effective way of redressing power asymmetries with winkas, eventually reconfigured all modes of sociality unfolding in more intimate settings, such as those within one's comunidad revolving around kin and neighborly relations. The operational impossibility of adopting documents without being affected by daily reliance on them indicates that the domestication of otherness is a historical process that can, and often does, backfire. Nonetheless, while land formalization has contributed to the spread of the phenomenon of becoming winka, ideas and practices of land ownership reflecting a logic of land-belonging other than that of property theory have not been simply eradicated. The second part of this book will show the practical manifestations of these ideas in land claims, where settlers' jural entitlement to land is openly contested. For now, let us conclude the analysis of land ownership and property that I have carried out in this chapter by examining those practices of land ownership within Mapuche settlements that simultaneously reinforce and contradict existing legal frameworks.

## Land Ownership as Property and Belonging

The dual nature of land ownership is a well-known theme in anthropological writing. In any social scenario, land is both a site of belonging and a resource onto which property claims can be laid (Strathern 1996, 531). Ideas about moral entitlement to land might thus validate legal recognitions of ownership or deny them. Regarding a tract of land as one's own depends not only on rights bestowed by a title of property but also on other factors as well, such as kin membership and soil use (Verdery and Humphrey 2004, 12). As suggested by Strathern (1996), proprietorship remains an essential feature of human connections with nonhuman beings, including land, for its severing effect, which constantly reinstates boundaries in what could otherwise be conceptualized as a limitless network of affect linking humans and nonhumans. In Indigenous southern Chile, the dual nature of land ownership as a matter of belonging and property materializes in certain patterns of land transactions and use. In the comunidades I had the chance to know, legal ownership is unconditionally seen as an essential individual right. Property transgressions, such as leaving cattle to graze on someone else's land, are promptly acted upon. Yet tendencies in land transactions, such as a widespread resistance to buying or selling land to individuals from comunidades other than one's own, reflect the central role that the idiom of geographic belonging—tuwün—holds in ideas about land entitlement. The consequences of those transactions involving Mapuche landowners from different comunidades illustrate this point clearly.

As established by the 1993 Indigenous Law, only holders of a certificate of ethnic affiliation, the Calidad Indígena issued by CONADI, can purchase and sell land within a Mapuche settlement. Cases of non-Indigenous landowners who have legally acquired land within Indigenous communities through such certificates are quite common. This possibility typically reinforces a perspective common among residents of comunidades that CONADI is a bureaucratic machine unsympathetic to farmers' needs and is exposed to manipulation by politicians and functionaries. However, restrictions based on certification have certainly helped to reduce the extent of land purchases by non-Indigenous individuals. Such restrictions have also ensured that properties within Indigenous communities are cheaper than others. This market tendency has two explanations. Firstly, Mapuche people have less purchasing power than non-Indigenous people after a long history of exclusion and institutional racism. Secondly, land within communities cannot be seized by large creditors such as banks.

Among residents of comunidades, moving to an unrelated community is generally seen as an unviable option, unless access to land is undermined. The prospect of losing networks of mutual assistance involving consanguineous relatives is a fundamental deterrent in relocation. In line with the customary observance of the virilocal residential pattern, patri-relatives are in fact expected to provide and reciprocate help (*kelluwün*) in agricultural and domestic work (Course 2011, 51). More broadly, land is understood as a stable base for life. We have seen that in contrast with the volatile nature of cash flow and agricultural goods accumulation, land is a reliable provider whose productivity is ensured by the establishment of relations of mutuality and care with farmers. For this reason, land sale is considered a potentially beneficial option only in the short run, as future misfortunes will follow such decision. The reader might remember an anedocte that I presented earlier in this book about a Mapuche man who decided to sell his land without consulting his sons and heirs. Soon after selling his property, this man moved to the nearby town of Traiguen in search of a better life. His hopes were eventually crushed. He spent the rest of his life in the town, but in extremely poor conditions and complete abandonment from other family members.

Despite resistance toward land transactions, cases of Mapuche people moving to unrelated Indigenous communities are frequent. The relatively low price of community land has allowed many Mapuche urban residents to purchase land within communities located around major urban centers, mainly Temuco, so that they can commute on a daily or weekly basis. More commonly, newcomers are from nearby rural settlements from where they had to move mainly as a consequence of land shortages emerging from inheritance partition. In some cases, the presence of these newcomers is highly valued by local residents. Commuters from urban areas, for instance, might have professional skills that could be put to use by community boards and local organizations. However, more frequently they might feel unwelcome, as their presence often raises rumors and suspicions among local residents. This was the case with two friends of mine, Carlos and Ruby, who moved to Comunidad Contreras with their family a few years ago to start a new "life project" (*proyecto de vida*) away from Santiago. Ruby had just inherited a plot from her family, and some of their new neighbors were known relatives. Carlos was frequently recognized as a winka by his new neighbors, as his genealogical links with Mapuche antecessors were unclear. Unfriendly attitudes from their neighbors were clear in the months immediately following their relocation. A couple of neighbors, for instance, used to log in a forested section of their property, an occurrence that had begun years earlier when this particular property was not inhabited. Carlos and Ruby's position in the comunidad, however, began to change. They became actively involved in community activities, especially those concerning land claims and local development projects. For Carlos, his commitment to community politics was key to the profound changes that he experienced in relating to his neighbors: "They used to treat me as a winka; now I am one member more of this comunidad." Some suspicions about newcomers from other communities are harder to dissipate. While for local residents it is clear that urban residents move to an Indigenous community because they are attracted to country life, the reasons that newcomers from other comunidades had left their settlements often remained unclear, so that rumors among neighbors spread quickly. I was told by some friends at Comunidad Contreras about the case of a machi who moved to the community decades ago. Rumors that an unresolvable family dispute had forced her to move away from her settlement began circulating as soon she settled in her new home. These rumors were fed by the fact that none of her patients were former neighbors, but only Mapuche and chilenos from other rural areas. Eventually, after a few years, she moved back to her comunidad.

Experiences of migration to genealogically unrelated comunidades demonstrate the inherent duality of land ownership as a matter of belonging and property. Among Mapuche rural residents, the right of newcomers to buy land and move to a comunidad is not denied. This arrangement can be made possible by a consensual transaction between a buyer and a landowner, which is not—and should not be—a public concern. However, land ownership by newcomers is resisted in practice through hostile attitudes toward newcomers and a more general resistance to selling one's property. Ideas and practices of land ownership originate in the entanglement of Mapuche expressions of geographic belonging centered on the notion of tuwün on the one hand, and a general reverence toward private property on the other hand. Such an entanglement explains why private property might be overtly contested when associated with settler expansion and land grabbing, while being understood as a basic right among residents of the same comunidad.

The duality of property and belonging in land ownership is a reflection of the general analytical distinction between Indigenous and legal land ontologies, a disjunction I raised at the very beginning of this book. My use of this distinction allows me to express differences in the ways land connections, of which ownership is an integral part, operate in the legal realm and in notions and practices of land connections in the Mapuche lived world. In legal property theory, ownership depends on a type of formal recognition independent from all existing connections between land and its dwellers. Property relations are "linked to the jural context under whose jurisdiction the strength of each property, no matter what its history, rests upon the legitimacy of contemporary mediations rather than the authority of the past" (Abramson 2000, 8). The discontinuous temporality of property is intimately related to another key notion—that of the intentionality of ownership. Western property theory is loosely based on the premise that possession sanctioned through property rights originates as an intention independent from social bonds connecting the owner not only with other human beings but also with the owned object. This idea emerged as early as the first systematization of property rights, the Roman law. Here, the legal recognition of individual entitlement over a thing (*res*) is known as *possessio*. This notion presupposes that the owner has *animus possidentis*—that is, the intention of possessing an object. This intention coexists with others, such as *animus detenendi*—that of using an object while recognizing the legal ownership by another individual (Clarke and Greer 2012, 170). The principles of Roman law have pervaded much of Western property theory in reinforcing land ownership as a relation dependent exclusively on individual intention and mutual agreement between parties involved in a transaction. The inherent features and qualities of land might influence exchange values, but not the act of owning it. The principles of legal land ontology contrast with the model of Mapuche land ontology that I have sketched earlier in this book. Rather than an object of human intentionality, the notion of tuwün presupposes land as a sentient subject. Land is topologically differentiated as different places of origin engage actively in self-making, acting as a potentiality genealogically transmitted among its dwellers.

The distinction between Indigenous and legal land ontologies allows me to highlight the divergent principles between the configuration of land connections in property theory and Mapuche thought. It should be apparent by now, however, that in Mapuche rural life, land connections can be reduced neither to an intersubjective relation of affect nor to a subject/object relation of ownership. Nowhere is the ontological instability of the subject/object divide as clear as in claims of ownership over land that is understood as sentient by its owners. Generally, modes of land ownership and, to a lesser degree, property systems vary in relation to different notions of personhood and agency associated with the "owner" and the "owned." Divergent understandings of the owner as a collective identity, an individual, or a sum of individualities necessarily converge in differences in land ownership (Verdery and Humphrey 2004, 6). The qualities of the owned object also shape understandings of what it means to be an "owner." When owned objects possess the owner, property emerges in a bundle of relations in which the owned is simultaneously subject and object (Strathern 1999). This is certainly the case of land ownership in Indigenous southern Chile, where everyday environmental and social relationships are deeply structured by naturalized legal principles, and yet sentient lands resist becoming objects.

---

This chapter concludes the first part of this book, where I have examined the historical, experiential, ecological, and legal processes through which ancestral land emerges as a relevant ontological and political category. We have seen that in Indigenous southern

Chile, the affective properties of land connections are inextricably intertwined with property theory. The historical introduction of property stands as a key dilemma. As with other features of colonial culture, such as formal education, property formalization was desired by Mapuche farmers as a means of self-defense against land grabbing. Instrumental adoption of winka practices, however, entailed a domestication of alterity that was not always possible. The adoption of property notions and practices, which was aimed at preserving connection with one's tuwün, a key element of Mapuche self-determination, has also led to the gradual decline of values and practices of sociability upon which Mapuche identity is predicated. The historical intersections of legal and Indigenous land ontologies examined in this chapter not only reveal the ability of property theory to exclude nonmarket forms of values assigned to land, but also help us to realize the malleability of legal understandings of land as local conceptions. In the second part of this book, I continue to explore the entanglement between legal and Indigenous land ontologies. I do so by examining Mapuche claimants' and state actors' involvement in land claims.

# PART II
# LAND CLAIMS

# CHAPTER 5

# MAPPING ANCESTRAL LAND
*The Power of Documents in Land Claims*

ON A COLD WINTER SUNDAY, A CROWD OF PEOPLE OF ALL AGES GATHered in a large wooden house that served as a community center for the monthly meeting of Comunidad Contreras. After all attendees took their seats, a community board member informed his neighbors of recent difficulties with the review of their land claim by CONADI. Among other problems, the misplacement of key documents by state officials was slowing down the process. Upon hearing this news, several attendees voiced their opinions about how to respond to the delay. At one point, Segundo, an older resident, reported a conversation he had had with a friend from a nearby Mapuche settlement a few days earlier: "He told me there is another property not far from here that the owner wants to sell. We could ask CONADI to buy it for us. He asked me why we were fighting so hard for El Huadaco. [That] fundo [estate] lacks irrigation and all trees have been cut down." A heated debate soon followed. Many attendees made clear that they would not accept any land subsidy from the government to settle their demands. Others favored a quicker solution to their claim, since the restitution of the properties they demanded appeared a distant prospect. At one point, Juana firmly stated, "We are here to get our ancestral territory [*territorio ancestral*] back. Even with my eyes closed, I can see El Huadaco; this is our land." Episodes like this one are common across the southern Chilean countryside. Like many other Mapuche claimants, the residents of Comunidad Contreras confronted numerous dilemmas when they embarked on the long and uncertain land claim process. The most pressing was how to convince state officials that the land whose restitution they were seeking was ancestral territory. Since the land program privileges colonial titles and archival sources over other forms of evidence, Mapuche claimants are paradoxically forced to validate claims to their ancestral land through documents that were designed to legitimize their dispossession. The question for me and for friends at Comunidad Contreras, albeit from different positions, was how to turn property from a constraint into an opportunity.

As many authors have shown (Fay and James 2009; James 2007; Monet and Ska-nu'u 1991; Nadasdy 2003), Indigenous land programs promise restoration of precolonial geographies while instituting new geographic constructs that are often at odds with claimants' intentions. In Chile, as elsewhere, the contradictions inherent in Indigenous land programs have been at the core of often conflicting critiques. On the one hand, conservative critiques question the significance of place and territory in Mapuche culture by invoking the precolonial mobility of the Mapuche people. On the other hand, progressive perspectives insist that community land restoration is a form of state co-option of Indigenous politics and a distraction from the broader struggle for regional and ethnic autonomy. The saliency of ancestral territories is thus delegitimized on both fronts: either it is deemed a rhetorical strategy articulated by Indigenous organizations that is unsupported by historical evidence or, more directly, it is undermined by state intervention. In contrast, during fieldwork, I realized that far from being a mere rhetorical strategy by activists or a spatial conformation generated by the allotment of land subsidies, the ancestral territory formed through land claims is the result of the productive yet unequal relation between property and place instigated by claimants themselves.

In this chapter, I explore the tension between local notions of place and property in Mapuche land claims. In doing so, I show that the conceptual and material ramifications of articulating ancestral land through the jural language of property materialize not in the act of demarcating this territory but, rather, in the formation of new spatial constructs that reflect the particular logic of compensation at work in land claims. The analysis of the intersection between Indigenous and legal land ontologies that I advance in this chapter reframes some of the topics presented earlier in this book within the governmental context of land claims. In accordance with the notion of tuwün, the power of place resides in its agential role in processes of self-making rather than its historical consistency concerning either group membership or spatial demarcation. While maps and documents can serve as a means for Mapuche claimants to demarcate demanded tracts of land characterized by porous boundaries, they can also contribute to the legitimation of existing property regimes as a naturalized grid through which the ancestral territories can be approximated. This chapter depicts the dilemmas and actions undertaken by claimants in their relations with the complex bureaucratic machine of the Indigenous land program. The challenge here is how to recognize the specificities of state power and its relation to historical trajectories of colonial domination within land claims while acknowledging the opportunities and spaces of contestation offered by participation in the program to Mapuche claimants. In this task, I let the ethnographic analysis be guided by two complementary and opposing processes at work in land claims: those of transactions and those of translations. As Strathern and Hirsch (2004, 8) define it, a transaction entails any set of actions aimed at rendering something exchangeable by expressing one set of values in terms of another. Claimants' actions vividly illustrate the entanglement of legal and Indigenous land ontologies. In contrast, the allocation of land grants as compensation for historic land loss by the Chilean state entails a translation of the "ancestral territory" from a qualitative, topological, and sentient subject into a standardized object of exchange. This process serves to negate the fluid and sentient character of the ancestral territory derived from local geographic conceptualizations and embodied experiences in the landscape. Codification of the ancestral territory by the state apparatus illustrates what Gilles Deleuze and Félix Guattari (1987) describe as reterritorialization. In dialoguing with Deleuze and Guattari's view of state power and its conceptual antagonisms, I hope to show the concomitant positionality of Indigenous geographies against and within the state.

## Mapuche Land Claims: From Protection to Restitution

Contrary to conservative critiques of Indigenous demands in Chile, land disputes are not recent inventions prompted by a few radical activists with transnational connections and left-wing sympathies. As seen in the previous chapter, the first instances of property disputes involving settlers and caciques occurred in the aftermath of the introduction of the reservation system at the turn of the twentieth century. Since their establishment in 1931, the Juzgados de Indios (Indians' Court) served as the only legal space in which caciques could have their rights enforced. While feuds were generally resolved in favor of settlers, there were cases of legal success among caciques. For much of the twentieth century, state intervention was limited to offering legal means of protection against land grabbing. It was not until the 1970s that the prospect of the allocation of land subsidies directed to Mapuche residents surfaced within broader political debates about land reform, rural poverty, and inequality. While land redistribution to peasants was the major objective of the agrarian reform (1962–1973), in 1972 the Unidad Popular (UP) government introduced an unprecedented legal reform (Law No. 17.729) that instituted mechanisms for the restitution of reservation land expropriated by non-Indigenous landowners (Correa, Molina, and Yáñez 2005, 159–200). The measures introduced by this law, however, were never to be put into practice, as in 1973 the military junta led by Augusto Pinochet violently seized power and reversed all land reforms implemented by the UP government. As seen in the previous chapter, within the nationalist agenda of Pinochet's dictatorship, there was no space for the recognition of Indigenous collective rights over land.

With the return of democratic rule in 1990, land restitution emerged at the center stage of the political debate on democratization and Indigenous rights. Indigenous and human rights activists mobilized through tomas (land occupations) and protests to pressure the postdictatorship government of the center-leftist coalition of Concertación de Partidos por la Democracia to negotiate a solution for pending land disputes. Governmental responses to land demands have been twofold. On the one hand, acts of mobilization have been violently repressed by the police, and numerous activists labeled in the media as dangerous "terrorists" have been detained through the application of the Pinochet-era martial law, Ley de Seguridad del Estado. On the other hand, the Indigenous Law of 1993, Ley Indígena 19.253, instituted the first comprehensive Indigenous land program in the country. In the first article of this law, one can read an explicit recognition of the value of land for Indigenous culture: "For them [Indigenous people] land is the main foundation of their existence and culture." Yet as the rest of this chapter highlights, this promising statement has not resulted in a tangible acknowledgement of Indigenous notions of territory within the legal system.

The allocation of land subsidies and compensations to Indigenous claimants follows two procedures, each established by a separate clause of Article 20 of Indigenous Law 19.253, known as Letra A and Letra B (Senado de Chile 1993). Both procedures are implemented by a department within CONADI, the Fund for Indigenous Land and Water (Fondo Tierras y Aguas Indígenas). Letra A regulates the allocation of land subsidies to individuals or groups of applicants according to standardized levels of economic hardship. The individualized character of the Letra A subsidy scheme has come under strong criticism from human rights activists, who see the initiative as an attempt to disarm collective forms of political representation among Mapuche people (Aylwin 2002). As with other welfare programs of the new coalition government, reviews of Letra A applications are performed through a point system accounting for employment possibilities, income, and tangible goods. Applicants need to fall within established standards of poverty and provide evidence of ethnic affiliation through an official certificate (*certificado de calidad indígena*), issued by CONADI to citizens with Indigenous surnames, genealogical links to Indigenous ascendants, or their recognition as Indigenous people by the board of a comunidad indígena. In my area of study, land subsidies tend to extend for no more than fourteen hectares, an amount regarded by CONADI as minimal to ensure subsistence farming. This number rises in areas characterized by scarce agricultural production, such as forested areas.

While the Letra A subsidy scheme has been designed as a partial solution to land shortage and poverty in Indigenous rural areas, Letra B addresses pending land disputes more directly. This procedure was designed to provide funds to transfer land from non-Indigenous land owners to comunidades with proven cases of historic land dispossession. As specified in CONADI guidelines, a successful claim must have passed through thirty-two different procedures, divided into four phases. The first phase, Applicability (*Aplicabilidad*), concerns the initial assessment of the legal and historical evidence presented by an Indigenous community and can be concluded with approval or denial of legitimacy for the claim. The second phase, Viability (*Viabilidad*), refers to the selection of a suitable property to be later transferred to the claimants. In the third phase, that of Feasibility (*Factibilidad*), CONADI and the incumbent land owners negotiate the purchase of the demanded property to be transferred to claimants on the basis of market values. The last phase, Realization (*Concreción*), refers to the bureaucratic procedures necessary to record the property's new status in the local cadastre (Conservador de Bienes Raíces). This summary does little justice to the complexity of the land claim process run by CONADI. Its intricate bureaucracy has deterred numerous Mapuche claimants from entering land negotiations. All sorts of obstacles, including typographical errors in the registration of claimants' names, can dramatically slow the review process. The list of cases still under review is so long that claimants' exasperation occasionally turns into enraged protests and confrontations with state officials.

When I started fieldwork in southern Chile in 2008, the board of Comunidad Contreras was awaiting disposition of their land claim. The idea of forwarding a claim to CONADI was first discussed in 2005 after community representatives heard about the successful claim of a nearby Mapuche settlement. In any land claim, the first step is the recruitment of *socios* (members), who together constitute a comunidad indígena to act as a legal representative for all community members. The recruitment of *socios* is a primary concern, as a land claim is considered legitimate by CONADI only if the ratio between the area of land demanded and the number of signatories to the claim falls within a range of roughly fifteen to twenty hectares per signatory. In order to ensure equal redistribution of land among the claim signatories, an agreement was reached that there could be only one beneficiary from each generation within a household. During the first few months of the land claim process, divisions between those in favor and those against it were quick to surface. I had the chance to meet both active supporters of the claim and residents who were reluctant to participate in it. There are several reasons for the reluctance. Many residents feared that the financial outlay needed to organize meetings and finance their delegates' trips to the city of Temuco, where CONADI's head office is located, would go to waste. Signatories are indeed requested to pay fees (*cuotas*) to finance delegates' trips to the city and legal services. Another explanation is a general distrust toward state agencies. As seen earlier in this book, local politics in southern Chile are shaped by client relations involving both Mapuche and non-Indigenous farmers. This is particularly evident in relations with officials from CONADI, an agency that holds little credibility among Mapuche people. During fieldwork, I heard numerous rumors about CONADI functionaries involved in half-share agreements with communities that had been recently benefited with land subsidies. For friends at Comunidad Contreras, there was no doubt that these commercial agreements consisted of an exchange between an official's influence on the review process in order to favor a group of claimants on the one hand, and the prospect of working as agricultural partners on favorable terms for the official on the other.

Another factor influencing the recruitment of signatories among community members is to be found in the intersection of political affiliations with labor relations. Most *asalariados*, residents whose main source of income was yearly employment in nearby agricultural estates, were concerned about possible future tensions with their employers (patrones), whose property could be the subject of restitution demands. Not without a polemic tenor, Miguel, who relies on farming as his main source of income, once explained to me, "People around here have depended on patrones for many generations now. They no longer care about agriculture. For the *asalariados*, the patrón is like god." Friction over participation in land claims also reflected long-divergent political perspectives: residents opposing the claim tended to be supporters of conservative parties such as the Unión Demócrata Independiente (UDI), which have traditionally embodied nationalist ideals in the country. Community members working as estate owners tend to be right-wing sympathizers, an inclination that

FIGURE 12　CONADI headquarters in the center of Temuco. (Photo by author)

correlates with the fact that estate owners are often active members of conservative parties and seek support among their employees for local elections. Although divergences among community members concerning their land claim never disrupted kinship and friendship relations during the land claim process, they resurrected painful memories from the era of Pinochet's dictatorship. Elder members of those families spearheading the land claim had also been actively involved in the agrarian movement of the early 1970s and, as a consequence, had suffered military persecution after the coup.

The recruitment of *socios* took several months. By the end of this process in late 2007, eighty individuals had signed the land claim, while roughly a third of all community members had opted not to take part. Among the *socios* recruited for Comunidad Contreras's claim were members who had migrated to urban areas and maintained relations with family members and friends in the community. The participation of members living in the regional capital, Temuco, could prove to be key to the articulation of the land claim since some of them were members of NGOs and Indigenous organizations whose support Comunidad Contreras could rely on. The inclusion of immigrants residing in cities reveals the high mobility of Mapuche population between rural and urban areas, as well as the general principles of tuwün, according to which belonging to a place of origin is context specific and designated by both residence and genealogical links.[1] It should be apparent by now that since its very beginning, a land claim process is shaped by governmental definitions of the collectivities entitled to lodge territorial demands. The bureaucratic aspect of claim staking concerns not only engagement with the bureaucratic apparatus but also a bureaucratization of political life within Indigenous settlements (see also Nadasdy 2003). Yet in the process of recruitment, claimants are able to bend the regulations of the land program to creatively define group membership and reestablish relations with members who had migrated to urban areas. But recruitment is only the first challenge that claimants face upon staking their claim. In the following process of evidentiary production, community members have to deal with the thorny question of how to transform uncertain knowledge about ancestral land into proof of the existence of a demarcated ancestral territory.

## Territorial Restoration: The Question of Place and Memory

In Comunidad Contreras, knowledge about ancestral land was not in dispute, as all residents concurred that the ancestral territory extended beyond the reservation boundaries. Oral accounts transmitted by elder family members, as well as the existence of ancient sites beyond the present limits of the comunidad, are powerful reminders of past territorial extension. However, a recurrent topic of discussion during community meetings was the existence of clear boundaries for the ancestral territory. The land claim of Comunidad Contreras was indeed destined to fail unless a clear image of territorial partition was to be offered to CONADI officials. The major difficulty is that ancestral territory never functioned as a self-contained property in precolonial times. Before the invasion of Mapuche territories by the Chilean army at the end of the nineteenth century, tenure consisted of a complex set of collective and individual rights to land. As seen in the previous chapter, topographic features such as stands of trees and large ceremonial grounds generally served as spatial markers of land occupation for local kin groups, or lof (Durán 1998). This is the reason why many present residents consider certain topographic features as potential boundaries of land occupied by their ancestors (*los antiguos*). The presence of these boundaries reflects the broader principles of the notion of tuwün. As I have argued in chapter 2, tuwün is best understood as both a stable and relational component of selfhood since it articulates boundaries of sameness and otherness among Mapuche people from different localities, and with winka, or canonical others, in substantial rather than symbolic terms. The topological nature of tuwün, according to which space is a discontinuous and partitioned set of forces acting divergently with different human beings, is manifested in the landscape. Certain topographic features are regarded as potential boundaries of tuwün and thus are able to engender perceptions of temporal relatedness and unrelatedness toward different tracts of land. Among these topographic features, rivers are certainly the most effective markers of spatial differentiation.

For residents of Comunidad Contreras, two watercourses, the Quino River and Estero Huadaco, served as the boundaries of their ancestral territory. Both of them were indeed mentioned in the final report forwarded to CONADI. The large Quino River stands as the legal southern boundary of the community. The Quino is an essential source of water for agricultural activities of local residents, as cattle are taken to this watercourse to drink during the dry summer months. According to oral accounts, before the reservation era, this river marked the limit between the lof kin group genealogically associated with today's Comunidad Contreras and that of another Mapuche settlement. A neighbor of mine during fieldwork once recounted a story heard from his mother several decades ago: "There was a community on the other side of the Quino. Then the plague [*viruela*] began, and in a couple of months the entire community vanished." This case was not isolated. On several occasions, I was told by elder community members about the eradication of entire settlements as a consequence of the Chilean military invasion at the end of the nineteenth century. The role of the Quino River as a geographical boundary is experientially reinforced by the numerous threats associated with its crossing. Its banks are so steep that they can be accessed only through a few trails. Access to the other bank is even more difficult, as the Quino can be waded through only during the summer. Residents living in the proximity of the river have built two log bridges to reach an agricultural estate on the other side, where a few community members are seasonally employed. They recall numerous fatal accidents involving workers from both Comunidad Contreras and nearby settlements. Falling from these high log bridges is very likely to result in death due to the strong currents and the presence of rocks along the river. Dangers also can be found in the thick forestation extending along both banks. Mountain lions (*trapial*) lurk in this area and although contacts with humans are rare, residents who encounter them remember the sight as a terrifying moment. The Quino River is also the primary setting for encounters with *ngenko*, the spirit of water. As seen in chapter 3, *ngenko* manifests itself as a half-fish woman (*sumpall*) or as the floating skin of a bull (*kürü kullin*) along the banks of rivers. While some residents treat accounts of the appearance of *ngenko* with skepticism and quickly discard them as legends (*leyendas*), others recall numerous cases in which those who encountered the entities were struck by misfortune soon after. Despite discordant opinions among local residents about the presence of *ngenko* spirits along this river, the possibility of facing them along the banks of the Quino River reinforces a general perception of this watercourse as a vital and yet dangerous topographic feature. In accordance with experiences and oral accounts reinforcing a perception of this river as a spatial marker, no territorial claims have ever been raised on land located beyond it.

The other watercourse, Estero Huadaco, is located one kilometer from the northern boundary of the Indigenous community. Huadaco is a creek with little importance for agricultural and domestic activities as, according to its Mapudungun etymology (*weda-ko*, "bad water"), it is thought to be harmful to humans and cattle. Unlike its water, the vegetation surrounding this creek is highly valued among local residents. Around its banks lies one of the area's few native woods (*bosque nativo* in Spanish, *mawida* in Mapudungun). Native woods are also likely dwelling places for ngen spirit masters and other entities. During fieldwork, I have heard about the presence of a river snake, *culebrón*, living around Huadaco Creek. Among both Mapuche and chilenos, narratives about the *culebrón* emphasize the voracious nature of this creature, who would attack anyone attempting to unearth treasures guarded by it. This entity is generally not considered a manifestation of *ngenko*, as its origins are usually associated with Spanish mythology. Regardless of its origins, accounts about the *culebrón* contribute to the general perception of Huadaco Creek as a place with little interest for local residents, if not a dangerous place. However, the Huadaco still offers local residents with a high concentration of endemic plant and tree species serving as *lawen* (herbal remedies) and as features of collective rituals. Among the different native species located around this creek, one finds large numbers of canelo trees (*Drymis winteri; foye* in Mapudungun), an essential element in Mapuche rituals (Bacigalupo 2007,

75). When shaken during healing practices (*machitun*) or collective rituals, canelo branches serve to protect those present against evildoing and to infuse them with newen, a beneficial spiritual force. Canelo is also a crucial element of the rewe, a sculptured trunk of laurel (*triwe*) adorned with branches from different trees, which serves as the ceremonial centerpiece for Mapuche religious practices. I will explore in more detail the potentials of religious social practices, particularly those related to ngillatun, in the articulation of land demands in the following chapter. For now, it is sufficient to recognize the central role that this watercourse played in the context of collective practices held by residents of Comunidad Contreras.

Before each ngillatun, old canelo branches at the top of each rewe must be replaced with fresh ones, an activity described to me by my hosts as "the renovation of the rewe." The renovation of the rewe follows a group trip to the Huadaco, where a few volunteers cut new canelo branches under the direction of one resident, lonko Nelly, who has been acting as the community ritual organizer for a few years.[2] This activity is highly ritualized and is generally accompanied by a *llellipun* incantation, whereby permission to take branches is sought from the corresponding ngen spirit master. Community members generally describe trips to the Huadaco in preparation for a ngillatun as part of a body of ritual knowledge inherited from the ancient ones. For any ritual to be effective, its practices must be reproduced from one generation to the next as precisely as possible, leaving little space for improvisation. The same is true for the collective gathering of canelo branches around the Huadaco. By walking toward this creek as a collectivity, residents become aware that this apparently insignificant watercourse has been an integral part of community life since ancient times. As Christopher Tilley (1994) suggests, walking is an essential activity in structuring knowledge about landscape. In a similar vein, walking to Huadaco Creek in the completion of a ritualistic practice reinforces a sense of relatedness with the tract of land framed by this watercourse and of unrelatedness with the land beyond it.

Experiences around the Quino River and Huadaco Creek reflect the sentient character of land in Mapuche society. As seen throughout this book, one of the constitutive features of personhood is the mutual relation between the experiential and embodied significations of place and, according to the notion of tuwün, the existence of place as a given potentiality preexisting individual engagement with the environment. The foregoing suggests that the transformation of the ancestral territory into property carried out by claimants cannot be reduced to a forced eradication of their knowledge about land and local history, and more broadly, of the characterization of land as sentient. By adjusting knowledge about local history and perceptions about the landscape to the requirements of the land restitution program, claimants are able to demarcate and ultimately stabilize their uncertain knowledge of the ancestral territory. The use of documents and cartography in the claim-staking process can clarify this point.

## Documents, Maps, and Transactions in Land Claims

CONADI guidelines explicitly define deed titles and court decisions on property disputes as the primary sources of documentary evidence to prove ancestral land dispossession (see Bauer 2018). This principle has been supported by different governmental reports, including that of the Comisión de Verdad Histórica y Nuevo Trato of 2003, the largest commission on Indigenous social policies ever instituted in Chile. This commission recommended that compensation for land dispossession should be awarded only for those claims backed by evidence of loss of reservation land. This recommendation attracted the criticism of Indigenous activists for excluding demands over land lost prior to the introduction of the reservation system (Toledo Llancaqueo 2005). According to CONADI guidelines, archaeological and anthropological reports (*informes*) are accepted as complementary evidence in the review phase. The numerous difficulties of evidence production within the claim-staking process are the primary reason that claimants seek support from Indigenous and human rights organizations. For a claim to be successful, evidence indeed needs to be merged with a convincing legal argument. The board of Comunidad Contreras sought the legal support of two influential organizations in Temuco: Fundación Instituto Indígena, a nongovernmental agency affiliated with the local bishopric, and Observatorio de Derecho de los Pueblos Indígenas, the most renowned institute specializing in Indigenous rights in Chile. Community representatives also contacted an archaeologist to conduct a preliminary study on the possible presence of ancient cemeteries, or eltun, in the demanded territory. A preliminary study was carried out with the participation of a few local residents who helped the archaeologist to retrieve a few samples of stone tools in one particular site located outside the boundaries of the comunidad. The final archaeological report, which was included in the land claim, indicated the probable presence of an ancient site and recommended further excavation.

The claim of Comunidad Contreras was particularly complex. Their demand indeed concerned land whose loss preceded the institution of their reservation in 1884. It thus fell outside the more typical case of compensation of reservation land loss. The only evidence that could prove this particular case of land dispossession was cartographic documents anteceding 1884. As part of my involvement in their land claim, I joined the members of Comunidad Contreras in the search for maps of and documents about their community that predated the founding title of their reservation. I made several visits to the Archivo General de Asuntos Indígenas (AGAI), which brings together information about Indigenous people in Chile previously held in different archives. It was a common opinion among community members that, given ongoing discrimination against Mapuche farmers in state offices, it would be easier for a foreign researcher than it would be for them to gain access to historical documentation. As a council member stated during a community meeting, "People in CONADI treat us with great suspicion and look down at us for being Mapuche farmers. In contrast, they always welcome Piero. We should take advantage of this situation." During the review process, residents of Comunidad Contreras hoped that deep in some state archives lay key documents that would unequivocally prove the extension of their ancestral land. However, our search was not fruitful. Archivists at CONADI assured me that no official cartography had been carried out in the area around Comunidad Contreras until the introduction of the reservation system.

The lack of precolonial cartography did not prevent the board of Comunidad Contreras from presenting other documentary sources. The Título de Merced 18-B, the document that established the foundation of Reducción Contreras in 1884 (see fig. 13), was included in the land claim as primary evidence for the existence of their ancestral territory. This sets the extent of Reducción Contreras at 760 hectares. Given that the size of the reducción was recorded as 700 hectares in 2005, the map included in the *título* proved beyond doubt that 60 hectares of reservation land

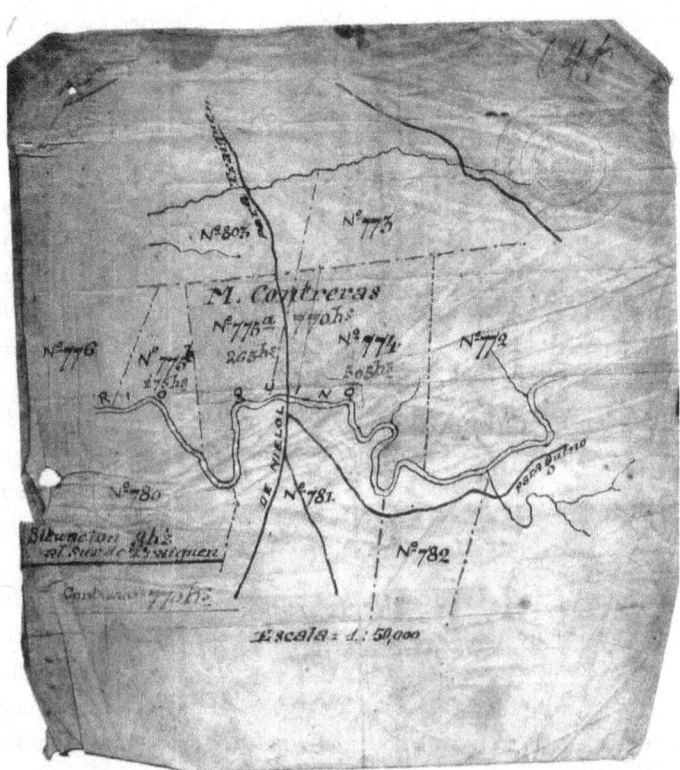

FIGURE 13  Map of the Título de Merced 18-B. (Archivo AGAI CONADI)

had been expropriated between 1884 and 2005. However, the board of Comunidad Contreras used this map as evidence for the historical dispossession of 1,200 hectares of land lying outside the limits of the original reservation. Clearly, the value of this cartographic document was not confined to its ability to prove the expropriation of land after the resettlement process. In its claim, the board of Comunidad Contreras argued that the depiction of the area surrounding the reservation in this map proved that state officials involved in the resettlement process were aware of the extent of the ancestral territory. While the latter is clearly shown on the Título de Merced map, its boundaries are not delineated. Besides the reservation's limits—marked in red— the only topographic features that appear on this map are the Estero Huadaco and the Quino River. The board identified these two watercourses as the northern and southern "natural boundaries" (*limites naturales*) of community land, a point consistent with the customary employment of rivers as boundaries for large landholdings in southern Chile. However, the Título de Merced map gives no indication of the western and eastern limits of this ancestral territory. Accordingly, on the map presented in the community claim, the eastern and western boundaries were squared off in such a way that the total amount of land for which restitution was demanded fell within the ratio of area-per-signatory established by CONADI. While many community members believed that the ancestral territory extended farther than the limits identified in the claim, the lack of clearly visible western and eastern boundaries required them to adjust their proposed demarcation to the criteria established by CONADI.

The demarcation of the ancestral territory by Comunidad Contreras exemplifies the dilemmas inherent in all land restitution programs. One such dilemma is that claimants are forced to prove dispossession through the means offered by documentary regimes initially designed to facilitate that dispossession. For colonized groups, historical cartography has had a double role as a strategy of colonial domination and a viable means for them to protect existing land access (Cohn and Dirks 1988). As Joanne Rappaport (1998, 11) has shown, among the Paez of the Colombian highlands, colonial land titles are represented as powerful Indigenous objects in mythohistorical narratives that openly challenge European narratives of conquest and assimilation. Dissident uses of colonial cartography by Indigenous groups, as exemplified by Mapuche legal claims over ancestral land, can also be explained with reference to the susceptibility of maps to divergent interpretations. The power of maps generally rests on their reification as self-evident representations of social reality (Ingold 2000, 224; Turnbull 2000, 1). Even when cartographic projects are well-intentioned, "The creation of maps that represent local land use in forms that are legible to the state bears the risk of displacing other, embodied ways of knowing one's land" (Kirsch 2006, 202). Yet like other written expressions, cartographic representations are characterized by a certain degree of malleability. As Benjamin Orlove (1991) suggests, the permanence of maps is what "makes their content public and subject to multiple interpretations" (4). The ambiguous nature of colonial cartography also reflects some of the general features of archival knowledge. While the power of archives depends largely on their role in delegitimizing knowledge that stands outside them (Zeitlyn 2012), their connection with promises of democratization and empowerment for citizens in grounding legal claims allows them to be interiorized and validated as regimes of truth by users themselves (Hetherington 2011, 166). As Hirokazu Miyazaki (2004) suggests, a key effect of the existence of archives is the generation of hope that they contain yet-to-be-discovered documents with the potential to validate other truth claims. Similarly, the engagement of the board members of Comunidad Contreras with archives illustrates that the veracity of the ancestral territory is not opposed to archival information as a contrasting regime of truth. Rather, a direct engagement with archives can stabilize uncertainties about ancestral land. The board members' fruitless search for a missing document that could settle state officials' doubts about their claim reinforced the suspicion among the residents of Comunidad Contreras that the state was jealously guarding knowledge about their ancestral territory and refusing to make it public in order to limit Mapuche demands for land.

Mapuche land claimants' critical engagement with documentary regimes illustrates the possibility not only for subversive readings of archival information but also for the employment of documents as tokens of power that could potentially invert the customary power dynamics between Indigenous and non-Indigenous people (Gordillo 2006; Veber 1998). On several occasions, community members told me that the success of their claim depended on their ability to gather together as many documents as possible, regardless of their content, so that the state officials reviewing their case would take them seriously. Such a point is consistent with the characterization of documents as a means to counteract power imbalances between Mapuche and winkas, as I have discussed in the previous chapter. Since winkas' power is commonly associated with their astute use of documents, narratives about the past emphasize the need for the adoption of documents—and for formal education in Spanish more generally—as strategies of self-defense. In such narratives, the ancient ones tend to be portrayed in contradictory terms. On the one hand, they are commemorated for their exceptional knowledge of natural phenomena and for the respect that characterized their social relations; on the other hand, they are accused of being superstitious and soft targets for winkas' tricks (*engaños*), such that they readily fell victim to land expropriation by estate owners. Similar ideas are apparent in claimants' interpretations of their engagement with the land restitution program. During a meeting, Roberto, a member of Comunidad Contreras in his fifties, stated with respect to the land claim, "We need to learn from the winkas. This is what Lautaro did. He was adopted by Valdivia, learned everything about the Spaniards from him, and then returned to his land to fight against him." Roberto is referring here to the relation between Lautaro, one of the most powerful *toqui* (war chiefs) in Mapuche history, and the Spanish conquistador Pedro de Valdivia. Lautaro had once been enslaved but became Valdivia's interpreter and assistant. After years of service, he escaped to southern Chile, where he shared the Spaniards' military secrets with Mapuche war leaders and sowed the seeds of the Spanish downfall.

As the foregoing discussion makes clear, the power of documents in land claims lies in their openness to subversive interpretations and their employment as a means to address power imbalances with colonial others. By emphasizing the possibility of pragmatic adoption of colonial culture, Mapuche narratives about literacy and documents challenge straightforward stories of colonial domination (Pels 1997), which ignore the creative ways in which colonized people grasp the logic of colonial states without sacrificing their own interests (Robbins 2004, 4). Indigenous groups in Latin America have a long history of both using colonial documents and producing their own documents as strategies to subvert power relations (Abercrombie 1998, 119). Official letters, for instance, have been a central mode of communication between Mapuche caciques and Chilean political authorities since the mid-1800s (Pavez 2008).[3] As seen in chapter 4, narratives about the adoption of documents by Mapuche land claimants highlight the paradox of needing to embrace elements of colonial culture to resist assimilation. While documents have historically served as a means of self-defense, their use is also associated with the phenomenon of becoming winka-like (awinkado), a status consisting in the loss of essential Mapuche practices and values. In particular, residents of Comunidad Contreras tend to see the ubiquitous use of documents in regulating social relations within Mapuche communities as evidence of loss of respect, a value understood as a central element of identity. But despite the threat of assimilation, land claims show that documents remain an effective means to beneficially shift power relations with outsiders such as state officials and estate owners.

Mapuche claimants can, thus, resignify the documentary regime at work in land claims and employ property titles and colonial cartography to frame local knowledge about ancestral land. Claimants' use of colonial maps and documents reflects some of the broader features of the notion of transaction, in Strathern's and Hirsch's (2004) sense. Such use establishes new relations between the sets of values associated with local geographic constructions and those established within the jural language of property. My definition of ancestral land demarcation as a form of transaction allows me to recognize the creative and critical agency of Indigenous claimants. However, such a definition should not be read as an attempt to underestimate the way the state translates the ancestral territory and makes it commensurable with existing property regimes. Before exploring the outcomes of governmental translations of Mapuche territories, I would like to draw attention to some of the key differences between transaction and translation that I have in mind. Transaction, we have seen, is a human facility as well a process inherent to social interactions that allow the transactability of items and ideas (Strathern and Hirsch 2004, 8). Translation, a key notion within anthropology's own self-analysis, is the process by which a phenomenon is transformed into a comparable phenomenon within a different context of intelligibility. Translation is not a mere act of linguistic conversion. It exceeds language exactly because it connects phenomena across separate ontological barriers, thus prompting their alteration (Hanks and Severi 2014, 8). Once taken as a transformative process rather than a mere facilitator of communication, translation becomes an intrinsically political process (Gal 2015, 225). Central to the politics of translation are the asymmetries between the different contexts of intelligibility that this process aims to abridge. Nowhere is this clearer than in the governmental translation of the ancestral territory into land grants defined around the existing legal language of property.

## Translations, State Power, and the Becoming of Ancestral Land

Deliberations on land claims depend on numerous factors, including the urgency to resolve land disputes and the support of state officials for specific Indigenous communities as part of political patronage in rural Chile. Staking a claim for land restitution is thus never an exclusively bureaucratic matter. For over five years, the board of Comunidad Contreras organized meetings with influential political intermediaries and carried out acts of mobilization, such as road blockades, to exert pressure on CONADI to find a resolution to their claim. As a matter of fact, a claim can languish for several years in CONADI offices before it is actually reviewed. In 2009, five years after Comunidad Contreras lodged its claim, CONADI deliberated in its favor and by 2012 had transferred two-thirds of the demanded land to the Indigenous community. By 2014, the annexed properties had been divided among the signatories to the claim.[4] In the final report of Comunidad Contreras's claim (*resolución exenta*), one finds general references to the consistency of documentation and archival evidence as the main reason for the positive deliberation. For community members, the claim's success depended largely on their ability to gather a substantial body of documentation and on their willingness to mobilize to demand a resolution to their demands. Most claims are disqualified early in the review process for lack of adequate supporting documents. The general feeling among them was that, rather than facilitating their claim, CONADI was responsible for all the obstacles that they had encountered. It is for this reason that functionaries of this agency were not invited to partake in the official celebration for the transferal of one of the demanded properties described at the beginning of this book.

Claimants' emphasis on their active role in the land claim process challenges any depiction of this process as a social policy imposed upon passive political actors. Rather than mere participation in a bureaucratic process, friends at Comunidad Contreras have generally described their actions to me as a fight (*lucha*) for "territorial restoration" (*recuperación territorial*). During fieldwork, I heard the use of the term *territorial restoration* to refer to processes as diverse as land occupations by Indigenous organizations, participatory land mapping (Hirt 2009), and legal claims regulated by CONADI procedures. Members of Comunidad Contreras tend to characterize their land claim as an instance of community struggle, a point consistent with the localized form of identity inherent in the notion of tuwün. For some of them, the local character of territorial restoration does not contradict the fact that land claims belong to a broader pan-Mapuche action aimed at fostering forms of autonomous governance (see Caniuqueo 2011). While claimants tend to characterize land claims as territorial restoration, this same phenomenon is conceptualized in different terms by state officials. I became aware of these divergences during my visits to CONADI. On one occasion, I asked an official about his opinion on the role played by CONADI within the process of land restoration. I was quickly reproached by my interlocutor: "The Chilean state does not recognize any form of 'territorial restoration.' The right term is 'purchase of land' [*compra de tierra*], which CONADI does to benefit Indigenous communities." This apparently trivial disagreement over words encapsulates a more profound tension: that between Indigenous agency and state control. Put in analytical terms, the question is how to recognize, on the one hand, claimants' own perspectives on the effectiveness and creativity of their action and, on the other, the extent of state power. A look at the compensatory mechanisms of the Indigenous land program can help us in approaching this question.

Since 1993, the Chilean state has allocated an unprecedented amount of public funds to land subsidies. Between 1994 and 2004, more than 416,000 hectares were transferred to Indigenous families nationwide. But behind these statistical accounts of success lie several shortcomings concerning the impact of the land program on the livelihoods of members of Indigenous settlements. Roughly 66 percent of land transferred to beneficiaries of this program from 1994 to 2000 corresponded to state-owned properties concentrated in mountainous areas that had never been involved in litigation over restitution (Richards 2013, 76). Given the shortage of state-owned land, the future prospects for the allocation of subsidies appear gloomy. Another limitation of the land program concerns the consequences of subsidy allocation. For instance, beneficiaries rarely have access to those technologies necessary to farm new properties, so that subsidized land is often rented to non-Indigenous agricultural entrepreneurs, a consequence that paradoxically reinforces dependence on non-Indigenous people despite promises of economic autonomy embodied by land subsidization. From the claimants' point of view, however, the most tangible shortcoming of the land programs concerns the compensatory mechanisms through which land disputes are conciliated. As prescribed by the 1993 Indigenous Law, land can be transferred to claimants only if the current owners are willing to sell their properties to the state. Accordingly, in the last twenty years, only a handful of Indigenous communities have secured the restitution of ancestral land, as many communities with a proven case of dispossession have been divided up and relocated through the endowment of land grants (Mallon 2005). Even if the claim of Comunidad Contreras was successful in comparison with those of other Mapuche settlements, its demands for restitution were never met in full. Roughly two-thirds of the demanded land has been annexed to the comunidad to date. The rest is still in the possession of an estate owner who has refused to negotiate the sale of his property with CONADI. To this day, residents reject open confrontations with the estate owner as a viable option for their claim. Occasional meetings involving CONADI representatives, board members, and the estate owner have been organized, but the restitution of this property remains a distant prospect. Community members have faced a dilemma shared by virtually all Mapuche settlements: to accept relocation to an "alternative property" (*predio alternativo*) or to pursue more radical forms of mobilization—and thus run the risk of suffering police repression—in an attempt to have all their ancestral territory returned. Another consequence of the compensatory mechanisms at work in the land program is that by accepting land grants as compensation, Indigenous communities exclude themselves from making any further claim. Given the limited funding currently available to CONADI, this agency has opted to prioritize claims from communities who have not previously forwarded them. Signatories to the Comunidad Contreras claim have been enjoying economic benefits from the annexation of land following the resolution of their case. However, they will have little chance to pursue further restitution in the future.

The implications of the compensation process suggest that Indigenous land claims in Chile may paradoxically contribute to a disruption of the link between local residents and their ancestral territory, which is usually what motivates demands for land restitution in the first place. The allotment of land grants as compensation for historical dispossession is not a new phenomenon in Latin America. Land reforms and cartographic practices have long served to fix Indigenous land "as a stable, visible and readable stage" for state intervention (Craib 2004, 8). Indigenous land programs often lead to the formation of territorial constructs that are at odds with local modes of land use. In Latin America, Indigenous land reforms have created administrative units, such as ejidos in Mexico (Nujten 2003, 45) and *comunidades campesinas* in Peru (Nujten and Lorenzo 2009), where Indigenous identity has been dissolved in favor of a rural national identity. The allocation of land grants also shifts the discursive focus from restitution to endowment, allowing the state to co-opt the rural Indigenous population by portraying itself as a donor to which Indigenous people should be grateful (Nugent and Alonso 1994, 238). The fixing of Indigenous geographies through land endowment centers on one particular principle of statecraft, that of standardization. James Scott (1998) has illustrated how modern forms of statecraft have consolidated through the historic development of a metric that allows the state "to translate what it knew into a common standard necessary for a synoptic view" (2). Standardization thus consists of the imposition of a conceptual grid that transforms qualitative differences, such as disparate forms of land ownership, into quantitative ones, such as hectares to be transferred (15). The translation of ancestral territories into quantifiable land grants highlights profound divergences between Indigenous claimants' spatial and temporal conceptualizations on the one hand and the land grants they would receive should their claims be successful on the other. In particular, such a translation entails the introduction of a regime of temporality that contrasts sharply with the historical continuity implicit in Indigenous notions of territoriality. In legal understandings of property, the legitimacy of any form of land ownership rests not on the authority of the past but, rather, on contemporary mediations (Abramson 2000, 8). In this context, "Each change of ownership takes place as an event, disconnected from all others" (14). In contrast to conceptualizations of ancestral territory that emphasize continuity with the past, the formation of new Indigenous land properties as a result of land compensation emerges as a foundational and irreversible event that works to exclude those tracts of land that are not legally recognized as ancestral from future demands (Peluso 1995, 385; Wainwright and Bryan 2009, 163).

The translation of ancestral territory into land grants reveals the profound ontological differences between concepts of property, according to which land is an undifferentiated and quantifiable object, and the notion of tuwün, which presupposes land as a plenary and agential being. While the ancestral territory is the result of claimants' creative transactions in the process of demarcation, state power materializes in the translation of this geographic construct into land grants commensurable with existing property regimes. This tension is highly evocative of the notions of deterritorialization and reterritorialization introduced by Deleuze and Guattari (1987) in their analysis of state power. Deterritorialization can be summarized as a process through which indeterminate and creative forces constitute expanding networks of connections unfolding in an immanent plane of existence. In contrast, reterritorialization refers to any state or action aimed at recoding unrestrained movement associated with deterritorialization. Ultimately, deterritorialization and reterritorialization are mutually constituted, as any form of becoming is the deterritorialization of one term and the reterritorialization of another (Deleuze and Guattari 1987, 10). Becoming in this case can be said to be the movement by which a subject departs from its own condition by means of a relationship of affect that can be established with another condition (Goldman 2013, 21). In Deleuze and Guattari's formulation, the state appears as a power formation whose function is to capture energy through constant reterritorialization (Patton 1984, 68). Conceptually the state exists only through its opposition to stateless societies, which are characterized by multiple lines of deterritorialization and internal processes through which the accumulation of power and capital is resisted. This characterization of stateless societies stems from Deleuze and Guattari's engagement with Pierre Clastres's (1987) formulation of society against the state, a proposal that draws attention to the immanent nature of power in Amazonian societies as a form of internal opposition to state formation (Hage 2012, 298).

Deleuze and Guattari's (1994, 101–2) use of the term *territory* refers to a broad immanent plane of thoughts and relations among different forces, which is crossed by different forms of movement. Applying the notion of territory too literally in the analysis of postcolonial land politics clearly oversimplifies the conceptual ramifications of Deleuze and Guattari's perspective on the problem of immanence. Yet their spatial terminology provides me with a language to articulate the conceptual opposition between Indigenous and state geographies. Clearly I am not alone in this, as Deleuze and Guattari's notion of reterritorialization has been profoundly influential in the geographical analysis of statecraft (Patton 1984). For example, Gastón Gordillo (2011) has proposed that, rather than referring exclusively to state power, reterritorialization can be constructive in framing Indigenous processes of territorial codification as practices of resistance. Indigenous reterritorializations can thus produce "spaces through the horizontal spread of flat, connective, but relatively independent lines of spatial expansion" (859). In this chapter I have also drawn on Deleuzian notions of reterritorialization and state power. Rather than the reconstruction of Indigenous past geographies, as the term *reterritorialization* initially might be interpreted, I take this notion as a state process of spatial domestication. As I have argued earlier, property is not something that is merely imposed on a purely Indigenous territoriality, as its conceptual assumptions are integral parts of how claimants envision their ancestral territory. The subtle nature of Indigenous/state relations invites us to abandon an oppositional view forging a representation of the state as a monolithic entity (Abrams 1977; Alonso 1994; Gupta 1995). However, my acknowledgment of the embeddedness of property and Indigenous geographic notions in the actions of claimants should not be read as an attempt to underemphasize state power. I have suggested that by employing the means and technologies of an existing regime's property to their own ends, Mapuche claimants also validate them. To recognize Indigenous societies in the context of land claims as being simultaneously against and within the state can help us to uncover state power as an interiorized set of conceptual assumptions that can be simultaneously challenged and reinforced in practice.

In this chapter, I have explored the tension between Indigenous and legal land ontologies in Mapuche land claims, and in particular in the demarcation of ancestral territories. The ethnographic analysis of claim staking in southern Chile suggests that the conceptual and material ramifications of articulating ancestral land through the jural language of property materialize not in the act of demarcating this territory but, rather, in the formation of new spatial constructs that reflect the particular logic of compensation at work in land claims. A focus on the limitations and possibilities offered to Mapuche claimants by the technologies of property has allowed me to rearticulate a question central to the broader debate on multiculturalism and postcolonialism: Can the governmentalization of territorial disputes allow for the emergence of nondominant forms of spatiality? Analysts have provided different answers. For instance, in his ethnographic study of land claims of the Kluane First Nation, Paul Nadasdy (2003) has argued that "by accepting and adapting to governments' bureaucratic approach to Aboriginal state relations, First Nation people also tacitly accept the assumptions about the nature of lands and animals that underlie the rules and functions of that bureaucracy" (8). These assumptions run counter to existing perspectives on the environment, including the fact that land among the Kluane cannot be owned (Nadasdy 2002, 249). A similar scenario can be observed in Mapuche land claims, in which claimants are forced to prove the existence of their ancestral territory primarily through documents that have been designed to delegitimize local forms of land occupation. Yet as this chapter has shown, Indigenous and legal land ontologies are enmeshed in the experiences of claimants. In Mapuche areas, property is conceptualized as part of a broader struggle for protection against colonial encroachment. Furthermore, it has been historically incorporated in daily expressions of sociability, which are shaped around property relations. Any statement describing land claims in southern Chile as the imposition of a foreign set of ideas would misrepresent the hybrid position of Mapuche rural residents within the Chilean nation. The dual connotation of property for Indigenous people—as a means of both domination and self-defense—might explain why notions of property introduced as part of colonial enterprises can simultaneously be interiorized as a set of rights and discourses on morality and openly defied in practice, as land claims show. The ability shown by the members of Comunidad Contreras in using archival sources to their own ends clearly illustrates this possibility. Yet the compensatory mechanisms of the Chilean land program reveal the potential of property theory to delegitimize Indigenous forms of territoriality. The lessons provided by Mapuche land claims to the broader debate on legal pluralism are further discussed in the following chapter. Here, I focus on frictions and misunderstandings between state officials and Mapuche claimants in the negotiations concerning the resolution of land disputes.

# CHAPTER 6

# NEGOTIATING ANCESTRAL LAND

*Claimants, Bureaucrats, and the Realpolitik of Sacredness*

"MAPUCHE BLAME THE GOVERNMENT FOR DISPUTE OVER AGRICUL-tural estate." Under this headline on September 16, 2008, *El Mercurio*, a widely read conservative newspaper, reported the declaration of José Contreras, spokesperson (*werken*) of Comunidad Contreras: "We cannot reach the point of killing ourselves among brothers due to government's fault" (Fredes 2008). José's words referred to a recent event involving a few members of his community and those of another Mapuche settlement. A brawl had erupted, resulting in minor injuries to four individuals as a consequence of an attempted arson at a particular site—a rewe, a step-notched tree trunk serving as the ceremonial centerpiece for Mapuche rituals. Members of Comunidad Contreras had installed a rewe a few months earlier on a property, Fundo El Panal, which was in dispute between the two parties. This confrontation was the last straw in several months of mounting tensions. In 2006, CONADI had taken the controversial decision to assign El Panal—which was part of the Comunidad Contreras claim—to a group of Mapuche grantees who were originally from a settlement located ninety kilometers away from it. The spokesperson's words stood as a ringing accusation against the Chilean state, first for instigating a confrontation among Mapuche people and second for failing to provide a satisfactory resolution to this legal controversy. Soon after the dispute over El Panal estate broke out, delegates of Comunidad Contreras led negotiations involving members of the two communities, high-ranked officials from CONADI, and influential intermediaries to find a resolution for the dispute. Among the most pressing issues discussed during negotiations was the contentious presence of the rewe. During fieldwork I often heard sarcastic comments by chilenos about the sudden appearance of sacred sites across the southern

Chilean countryside ever since the Indigenous land program has been in place. This opinion was echoed among some of the state officials involved in the negotiations over El Panal, for whom the rewe was nothing more than a show prepared by Comunidad Contreras.

The strategic use of sacred sites, and their role in strengthening claims over ancestral territories, has long been observed in Chile, as in many other postcolonial contexts. An overarching question reverberates in governmental offices around the world: Can sacred sites evoked in Indigenous land negotiations be more than performative political claims? This question is at the very core of misunderstandings and other epistemic failures at work in land negotiations. Its answer lies beyond academic interest, as the chance for Mapuche claimants to restore their land depends on it. In this chapter, I focus on the intricate case of the El Panal dispute in order to show the general role of sacred sites in Indigenous political action and negotiations with state officials. Attention will be drawn to some of the reasons that misunderstandings originate and their implications for the broader framework of multicultural governance. Common explanations for misunderstandings in land claims point to their strategic nature and to the postulated impossibility of mutual intelligibility. Thus, state actors would simply be unable to understand Mapuche claimants or refuse to do so in the name of personal or institutional benefits. While these two explanations certainly resonate in land negotiations in southern Chile, they also fail to grasp the interethnic and Indigenous/state subtleties. Officials involved in Indigenous issues are often well-intended, and their actions cannot be reduced to vehicles of official discourses. The scenario is further complicated by the fact that in southern Chile, it is very common to find Mapuche people working in state institutions.

In this chapter I intend to show that misunderstandings in Mapuche land negotiations in Chile do not originate as strategic refusals to understand or lack of mutual communication, but rather in a form of understanding that aims to make radical differences commensurable within the logic of statecraft. This particular form of comprehension, which I call "understanding by domestication," depends on the extension of familiar meanings and expectations onto homonymic phenomena—that is, concepts such as sacred sites, which might look or sound the same, in fact reveal the existence of ontological divergences (Viveiros de Castro 2004). In the process of cultural translation, the ontological principles that make certain places sacred in the Mapuche lived world are not recognized, and this results in the sites being interpreted as symbols of identity that are strategically employed for political ends. The sentient character of the ancestral territory is reduced to a cultural attribute, thus allowing for the commensuration of ancestral land as a form of property dependent on existing market configurations. Far from being neutral instances of failed communication, misunderstandings contribute to and reflect late liberal ideologies of public reason, which aim to domesticate radical difference by making incommensurable worlds appear unremarkably similar (see Povinelli 2001). Looking at misunderstandings in land negotiations helps me to go deeper in the analysis of state translations of ancestral territories that I began in the previous chapter. The suspension of radical difference in land negotiations ultimately reflects the ideal of neoliberal multiculturalism, according to which cultural differences can be values insofar as they are organized on the basis of market values.

## Land Compensations Gone Wrong: The Case of the El Panal Dispute

In the previous chapter, I showed the inherent difficulties of evidentiary production in land claims and the creative solutions that claimants conceived to bolster their demands. The need to provide convincing evidence of historic dispossession, however, is not the only major obstacle that Mapuche people face upon entering the land program. Claims also fail as a consequence of disagreement between three parties— Indigenous communities, non-Indigenous landholders, and state officials—on the purchase and transfer of properties subject to the demands of restitution. The absence of a principle of expropriation in Ley Indígena 19.253 makes all land claims exclusively dependent on the will of landowners to negotiate the sale of their properties to CONADI. As seen earlier, Mapuche claimants with a proven case of dispossession are thus forced to accept the allocation of an "alternative property" in order not to miss out on compensation. Claimants are often relocated to land according to availability in the estate market. Indigenous beneficiaries are asked to indicate their preference for properties to be negotiated. Proximity to one's settlement and quality of soil are key factors in claimants' choices. Given the shortage of properties whose owners are willing to sell to CONADI, Mapuche claimants are forced to compete among themselves for land opportunities. News about local estates for sale circulates quickly across Indigenous settlements. The reconfiguration of the estate market produced by the particular compensatory mechanisms at work in the land program has produced an increasing number of Mapuche and non-Indigenous brokers. Their role consists mainly in striking agreements between landowners and Mapuche communities that could be beneficial to both parties. Furthermore, there are widespread suspicions that estate owners are increasingly interested in escalation of conflicts, as the price of properties under dispute rise in negotiations with CONADI. Among large landholders, this state agency is known as a reliable buyer in comparison with other potential purchasers.

Tensions between Indigenous communities can arise when two or more community boards set their eyes on the same properties. The members of Comunidad Contreras faced the prospect of having to compete for land grants with other claimants on two occasions. In 2006, the community board found out that they were not the only ones interested in two estates, El Huadaco and El Panal, both adjacent to their settlement. A section of each of these two properties was indicated as part of their ancestral territory in the claim forwarded to CONADI one year earlier. Claimants from Comunidad Molco, a nearby community, visited the two properties on numerous occasions after being granted right to a land subsidy by CONADI. As soon as the board of Comunidad Contreras knew about this potential conflict of interest, they began negotiations with their potential new neighbors. The two parties finally reached an agreement according to which claimants from Comunidad Molco would express their preferences for land grants in relation to only those tracts of land from the two properties that were not demanded as part of the ancestral territory by Comunidad Contreras. The other conflict of interest over land proved more intricate. At the end of 2008, CONADI assigned the estate El Panal to Comunidad Paillacoy, an Indigenous community located ninety kilometers from this estate. A few weeks later, escorted by police, less than twenty residents from this community moved to three former estate workers' houses within this property. For residents of Comunidad Contreras, this decision was unsound as it infringed on their ancestral rights over El Panal estate. They immediately appealed to CONADI to annul the allocation. However, officials were reluctant to take action, because a reversal of the legislation would have been equivalent to an admission of guilt for their incorrect decision.

During my stay in southern Chile, I heard numerous accounts of state functionaries favoring land grants to Mapuche claimants with whom they would later form a partnership in agricultural activities. For people at Comunidad Contreras, the relocation of other Mapuche grantees to land they had put in a claim for, and CONADI's unwillingness to take action in the resultant legal dispute, was not caused simply by a bureaucratic deficiency. Rather, everything pointed to the existence of cliental relations between CONADI officials and the relocated land grantees. This hypothesis gained strength a few months later when residents of Comunidad Contreras heard rumors from connections at CONADI about cases of influence peddling implicating at least a couple of functionaries. While rumors were never confirmed in court, doubts about the inexplicable action of relocating Mapuche claimants to land demanded for restitution by others were never cleared up. Soon after the relocation of claimants from Comunidad Paillacoy to El Panal, the board of Comunidad Contreras took action on several different fronts. First, they met with their new neighbors to seek an agreement about their possible relocation. However, the new residents of El Panal estate rejected invitations to negotiate their further relocation as they were justifiably concerned about losing their land grants. It soon became evident to the board of Comunidad Contreras that pressure was needed to force CONADI to reverse their decision. To this end they staged numerous road blockades around their settlement and protests in the nearby city of Temuco.¹ To further publicize their case, the community board wrote several letters to newspapers and online magazines.² Mobilization was instrumental in establishing a large network of local politicians and human rights organizations who could act as intermediaries in negotiations with CONADI officials. An intense agenda of meetings, mainly in the city of Temuco, was set up and hosted by high-ranking officials from institutions other than CONADI, including NGOs such as the Fundación Instituto Indígena, which was affiliated with the regional bishopric.³ For local residents, the most memorable of these meetings occurred in 2007, when a few delegates traveled to the capital, Santiago, to present their case to then president Michelle Bachelet during a public hearing. During fieldwork, I had the chance to attend numerous meetings in Temuco. They generally concluded with CONADI officials promising a prompt resolution that, nonetheless, never materialized. The reason officials could constantly make empty promises in the dispute over El Panal can be found in the administrative structure of CONADI. High positions in CONADI were generally distributed among members of national parties in line with national elections. Furthermore, these positions rotated so quickly that it was unfeasible to establish long-term relations with anyone, as the delegates of Comunidad Contreras were attempting to do.

FIGURE 14  Sit-in at regional government building (Intendencia Regional) in Temuco. (Photo by author)

The dispute over El Panal seemed to have ground to a halt. Not until October 2007 did an unforeseeable development bring new hope to the residents of Comunidad Contreras. A group of residents from Comunidad Paillacoy approached José, the *werken* of Comunidad Contreras, and revealed that only a few members of their community had moved to El Panal, while the rest had remained in their settlement. Thus it emerged that Comunidad Paillacoy was divided into two factions—the one that had moved, and one that was willing to negotiate that relocation and leave El Panal estate to Comunidad Contreras. Negotiations subsequently began between CONADI officials and a few delegates from Comunidad Paillacoy, who came to be considered allies by people from Comunidad Contreras. For both parties, the relocation of the Paillacoys was a mess caused by the state, and yet a solution to this legal dispute could only come from them. Back at El Panal estate, tensions were quickly escalating between Comunidad Contreras and the relocated land grantees from Comunidad Paillacoy. On two different occasions, the hostility erupted into brawls, though there were no serious injuries. The cause of these episodes was clearly identifiable in the mounting frustrations experienced by both groups. However, the hostilities also had a specific focus: the rewe that Comunidad Contreras members had placed on the property a few months earlier. A machi from a nearby settlement officiated an *amunrewe*, a ritual that can be roughly translated as "the making of the rewe."[4] Community delegates had been invited to be vigilant for possible threats against their new sacred site, which materialized a few months later when residents of El Panal estate set the rewe on fire and removed it by truck. The history of the rewe at El Panal raises several questions. How could the members of Comunidad Contreras care so much about it, while explicitly acknowledging it as part of their political strategy to attain land? How can this site be truly sacred if it is attacked by other Mapuche people? And how can a site so recently installed, even on a tract of land claimed as ancestral in negotiations with the state, be truly sacred? These questions were frequently asked during meetings with CONADI functionaries and intermediaries. They were also raised by many townspeople I met during my stay in Traiguen, who in some cases used them to reinstate racist stereotypes about Mapuche people as hot-blooded and conflictive. In the rest of this chapter, I will try to answer these questions by illustrating both state actors' doubts and ethnographic observations on those premises and practices that make rewe sites sacred in the Mapuche lived world. Before moving on, however, I need to warn the reader about a potential partiality of my interpretation of the events related to the controversial presence of the rewe in El Panal estate. In particular, the reader will certainly notice a certain bias of mine toward the point of view of friends at Comunidad Contreras in comparison with other actors involved in negotiations, and especially those residents of El Panal estate with whom they eventually entered the property dispute. Following my hosts' recommendations, I refrained from meeting with people involved in the brawls aforementioned, as their relations were severely deteriorated at that time. With this in mind, let us now explore what might make a sacred site sacred in the context of land disputes.

## The Rewe as Sacred Site: Agency and Exchange in the Mapuche Lived World

Mapuche sacred sites can be found scattered throughout the landscape of rural southern Chile. They can be topographic features, such as hills (*mawida*) and large stones associated with spirit masters (*ngenkura*) and ancient sites, as in the case of eltun burial grounds I have described earlier in this book. Most Mapuche people I have met during fieldwork would agree that the most common of all sacred sites is the rewe. The rewe consists of a step-notched tree trunk of laurel (*triwe*) adorned with branches of *maki* (*Aristotelia chilensis*) and canelo. According to its etymology, the *re* (real) *we* (place) is the purest of all places. In my area of study, this site may occasionally be referred to as *altar* (altar) in Spanish. *Rewe* is also a polysemantic term, as it refers to the sacred site standing in the middle of a ceremonial ground (*ngillatuwe*), where ngillatun rituals are officiated, and the ritual congregation celebrating them. In accordance with the meaning of the term *nguillan*, "to ask for" and "to elevate" (Alonqueo 1979, 23), ngillatun can be taken as a ritualistic action aimed at the fulfillment of a vast array of appeals. As explained by friends at Comunidad Contreras, it also serves to express gratitude (*dar la gracia*) toward the main deity, *chao ngenechen*, or Chao Dios, as it is often referred to in my area of study. Most residents in Comunidad Contreras identify *chao ngenechen* with the Christian god, to whom prayers are offered according "to the Mapuche way" (*a lo Mapuche*). Some scholars have defined the ngillatun as a fertility ritual (Dillehay 2007; Faron 1964; Hassler 1979). This definition seems to be confirmed by the fact that ngillatun tends to be celebrated in the weeks immediately anticipating the harvest. However, at least in my area of study, petitions made during ngillatun extend to a wide range of concerns, including physical well-being of the participants and specific events affecting them all, such as land claims.

Any attempt of mine to describe the ngillatun would do little justice to the complexity of the ritual. Even among Mapuche people, only certain elders are felt to be sufficiently qualified to explain all norms and symbolic elements of a ngillatun.[5] Hence, I do not even try to explain the multiple meanings of this ritual, especially since most remain unknown to me, and furthermore, ritual organizers, both in Comunidad Contreras and other rural areas in southern Chile, prefer their ritual practices to remain unrecorded. A friend of mine once explained that elders can be "jealous [*celoso*] of their knowledge" and refuse to pass it on to their descendants. Accordingly, for the scope of my discussion, I would simply contextualize the role of rewe sacred sites within ngillatun in order to show the relation between the only apparently unrelated domains of land claims and rituals. The ngillatun ritual is characterized by numerous regional divergences. The number of participants may vary from a few dozen to hundreds. It can last two or three days, as in the case of Comunidad Contreras. Here, clothing etiquette, including the obligation of being barefoot, is not as strictly enforced as in other areas of southern Chile. However, most attendees dress according to custom, which for women prescribes the use of a skirt, a *chamal* (large black shawl), and headband known as *trarilonko*, and for men, ponchos (*makuñ*). Ngillatun can either be officiated by *ngenpin* (ritual orators) in those areas where machi (shamans) are not present or by machi themselves. Central features of any ngillatun are music and dances, such as the *purrun*, in which dancers organized in lines move with cadenced steps in a circle around the rewe altar.[6]

Numerous activities are carried out in different phases during the two-day event. Some phases can be said to have a more festive character. This is the case of *misawun*, a large meal taking place at the end of each ngillatun. Each household prepares dishes, such as grilled pork, that are consumed among friends and relatives in the *ramadas*, temporary shelters built a few days before the ngillatun on the one side of the ceremonial ground.[7] Other phases of the ngillatun are more ceremonial, and attendees show reverential attitudes. This is the case of the *llellipun*, a key moment that can take place on more than one occasion during the ngillatun. During a *llellipun*, male and female participants gather in two lines and kneel facing east, the ritual cardinal point in Mapuche society. Meanwhile, ritual orators initiate a rhythmic incantation in Mapudungun, staking collective petitions as diverse as the health of individual members and the positive outcome of a land claim. In some ngillatun, machi can enter a trancelike phase known as *küymi*. During the *küymi*, an assistant known as *dungumachife* engages in a conversation with the machi in order to elicit information about the machi's experiences and provide an interpretation for the rest of the attendees (Bacigalupo 2007, 196–204). As I was told by friends at Comunidad Contreras, the message revealed during the *küymi* often concerns contingent events affecting congregants, including those processes unfolding within the land claim process.[8] After a ngillatun, organizers discuss whether or not their ritual was successful (*salió bien*), a condition necessary to attain divine intercession concerning the congregations' petitions. Petitions can be satisfied—or not—a few days after the ritual, as in the case of appeals for good harvest, or several months later, as for land claims. For any ngillatun to be successful, three basic conditions need to be fulfilled. As it was explained to me during fieldwork, firstly, participants need to show faith (*tener fe*) toward the effectiveness of the ngillatun. Secondly, organizers need to dedicate substantive amounts of time, energy, and economic resources for the ngillatun to be as opulent as possible. For this reason, in my area of study this event tends to be described as a sacrifice (*un sacrificio*). Thirdly, a ngillatun is successful only if the different ritual practices that constitute it are carried out in ways consistent with past rituals. Nelly, the ritual organizer, once explained to me, "Everything I know about the ngillatun comes from the ancient ones. I follow everything strictly, according to what my family taught me." Little space is thus given to improvisation in the ngillatun.

It should be clear by now that the significance of rewe is predicated upon its essential role in ngillatun rituals. The main motivation for the members of Comunidad Contreras to place a rewe in El Panal was to carry out rituals specifically in this disputed property. For the past forty years, in Comunidad Contreras ngillatun had gradually decreased in number of participants and frequency to the point that they were celebrated only occasionally, and by members of only four households. Among the reasons for this decline were the death of experienced ritual organizers and the growth of evangelical churches in rural southern Chile, with their consequent pressure to shun activities defined as pagan (*paganas*)—and thus antithetic to Christian values. Since 2006, however, the land claim process had contributed to the regeneration of collective activities, many of them carried out to celebrate Mapuche heritage. In this context of growing political activism, ngillatun was revived as a community activity. There are two other fundamental reasons to explain why ngillatun came to be celebrated on this disputed property and not elsewhere. When I discussed the importance of the rewe with friends at Comunidad Contreras, I was told that this sacred site served to strengthen the Indigenous community in their struggle for land restitution by way of divine intercession. At the same time, the specific location of this sacred site served as a symbolic form of land occupation and a marker of Indigenous identity that could help the claimants from Comunidad Contreras to express their demand for territorial restoration in unambiguously cultural terms. Antonio, a neighbor of mine at the time, once explained to me, "We need the rewe to show CONADI that we are Mapuche."

Is the sacredness of this particular site at odds with its strategic use? This reasonable question can be asked by looking at the specific properties constitutive of the sacredness of a rewe for its related congregation. The sacred character of rewe has been generally ascribed to the role of this site as *axis mundi*, a term that Mircea Eliade (1961) used to refer to those symbolic centers connecting one plane of existence with another. Rewe stands as the bridge between the world inhabited by humans and the spiritual world known as *wenumapu* (literally, "the land of above"). This characterization is further confirmed by the practice carried out by some machi who can climb along the steps of the laurel trunk during healing rituals (Bacigalupo 2007, 52–53). The power of the rewe, however, is predicated not solely upon its ability to connect different planes of existence but also on its relation of exchange with different people interacting with it. My explanation for the central role of rewe in land claims beyond their strategic use posits that the sacredness of these sites is predicated upon one major property—namely, its engagement with the rewe ritual congregation in exchanges of newen. This term, also referred to as *fuerza* in Spanish, is a spiritual entity consisting of multiple volitional forces. The existence of this collective force is to be traced to the power ascribed to *chao ngenechen*. This deity is generally conceptualized as the determinant of all occurrences and actions in the cosmos, an idea that is sustained by the frequent utterance of sentences like "It all depends on God" in conversations among Mapuche rural residents. Yet newen is not exempt from human control, as it can be passed between people through various modalities. In the case of the rewe, ritualistic practices, such as *purrun* (circular dances) and *llellipun* incantations are performed by members of the local congregation in order to "give newen to the rewe" (*dar newen*). Similarly, the rewe is thought to give "force" to the ritual congregation in their land negotiations as long as it is protected from evildoing by potential enemies. Newen is thus an extremely fluid force that can be exchanged in a complex web of relations involving both humans and inanimate things.

The dynamic way in which newen travels across boundaries between different beings is also reflected in the possibility that evildoing can be transferred between people through the mediation of the rewe. As reported in numerous ethnographic works (Course 2011; Faron 1964; Foerster 1993), exposure to evildoing by enemies, including humans and malevolent beings such as the *wekufe* spirits, is a widespread concern in rural Mapuche society. In a manner similar to that found in the phenomenon of assault sorcery observed in other Amerindian societies (Wright and Whitehead 2004, 13), spiritual aggression in Mapuche society can be perpetrated through the manipulation or physical destruction of material substances. In meetings following the first attack against their rewe, residents of Comunidad Contreras often mention the need to protect this site against possible further acts of aggression by their rivals and thereby ensure their success in the land dispute. The physical attack against their rewe was thought to affect them by potentially provoking diseases and obstacles in the process of land restoration. A similar concern was also voiced by the machi shaman who officiated the *amunrewe*—installation of the rewe—about the possibility that a witch (*kalku*) could act against the rewe in order to inflict harm on her and her family. Soon after finding out about the aggression toward the rewe, the local machi asked local residents to remove all the burnt branches that adorned the main body of the site, since their presence could directly harm the members of Comunidad Contreras. The machi suggested that collection of the burnt branches should be carried out by volunteers who were not Mapuche. Since the harm was directed against Mapuche people, winkas would be immune from any negative consequences of contact with the burnt ashes. In the night before a ngillatun, the community board thus asked me and a chileno married to a local Mapuche resident to gather the burnt branches in sacks and throw them into a nearby river. Following instructions, we loaded a pickup truck with farming sacks, then drove to a nearby river and walked back and forth to dump the burnt branches in the river. The reason for this specific form of disposal is that the potential harm of the burnt parts of the rewe could only be annulled through the purifying action of running water (*witrunko*), an idea found in other healing practices performed by machi.[9] The particular method of disposal that I was involved with reveals that in Mapuche society, evildoing, as well as newen, does not simply exist on an immaterial plane but can be transmitted through material substances, such as burnt ashes. Far from being exclusively the potential object of evildoing, rewe can also actively react against malevolent actions. Months after the assaults, the aggressors of the rewe in El Panal suffered several misfortunes, including the emergence of internal feuds among them and, finally, the legal success of Comunidad Contreras in attaining the disputed property at the beginning of 2012. For most community members, these events were indications of the rewe's response to the attacks made against it.

My description of some of the interactions between rewe and people around them suggests that the agential nature of this sacred site is predicated upon its ability to engage in exchanges of both newen and evil with humans around it. Characterizing the rewe as an agential subject does not mean adhering to a universal recognition of nonhuman agency. This stance is most commonly associated with the work of Bruno Latour (2005), according to whom agency is dispersed across a network of associations involving both human and nonhuman components as actants. In numerous societies, only a few material objects are fully capable of embedding human action (Alberti and Bray 2009). This is true for most Amerindian societies, where only specific objects are endowed with the ability to communicate with humans. For instance, baby hammocks and shamanic stones among Urarina people in the Amazonian lowlands (Walker 2009), and carved figures known as *illas* among Andean Quechua speakers (Sillar 2009), act as intermediaries between humans and divinities. In Mapuche society, an illustrative example comes from *kültrun*, drums made from laurel wood and sheepskin, which are typically played in shamanic healing practices and ritualistic dances. While *kültrun* are ubiquitously sold to tourists in handicraft markets throughout southern Chile, only those built by experienced Mapuche manufacturers are considered to be effective in the transference of newen. Lonko Nelly, the ritual specialist of this community, once commissioned a *kültrun* from a renowned maker. Upon receiving the instrument, she was asked by the maker to pass on her newen by breathing into the drum, a practice observable in rituals and shamanic practices as well. Once they receive newen, *kültrun* drums are able to exchange it with humans. One way to give newen to the rewe is, in fact, by playing *kültrun* drums around it.

The relation between the rewe in El Panal and the humans around them reveals an inherently Mapuche form of agency, which is predicated upon two ethnographically abstracted ontological principles—namely, the facility for action possessed by certain cultural objects and the porosity of borders between those objects and human beings. The type of agency associated with rewe entails that these sites engage in relations with humans from a subject-like position, a point initially suggested by the dual indexicality of the rewe, indicating both a sacred site and its associated ritual congregation. My point contrasts with interpretations of the power of sacred sites as being centered exclusively on their symbolic significance and the emotional attachment of the people around them. If we follow Gell's (1998, 24) proposal regarding art objects, agency in this case would be predicated upon the apprehension of the site by an emotionally affected recipient. It is certain that the biography (Kopytoff 1986) of Mapuche sacred sites and objects begins with human action in ritualistic contexts, as in the case of the *amunrewe*. However, as shown earlier, once these objects are consecrated, they are able to engage in exchanges of newen with human beings. Contrary to a definition of agency centered on reception, which implies the identification of a signifying subject (the social group, in this case) and a signified object (their sacred site), the relation between rewe as a sacred site and rewe as a ritual congregation unfolds rather as one existing between two subjects.

The agential nature of rewe reveals some of the ontological principles inherent to the Mapuche lived world. Throughout this book, I have referred to the term *ontology* to explore the origins, persistence, and transformation of being as it occurs in different lived worlds. A focus on the ontological principles at work in specific instances of nonhuman agency begins with the premise that human engagement with the world cannot be reduced to the ascription of symbolic categories on an inert background. Rather, humans and nonhumans participate in ongoing processes of world making through a set of practices, or an onto-praxis (Scott 2007). This point is much indebted to Isabelle Stengers's (2010) proposal for the subversion of the hierarchical articulation of idea and practice, according to which "the idea conceived as vision would precede, inspire and command practice, thus defined as application, a simple implementation" (39). To say that the rewe gives newen and receives it from its associated ritual congregation is thus not a discursive claim ordering reality for a group of people through a consensually legitimated religious institution, as is the case with a Christian congregation, for instance. Rather, the actions of the rewe and their consequences for the lives of the people are the initial condition from which the connotation of "sacred" is derived. Rewe, in other words, can be sacred only if they act as powerful and agential objects. Their sacredness is an a posteriori condition for their actions.

After seeing what makes sacred sites sacred in the Mapuche lived world, the two major doubts expressed by state actors concerning the authenticity of the rewe in El Panal estate can finally be shed. Firstly, how can this site be truly sacred if attacked by other Mapuche people? While rewe are found throughout the Mapuche region with little regional variation, their status as sacred sites is not predicated upon a consensual agreement or on the ascription of their status as sacred by a central religious authority.[10] Rather, their power depends upon their capacity to be actively involved in a complex web of relations involving localized human groups, such as the corresponding ritual congregation and their potential enemies. Secondly, how can this site, which has been installed only recently on a tract of land claimed as ancestral, be truly sacred? This question can be answered by pointing to the fact that the power of rewe to affect people around them is predicated upon relations and actions in the present. Rewe do not express spatial continuity with the past, since their locations can vary according to different contingencies, such as the preference for a flat field (more apt for the activities of the ngillatun ritual), the willingness of single residents to offer a section of their landed property to host such a ritual, and even the role of rewe as markers of land occupation, as in the case of that installed in El Panal estate. Furthermore, rewe are not the manifestations of ancestral spiritual forces embroiled in the land. In my area of study, the ancient ones (*los antiguos*) are regarded as sources of knowledge (kimün) indispensable in ensuring appropriate behaviors toward sacred sites. Therefore, their influence cannot be explained as a set of forces rooted in a particular site or place.[11] In attempting to explain how a site at the core of a land dispute can be sacred beyond its strategic use in the political arena, I have engaged in a form of "bracketing," a technique inherent to the phenomenological dimension of ethnography that one could call purposive naïvety; as Henare, Holbraad, and Wastell (2007) phrase it, "Rather than immediately assuming that things encountered in the field signify, represent, or stand for something else," one can attempt to take them "as they present themselves" (2). The power of the rewe necessarily emanates from relations with humans, who also represent and signify it. More than a concrete heuristical stragegy, to approach a rewe as it presents itself requires a shift from an interpretation of an event understood as belief responding to a presupposed divide between a transcendental signifier and an immanent signified, toward an understanding of a subject, such as the rewe, that presents itself by virtue of being part of an inherent field of relatedness. This second stance is what motivates my personal attempt in trying to understand the political implications of the rewe as a subject. Other ideals and objectives can be found in state actors' interpretations of the involvement of sacred sites in land claims. In order to explain them, it becomes necessary to look at the governmental and epistemic grid in which their actions and their interpretations of actions and motivations by others are inserted.

## The Rewe as Realpolitik: Analogies and Misunderstandings by State Actors

Ethnographic research on statecraft has shown that while bureaucrats and functionaries abide strictly by legalistic codes in order to reduce their personal accountability, they can also violate rules as a statement of dissent with governmental ideologies, or simply as a strategy to relate empathically or instrumentally with clients (see Gupta 2012; Herzfeld 1992). A similar scenario can be found among state officials in southern Chile. During fieldwork, I came to know several public service employees who had ongoing relations with Indigenous clients. They belonged to different agencies that specialized in the agricultural, housing, and health fields. In some cases they were directly employed by CONADI, with duties concerning the oversight and implementation of differentiated social policies targeting Indigenous people. CONADI employees ranged from high-ranking officials to technical workers. Some officials had managerial experience in public service and little knowledge of Indigenous issues. Their presence reflected the technocratic character of governmental agencies in Chile (Silva 2009). Others fit more into the profile of party members for whom work in CONADI was a temporary position among other appointments. Finally, many officials were Mapuche. For some, especially those whose genealogical links to Mapuche society were distant or who did not engage with the social movement, CONADI was simply a source of employment. Others, especially those workers with active participation in Mapuche organizations, saw their employment there as an opportunity to actively participate in and reframe the implementation of Indigenous social policies, despite their strong critique of them.

The presence of Mapuche civil servants within CONADI brings to the fore two issues central to state-sponsored multiculturalism: co-option and the hybrid position of Indigenous state workers. For the past few decades, the growing number of Indigenous workers within state agencies has been useful to governments as a means to legitimate themselves as democratic actors (Park and Richards 2007, 1320). Yet such a post allows for the validation and incorporation of the critical agendas of Indigenous activists within policy making only partly (Radcliffe and Webb 2015, 266). The position of Mapuche civil servants within CONADI is hybrid due to their potentially conflictive commitment to both state service and Mapuche interests. This dual affiliation is far from being symmetric, as critical voices against governmental agendas within CONADI can easily be silenced. High-ranking positions are appointed by the Ministry of Social Development (Ministerio de Desarrollo Social) and rotated quickly. Actions that do not fit within the minister's agendas can thus result in the reassignment of officials to different state agencies.[12] The marginality of Indigenous state officials also allows them to strategically defend themselves against claimants' critiques. In one instance, after a fruitless trip to CONADI head offices, the delegates of Comunidad Contreras were approached by an official who explained the difficulties concerning the resolution of their case: "The Mapuche, we are a minority here. I would like to help my *peñi* [brothers], but they always leave us on the side." It is likely that this official was looking for a personal excuse to avoid accusations of incompetence by the delegates of Comunidad Contreras while also trying to be empathic to their plight. In fact, the dual affiliation of Mapuche officials opens them to resentment from rural residents. A common perception among residents of Comunidad Contreras, for instance, is that the process of getting involved with the state apparatus entails the potential risk of acting like a winka. In one community meeting, a resident of a nearby Mapuche community sought the endorsement of Comunidad Contreras in the municipal election in which he was running as counselor. Attendees, who in some cases were previously acquainted with the candidate, lauded his commitment to Mapuche interests, but warned him about the risk of becoming a politician (*un politico*). Gabriel, the then president of the community, voiced his opinion: "Some Mapuche become politicians; they forget their people and act worse than the winkas."

My fieldwork experience has convinced me that the vast majority of state officials have good intentions. Yet their actions seldom meet the expectations of Mapuche clients. A general explanation for the discordance between CONADI officials' intentionality and their actions is that they are compelled to develop and adhere to technocratic routines (Li Murray 2007) in order to legitimate their practices and positions. Theses routines are inserted in frameworks of procedural efficiency that reflect the general features of audit culture (see Power 1997; Strathern 2000). As proposed by Gledhill (2004), audit culture is "deeply embedded in development agencies and NGOs, leading to a system of project evaluation in which what is really being evaluated is the procedural efficiency of action in terms of the agency's mission rather than its substantive impact on the lives of human beings" (341). Similarly, in the case of the land program, grants endowed to Mapuche rural residents serve as indicators of work performance while the long-term impact of land policies stays out of focus. The relocation of Mapuche land grantees to properties that are distant or genealogically unrelated is symptomatic of the audit logics directing state officials' actions. Nonetheless, while the routinization of their day provides us with a general explanation for the failures in land negotiations, more specific reasons are needed to elucidate the origins of misunderstandings and other communication failures between Mapuche claimants and state actors. A look at the negotiations for the dispute over El Panal estate can help us to find these reasons.

Negotiations between CONADI officials and members of Comunidad Contreras proved particularly difficult. As seen earlier, the prospect for the resolution of this thorny legal dispute materialized only when the newly elected council of Comunidad Paillacoy decided to negotiate with the board of Comunidad Contreras over the possibility of leaving El Panal estate to its "ancestral owners." Members of both parties celebrated their collaboration as an example of cooperation that defied the divisive consequences of the land program for Mapuche people. In one meeting, Juan, a delegate from Comunidad Contreras, stated, "Our agreement showed that we can have a *visión de pueblo*." This term, widely circulating among Mapuche organizations in

Chile, indicates the ideal objective of ethnic unity implicit in political activism and threatened by social policies (see also Richards 2004, 28). In 2011, under the pressure of the intermediaries involved in the negotiations, CONADI transferred the disputed property to Comunidad Contreras. In 2013, the last residents on the El Panal estate were evicted, and a few months later members of Comunidad Contreras began agricultural activities there. Legal contentions continued for the following month, but at the time of writing there was no indication that the legal status of this property would change. Comunidad Contreras was able to achieve its goals in spite of the difficulties posed by CONADI officials. The same cannot be said about many negotiations in Chile, which are destined to remain unresolved. Successful and fruitless negotiations share common difficulties. My participation in meetings between members of Comunidad Contreras and state actors made me aware that these difficulties could originate in the suspicious attitudes of CONADI officials against claims over sacred sites and ancestral territories. Ultimately, land claims could be delegitimized by state officials according to their judgments on the cultural significance of the demanded ancestral territories. Sacred sites in particular are fundamental elements in most land claims, as their presence can direct the final outcome of any resolution. This is certainly the case of the rewe on El Panal estate. Its ambivalent interpretations were responsible for prolonging negotiations over several months, and only the discovery of irregularities in the transference of El Panal estate to Comunidad Paillacoy paved the way for the resolution of this property dispute.

The vast majority of state actors involved in this negotiation were winkas. However, Mapuche and non-Indigenous officials alike had doubts about the weight of the role of the rewe in the legal contention over El Panal. During negotiations, the presence of this site was a major topic of conversation. When the details were discussed, state functionaries consistently voiced doubts about its authenticity. First, they were generally surprised that the rewe was installed only in 2006, as its newness appeared to them to be a contradiction of its relatedness with ancestral land. The second major doubt about the sacred nature of the rewe concerned how it was possible that a sacred site could be attacked by members of the same ethnic group. The members of Comunidad Paillacoy residing on El Panal had also erected a rewe on the disputed property; theirs was roughly a kilometer away from that installed by Contreras. The simultaneous presence of two new sacred sites seemed to suggest that they were both inauthentic. This point reflected the impression, which I have often heard from state officials during negotiations, that the rewe in El Panal estate was only a "show." In negotiations between the members of Comunidad Contreras and state actors, the same object, the rewe, was seen from very different angles. The reasons for sacred sites involved in land negotiations appearing so differently to Mapuche claimants and state functionaries are better unfolded if we explore the possibility that the same concepts

FIGURE 15 Community members signing a land transference agreement. (Photo by author)

can be employed by both parties to refer to radically different worlds. Two notions in particular, "Mapuche" and "sacred," are subject to divergent interpretations.

For state officials, "Mapuche" is a category that encompasses an ethnic group and a religious congregation. In accordance with this assumption, the attack by the residents of El Panal on the rewe of Comunidad Contreras can only be explained by presupposing that this sacred site is not authentic. The conceptualization of Mapuche as a rigidly demarcated ethnic and religious group might be of little help, however, in explaining how this ethnonym is understood in Indigenous rural areas. While figurative consanguinity is extended to virtually all Mapuche people through the expression "people of the same blood" (*gente de la misma sangre*), in rural areas this category always appears relative, since it emerges from the particular context in which the term is employed (Course 2010b, 49). Hence, the Mapuche-ness of an individual can be judged according to their relative position between two poles: on one hand, someone may be "very Mapuche"; at the other end of the scale are the awinkados and individuals with behaviors similar to those of winkas. Moreover, as seen earlier in this book, "Mapuche" is a category that can be extended to individuals belonging to other Indigenous groups outside the Southern Cone. The open and fluid character of Mapuche identity contrasts with the assumptions of state actors, for whom "Mapuche" is the conflation of a clearly defined ethnic boundary with an extended ritual congregation.

The other major source of misunderstanding concerning the rewe on El Panal estate refers to the meaning of "sacred place." While in theory all sacred sites are characterized by the imposition of restrictions and prohibitions on human behavior, what makes something sacred in one society might have none of the characteristics of things and places regarded as sacred in other cultures (Hubert 1994, 10). As proposed by Roy Wagner (1981), culture is a relational category that is necessarily invented when a foreign set of conventions is brought into relation with one's own. Conventions constitute "the collective viewpoint or orientation of a culture, the way in which its members learn to experience action and the world of action. . . . [They persist] through being constantly reinvented in the form of conventional contexts" (51). In any instance of cultural translation, such as anthropology or land claims, analogies are necessary to translate one group of basic meanings into another, thus allowing for the understanding and objectification of alien cultures (9). However, the unreflective use of analogies might lead to the imposition of standards of sacredness from one society on sacred sites in other social contexts, thus contributing to misunderstanding. During my stay in Comunidad Contreras, I was told the meaning of the rewe through analogies. Arturo, a neighbor of mine during fieldwork, once told me, "The rewe is like the church for the Mapuche people. Here, we come to pray." The analogy between this Mapuche sacred site and the church, a familiar image for non-Indigenous Chileans and Mapuche, served to immediately convey the sacred nature of the rewe on El Panal estate. However, accusations of inauthenticity were also grounded in this analogy, once the standards of sacredness of Christian churches were applied in the understanding of this site. As a CONADI functionary once phrased it, "How can this rewe be sacred if other Mapuche have attacked it?"

The interpretation of Mapuche sacred sites involved in land disputes is illustrative of the inherent limitations of cultural translation and, in particular, of the problem of translating and interpreting terms in which profound semantic differences may be concealed behind apparent phonic similarity (Davidson 1984, 100). For Viveiros de Castro (2004, 5), anthropology as a form of cultural translation is inevitably exposed to the effects of equivocation, a set of potential misinterpretations arising from the translation of the practical and discursive concepts of the "Natives" into the conceptual apparatus developed by anthropology. Rather than attempting to annul it by way of grouping ostensibly equivalent phenomena, such as sacred places, into universal categories, an ideal form of cultural translation should attempt to make the most of equivocation by emphasizing radical difference. Controlled equivocation unfolds as "an operation of differentiation—a production of difference—that connects . . . two discourses to the precise extent to which they are *not* saying the same thing, in so far as they point to discordant exteriorities beyond the equivocal homonyms between them" (20). An uncontrolled equivocation can be said to occur whenever differences between discordant exteriorities are played down in order to allow them to be subsumed under the category of a universal concept—in this case, sacred sites. This is also the case when state actors find that the sacredness of Mapuche sites implicated in land claims is questionable based on their failure to accord with the state actors' expectations of what sacred sites should be and do. Different misunderstandings of and reservations about the sacredness of the rewe on El Panal estate led to the erroneous conclusion that this site could only be another example of an expedient use of symbols of Mapuche identity, or, as commonly heard throughout fieldwork, a show.

In virtually all Indigenous/state relations, unambiguous perceptions of nonconflictual Indigenous identity by state representatives are critical in ensuring a successful claim. In negotiations, the use of cultural objects by Indigenous people as a form of symbolic capital serves as a marker of difference, legitimizing Indigenous demands in the eyes of state officials. The strategic use of cultural objects, however, can prove to be a double-edged sword. Indigenous activists often run the risk of being perceived as no longer truly living their identity when their actions are seen as deliberate exploitations of symbolic capital (Warren and Jackson 2002, 35). As argued by Povinelli (2002), multicultural forms of recognition work to inspire "subaltern and minority subjects to identify with the impossible object of an authentic self-identity, [i.e.] a domesticated, non-conflictual traditional form of sociality and (inter)subjectivity" (6). For Mapuche claimants, the fact that sacred sites can be employed instrumentally as markers of Indigenous identity does not contradict the characterization of these places as powerful and agential. In marked contrast to this, accusations of inauthenticity made with regard to Mapuche sacred sites involved in land claims derive from the supposition that political pragmatism and sacredness are mutually exclusive.

The preceding analysis of the interpretations of sacred sites by state actors shows that misunderstandings emerge through the uncontrolled use of analogies and unexamined expectations about what sacred sites are and do. This particular form of interpretation leads to the transformation of objects responding to divergent ontological principles into symbols of identity employed for political purposes. This point bears one significant implication with regard to power relations between national majorities and Indigenous people. A commonly held view in social science is that interethnic conflicts can be reduced to "radical ontological misunderstanding, as the cognitive and affective worlds of dominant and dominated remain unknown to one another" (Clammer, Poirier, and Schwimmer 2004, 8). However, as shown throughout this book, such a scenario finds little correspondence in contemporary southern Chile. We have seen that land negotiations are carried out in Spanish, the first language of both parties; many Mapuche residents regard themselves as Chileans, and in many cases identify as Christians or Catholics as most Chileans do; ties of friendship and kinship between winka and Mapuche are also very common; and, finally, many state officials have direct genealogical links to Mapuche society. Misunderstandings in interethnic relations are thus best understood without presupposing rigid ethnic boundaries, which would make mutual understanding impossible. Quite the contrary: land negotiations in southern Chile indicate that failures to recognize radical difference originate in those interethnic contexts where visible signs of Mapuche alterity are not easily apparent to the non-Indigenous observer.

The foregoing discussion allows me to venture a tentative explanation of misunderstandings in negotiations over land and the delegitimation of Indigenous demands. Rather than presupposing irreconcilable communication differences, or state actors' strategic refusal to understand, misunderstandings can be explained as particular instances of a more general type of comprehension according to which mutual communication is possible only through the erasure of radical difference as the necessary condition to favor mutual understanding between divergent parties. I call this particular form of comprehension of difference "understanding by domestication." State actors' interpretations are thus inserted in a broader epistemology aimed at valorizing cultural difference by domesticating the political threat that it poses to existing market configurations and ideologies of nation making.

## Statecraft and the Problem of Incommensurability in Liberal Multiculturalism

By challenging current systems of land tenure and property relations, Indigenous demands for their rights to land highlight a central concern of statecraft in postcolonial contexts. On the one hand, historically conflictive relations between Indigenous groups and national majorities can in fact be ameliorated by responding to

Indigenous claims. On the other, demands for collective rights pose a threat to the national cohesion that multiculturalist policies aim to achieve by celebrating Indigenous culture as part of a shared heritage. This tension reveals the centrality of the demarcation of acceptable difference within legal debates on multiculturalism. The definition of acceptable difference, which unfolds primarily in the public sphere, consists in the establishment of a horizon for cultural difference that can be shared and accepted by both Indigenous and non-Indigenous interlocutors. While the positions of non-Indigenous and Indigenous actors are hierarchically organized, public debates about multiculturalism would, theoretically, increase the possibility for Indigenous participation in the demarcation of acceptable difference. The implementation of state multicultural policies offers a much clearer hierarchical relation. Through different forms of intervention, the state itself sets the conditions for acceptable cultural difference. Demarcation in this case depends on the possibility for the state to make differences commensurable with existing technologies of governability and market configurations.

*Commensuration* is a term most commonly associated with the question of mutual communication and understanding, a central theme in the philosophy of language. For analytical philosopher Donald Davidson (1984), radical interpretation—that is, the interpretation of two or more beliefs that cannot be made commensurate by way of a third system of reference—can be successful only through the employment of a theory and practice of translation that maximizes agreement between interlocutors. Agreement in this case leads to an inevitable paradox: "Just as we must maximize agreement, or risk not making sense of what the alien is talking about, so we must maximize the self-consistency we attribute to him, on pain of not understanding him" (27). The dilemma of agreement at the cost of mutual understanding is central not only to the philosophy of language but also to liberal ideologies of multiculturalism and public reason. Both views share the potential limitations of giving the impression that mutual communication unfolds as the result of equal agreements between two parties. This is certainly not the case with public debates on multiculturalism, in which ideals of reconciliation among different groups conceal their asymmetric positionalities. For Elizabeth Povinelli (2001), liberal ideologies of multiculturalism are inspired by the ideal that the state can accommodate difference by mimicking the self-correcting movement of reasoned public debate (327). The main principle behind liberal ideologies of public reason is indeed the search for a shared agreement, a value coherent with the ideals of national cohesion and peaceful interethnic relations promoted by the liberal state. The extent of what can be agreed on, however, is only apparently the result of mutual agreement between state actors and Indigenous claimants. The ideal of agreement conceals the fact that the establishment of acceptable difference essentially falls within the responsibility of the state. Cultural difference that cannot be addressed as the naturalized outcome of mutual agreement between minorities and majorities is marginalized.

In Chile, public policies targeting Indigenous groups are legitimized in accordance with liberal ideologies of multiculturalism centered on the ideal of agreement and are ultimately implemented through and around the principles of standardization. On the one hand, the land program is designed as an open competition, in which Indigenous communities must go through approximately thirty-two procedures in four phases before they can receive land compensations. The language used by this program is evocative of that used by welfare systems, as land subsidies are assigned to applicants (*postulantes*) participating in open competitions (*concursos*). On the other hand, as commonly described in the national media, negotiations over land disputes involving state representatives, such as cabinet members, are said to result in "agreements" with Indigenous claimants (see *La Tercera* 2011). "Agreement" and "competition" are thus interrelated notions in this particular form of governmentality. The emergence of the Indigenous land program in Chile as simultaneously a system of standardized subsidization and a space for mutual agreements between the state and Indigenous claimants reveals the profound link between liberal strategies of commensuration and the principle of standardization. We have seen in the previous chapter that governmental practices of standardization allow for the translation of qualitative differences into quantitative ones. In other words, the compensatory mechanism of the land program makes possible the transformation of the ancestral territory into land grants unrelated to those Indigenous geographic perspectives that animate demands of restitution in the first place. Standardization can be achieved only insofar as a form of understanding that annuls radical difference is at work. In the liberal imagination promoted by multiculturalism, "State apparatuses, as well as its law, principles of governance, and national attitudes need merely to be adjusted to accommodate others" (Povinelli 2001, 184). Only once radically different worlds are made unremarkable can they be commensurate within existing grids and practices of governability.

The ideas of standardization and domestication help me to clarify the concrete manifestations of the political imagination through which Mapuche demands are evaluated in both land claims and the Chilean public arena. Political imagination is a concrete social process through which the conceptual horizons of social thinking are established, contested, and occasionally subverted. It extends beyond individual intentionality to engulf all those disputed frameworks of intelligibility in which persons, things, and ideas are granted political legitimacy. Under neoliberalism, we have seen, the legitimacy of any form of life depends largely on its translatability into the language of market and property. If we take political imagination as the process by which the legitimacy of any claim is recognized, then state power appears as both cause and effect of this phenomenon. On the one hand, the state molds political imagination by providing its representatives with technologies of commensuration through which they can morally weight heterogeneous claims; on the other, the state is shaped by existing political imaginations that are reinforced and contested at once by different actors partaking in often ambivalent governmental practices. The mutuality of statecraft and political imagination that I observe in land negotiations reveals the embeddedness of the state within broader frameworks of intelligibility, or modes of objectification, as Foucault has defined them (1982). Objectification consists in the transformation of human beings into subject (777), a process made possible by the demarcation of the conditions under which specific subjects can legitimately exist. Objectification is inherently open to contestation and contradictions. In chapter 2, we saw some of the ways in which two subjects, Mapuche and land, historically have been formed not only as part of a narrative of nation building but also as the result of contestation by Mapuche people. Land negotiations show that state actors reproduce broader frameworks of objectification in their attempts to match categories, such as the ancestral territory, within existing legal codes. From the analysis of land negotiations, it is clear that the state lacks any inner coherence and yet can implement effective strategies of governance (Foucault 2008, 77). As land negotiations indicate, the state's lack of inner coherence does not prevent its technologies of codification from having a compelling impact on the domestication of radical difference. Being both cause and effect of political imagination, the state constitutes a source of heterogeneous forms of governance that is nonetheless able to provide a coherent effect on the codification of Indigenous geographies.

In this chapter I have explored some of the creative actions through which Mapuche claimants are able to reconcile political pragmatism with concerns over the decline of religious practices necessary to sustain Indigenous land ontologies. In the process of translation of sacred sites inherent to land claims, misunderstandings by state actors serve to delegitimize the ontological principles that make certain places sacred in the Mapuche lived world. Misunderstandings do not originate as strategic refusals to understand, I have argued, but rather as a form of understanding that aims to make radical differences commensurable within the logics of standardization. While Indigenous and state actions are evidently asymmetric, Mapuche claimants are not mere spectators of governmental action. The story of Comunidad Contreras reveals that governmental failures to accommodate the principles of Indigenous land ontologies into the land claim system can be overcome, at least incompletely. Through engagement with the state apparatus, land connections can be reactivated; at the same time, new relationships between humans and agential features of the landscape—rivers, forests, hills, and sacred sites—are entangled in ways that openly defy the topographic spatiality of the jural language of property. In the concluding chapter of this book, I continue to explore the implications of land claims in the ongoing struggle for world making by Mapuche people. In looking at some of the consequences of land restoration on the life of claimants and their projections, I intend to show how uncertainties behind the promises of neoliberalism and anxieties over environmental destruction are recast in ways that an alternative future might be at least possible to imagine.

# CHAPTER 7

# THE FUTURE OF ANCESTRAL LAND
*Uncertainties of World Making in a Reclaimed Territory*

ONE HOT SUMMER AFTERNOON OF 2016 I WAS IN A CAR WITH JOSÉ, the *werken* (spokesperson) of Comunidad Contreras, and two relatives of his. We were driving through El Panal, the land annexed to this community in 2011 after the long legal and political battle described in the previous chapter. "Do you see how the landscape has changed? It's no longer just fundos. There are people everywhere now; they are building their houses little by little all around the comunidad." As José was pointing out the profound transformation of the landscape around Comunidad Contreras, his cousin Miguel turned left onto a dirt road that cut through large fields of uniform yellow ears of wheat interrupted only by a few ordered lines of elm windbreaks. This road, unknown to me, had been built by the local municipality only a few months earlier to connect an area where land beneficiaries were building their new houses to a main thoroughfare crossing the comunidad. Scattered along this road were several houses under construction. Some of them were nothing but a wooden frame; others already had painted wooden walls and zinc roofs. During our trip, I was told that it was not only in Comunidad Contreras that new houses were appearing. Mapuche people from other rural areas were converging into different fundos outside the town of Traiguen. Changes brought by the land restitution program reflected the profound transformation that life for many Mapuche claimants went through once they were awarded with land compensation. Ever since the transference of the first tracts of demanded land in 2011, many of my friends from Comunidad Contreras had seen rapid improvements in their economic conditions. More land equates to more revenue from bigger harvests. Yet the changes experienced were not as simple as an increase in household income. The land transference soon began profoundly restructuring relations among community members and with authorities in local governments.

The first challenge for land beneficiaries was the administration of the newly annexed properties. As previously agreed by signatories of the land claim, the annexed properties were to be held collectively for at least three years and later demarcated and assigned to beneficiaries. Undivided land was put to two uses. Some sections of the new properties were designed as areas for cereal production, while others were left as commonage so that signatories could leave their cattle there and thus avoid overgrazing their own properties. The two types of field were separated by barbed wire fences left by the previous owners and repaired by community members to prevent cattle from feeding on growing crops. The major apprehension over the administration of collectively held land concerned cereal production. Residents of Mapuche settlements rarely own large machinery, such as a tractor or a harvester, necessary for the sowing and harvesting of such extended fields. Furthermore, the CONADI land program offered little training and technological transfer programs to land beneficiaries. Given the infrastructural difficulties of Mapuche farmers in making use of large properties, land beneficiaries were left with little choice but to find a partner, a *socio*, in the administration of collective land. Since the 1993 Indigenous Law prohibits the rental of land subsidized by CONADI, a sharecropping agreement is typically struck so that harvested crops are redistributed between land claim signatories and a machine owner. In Comunidad Contreras, collective harvesting was practiced with the participation of all land beneficiaries, who were given duties such as weighing, keeping records, and storing the wheat and barley that had been threshed. Generally, *socios* are non-Indigenous agricultural entrepreneurs who complement income from their own land with work on rented properties. Given the limited numbers of potential partners, Mapuche beneficiaries have very little control over the conditions of sharecropping agreements, which depend largely on the prices set by wealthier winkas, including patrones by whom they could be employed. Not all *socios*, however, act like patrones. Members of Comunidad Contreras considered themselves lucky to have found a partner with whom they could establish a trustworthy relationship and a satisfactory sharecropping agreement. Their partner, Julián, showed a genuine interest in Mapuche culture. He was often seen having teatime meals (*once*) with his friends from Comunidad Contreras, an act very unusual within the rigid class and racial hierarchies of the southern Chilean countryside, and for this reason much appreciated by local residents. The creation of a cooperative was just one of the many plans that the members of Comunidad Contreras and their *socio* had in mind. Sadly, Julián's sudden death in 2013 left community members without a friend and an honest partner. They were left to keep looking for possible partners year by year, knowing that it would be very unlikely to establish a commercial relation as fair as the one they'd had.

After three years of collective land use, land redistribution among the signatories of the land claim was finally under way. All beneficiaries were to be assigned the same amount of land, fifteen hectares. However, as previously agreed, they were going to be divided into groups with different levels of priorities over choices of property. Participation in the land claim process, as we have seen, was demanding. Signatories had been involved in time-consuming meetings and protests. They were also bound to pay membership fees to finance legal counseling and board activities. Those residents who bore the costs of the land claims more than others were rewarded with the chance of choosing their plots earlier than anyone else. Selection of specific tracts of land depended mainly on access to watercourses and proximity to roads. While all community members agreed with the rationale behind the preferment of certain people, this did not render the demarcation process immune to animosity, especially if it was nourished by rumors about supposed favoritism by board members toward close relatives. Once demarcation was completed, tensions lessened, most likely because beneficiaries were shifting their attention toward planning economic activities on their new properties. Some community members had specialized in farm food production, hoping that their activities would consolidate into a small business, or PYME, an acronym referring to small enterprises (*pequeñas y medianas empresas*) known throughout Chile. An aspiration held by most community members was to be able to provide for their families without having to depend on the precarious employment offered by nearby agricultural estates. In the past thirty years, the number of seasonal workers (*temporeros*) among residents of comunidades had been on the rise. Starting one's business was seen as a route toward economic independence and a chance to encourage healthy lifestyles through the production of organically grown food, and even to promote Mapuche culture, as in the case of those residents embarking on projects of rural tourism (*turismo rural*). But the new possibilities opened by the land grant also brought some negative consequences: in the already-strained relations between signatories of the land claim and a minority who had decided to withdraw from the claim, the gap widened. Land transference in fact amplified intracommunity economic gaps, which were previously narrow as a result of the history of land formalization in rural Mapuche areas. Beneficiaries were able to increase their harvests and possibly avoid overgrazing. For them, the economic benefits were evident. During my visits following the property transference, friends would point out the substantial increase in the number of pickup trucks owned by land beneficiaries as the clearest indicator of economic growth. Beneficiaries were also looking forward to participating in agricultural subsidy schemes for which they became eligible only after the endowment of the land grant. In fact, the more land one owned, the higher were the chances of being eligible for agricultural state programs. Among community members who had withdrawn from the land claim, feelings of regret were common. Their main hope of attaining land now was through the land subsidy procedure known as Letra A—a point-based competition that endowed land to applicants based on their level of social vulnerability. As seen in chapter 5, Letra A beneficiaries were usually assigned land some distance from their comunidad.

Despite some inevitable tensions among community members, the land claim process left residents of Comunidad Contreras with an invaluable experience in grassroots politics. Unlike middle-aged and older residents who had lived through the intense activism of the years preceding the military dictatorship, younger residents had their first experience in grassroots politics through the land claim. Many hoped that the reactivation of community action after decades of dormancy would provide them with a remedy against the depoliticizing effects of land redistributions. It was somehow expected that with land demarcation, residents' attention would eventually turn from unresolved claims over sections of their ancestral territory to the development of their new properties. While to a certain extent these expectations turned out to be true, the community board continued its activities, thanks partly to the return of young people to Comunidad Contreras from urban areas—another significant effect of land restoration. The land claim in fact provided many urban residents with the chance to leave the hostile and insecure space of the city and return to living off the land with family

FIGURE 16  A ceremony held to celebrate the land property transfer. (Photo by author)

close by. Returnees are often regarded as ideal candidates for the role of *dirigentes* for possessing some of the professional skills that Mapuche rural residents might lack. This reactivation of grassroots politics provided the community with the means and the skills to negotiate with local authorities for infrastructural improvements, such as the construction of a community health post and a new deep well.

In Comunidad Contreras, the reactivation of grassroots politics has also made possible a broader process of cultural revitalization. In the previous chapter we saw how a ngillatun could strengthen land claims by intervening in the complex web of relations in which ritual congregations are situated. In turn, the land claim helped to transform the ngillatun from a small celebration organized by a couple of kin groups into a large collective event articulating a vast network of political allies and reciprocal guests from nearby comunidades. Year by year, the number of *ramadas*—temporary shelters occupied by kin groups during the event—have increased. Even the Evangelicals, swallowing their concerns about the "pagan" nature of Mapuche rituals, increasingly participated in collective events, such as the intercommunity *palin* tournaments. Such a renewed interest in Mapuche culture (*cultura Mapuche*) has helped residents to reverse assimilatory processes after decades of racial discrimination and self-hatred. The concurrence between land endowment and cultural revitalization processes can be taken as a reflection of the transformative nature of indigeneity (see De la Cadena and Starn 2007; Merlan 2009). The land claims undoubtedly show how political action is motivated by a desire to reactivate Mapuche values and practices associated with past generations at the same time as it leads to the articulation of new forms of attachment and belonging

The recent history of Comunidad Contreras is one marked by hope, creativity, success, and frustration. For me and many residents of Comunidad Contreras, this history is a testimony to their extraordinary achievements within the often bleak context of Indigenous land politics in Chile. I have always felt privileged and at times anxious about the burden that my inevitably partial and incomplete depiction of the events described in this book represents for their protagonists, and for Indigenous rights actors in Chile. I share a sense of pride with the residents of Comunidad Contreras for their outstanding successes. Yet, irremediably, my feelings toward land claims continue to be mixed. In the previous chapters, I have shown how the politically destabilizing potential of the idea of ancestral territory is domesticated through the redistribution of land grants framed within existing market configurations. In this view, the new ancestral territories would not constitute a new political category. They would simply be more of the same, where "more" refers to hectares owned by farmers and "same" to the existing labor, property, and environmental relations in which members of comunidades find themselves. Yet if we look at the longer history of land claims from the perspective of the actors involved, another scenario can be imaged: that the new ancestral territories are not simply the outcome of governmental codification but also the result of claimants' attempts to create a space from where affective relations between two sentient subjects—the land and its dwellers—can be reactivated and maintained in the future. Territorial demands, such as those articulated by Mapuche people in Chile, are simultaneously backward- and forward-looking, as they reconfigure both memories of the past and expectations about the future (Kolers 2009, 101). Land claims can thus be understood as processes able to foster new actions of world making, a term I use in reference to practices that transform the multiple connections involving human and nonhuman forces that compose the world.

In this chapter I ask what types of future are projected through Indigenous land politics. Land claims, I propose, engender the articulation of social projects inspired by ideals of autonomy and respect while allowing for new forms of dependency on market and state. Moral discourses on practices and ideas emerging from the new ancestral territories cannot be naïvely thought of as projections of alternative futures. Rather, they allow for the projection of forms of social life that stand at once within and outside the market and the state—the two forces that more than others are not controlled by Mapuche rural residents and yet determine much of their existence. The new ancestral territories appear as truly interstitial spaces, where new instances of world making can be carried out in opposition to and alongside state and market forces. The interstice I am referring to here is not simply a space in between others but one where dominant geographies, such as those associated with state and market in southern Chile, are at once interiorized as ineluctable destinies and bracketed as just some of the possible ways in which the world can be thought of. The interstitial nature of the new ancestral territories resembles the enabling qualities that Foucault (1986) has notoriously ascribed to a particular type of place—the heterotopia. This space is "a kind of effectively enacted utopia in which the real sites, all the other real sites that can be found within the culture, are simultaneously represented, contested, and inverted" (24). Heterotopias are not utopias, because they are able to juxtapose utopic and concrete spaces within them. Examples of these sites are museums and ritual grounds. Unlike heterotopias, the new ancestral territories do not function as illusory spaces exposing real spaces or as real-yet-ordered mirror images of a messy world (27). Yet they also present some of the features that Foucault saw as distinctive of such spaces—in particular, the ability of engendering new ways of representing, contesting, and inverting the customary features of socioecological life unfolding around Mapuche communities. The new ancestral territories ultimately project images of a future in which Indigenous geographies might be entangled with non-Indigenous dominant ones and yet are able to endure in opposition to them.

Projections of world making stemming from the new ancestral territories offer a critical response to the two most pervading images of the future in southern Chile.

The first one, deeply embedded within neoliberal ideas of time, consists of an optimistic narrative rotating around prospects of self-realization within the market, here understood as a field of possibilities rather than dispossession and accumulation. This future of possibility is captured by the aspirations of becoming an entrepreneur free from dependency on paternalistic state support. The second image of the future is much gloomier. It is one that anticipates ecological destruction at the hands of humankind. Pessimistic views about the environment are common in the southern Chilean countryside, and they are consistent with historical consciousness about environmental degradation and *awinkamiento*. What is more, such a foreseen future resonates with the notion of the Anthropocene centered on an understanding of humans as a geohistorical force in their own right responsible for irreversible earth system alteration. In concluding this book I explore some of the enduring lessons that can be taken from the uncertainties of world making in reclaimed territories. The images of other futures elicited from the new ancestral territories are compelling exactly because they constitute a critical response to both the optimistic projections embedded in neoliberal accounts of self-realization and the gloomy predictions associated with the idea of the Anthropocene.

## Land Restoration and Self-Making Under Neoliberalism

Images in the media of land takeovers and arson attacks against timber companies have helped to consolidate a representation of the Mapuche people as the leading actors in grassroots contestation against neoliberalism. While many in Chile fear Indigenous mobilizations as a danger to national cohesion, to the point where they want them treated as a terrorist threat, some see them as the most creditable expression of a nationwide dissatisfaction with neoliberal economics. Contestation, however, is only one side of the coin. Neoliberal ideals and values pervade daily life in rural Mapuche areas, and in some cases, especially among sympathizers of right-wing parties, they can be willingly endorsed. Life in the new ancestral territory entails, among many things, learning how to cope with unprecedented effects of neoliberalism with both complicit and defiant attitudes. In this book I contextualized the governmental practices and rationalities at work in Mapuche land claims within one particular expression of political imagination, that of neoliberalism. In neoliberal political imagination—in other words, the act of identifying with and reacting to political affairs (Comaroff and Comaroff 1999; Spencer 1997) specific to neoliberalism—forms of life that are not organized on the basis of market values are understood as potential security risks (Povinelli 2011, 22). Therefore, one of the key concerns in neoliberal governance is how to valorize cultural differences while disarming their potential to interfere with existing market configurations (Hale 2006a; Postero 2007). Property seems to provide the perfect answer to this problem. Under neoliberalism, political claims over tangible and intangible goods have become increasingly framed within the legal language of property (Hirsch 2010, 349). By providing conceptual limits for how specific entities can exist as property, neoliberal political imagination constitutes a compelling power-knowledge formation in the definition of the ancestral territory. Although the emerging regime of privatization associated with neoliberalism has come to define Indigenous land politics in Chile, property disputes in Mapuche rural areas remind us about the contested nature of this ideology and its potential continuity with past colonial projects. As suggested by Hirsch, the expansion of proprietorship under neoliberalism has prompted new conflictive perspectives: "As the neoliberal emphasis on the expansion of property continues apace, so too do the contests about the division of persons and things that property theory both presupposes and, necessarily, continually subverts" (357). In the new ancestral territories, property is at once a useful tool to frame entitlement to land among community members and a matter of ongoing contestation in the case of non-Indigenous large landholdings stemming from the history of settler expansion and displacement in southern Chile.

The pervasiveness of the neoliberal political imagination in Indigenous southern Chile is evident not only in its particular emphasis on property as the field through which political legitimacy is played out, but also in those everyday processes through which subjects embodying neoliberal values of individual accountability, financial rationality, and entrepreneurial inventiveness are formed (see Foucault 2008). Freedom in the market is the crucial feature of neoliberal processes of subject formation. Neoliberalism is in fact characterized by "a promotion of freedom as a means to self-realisation that disregards any questioning of the economic and social conditions that make such freedom possible" (Hilgers 2011, 352). The particular neoliberal emphasis on freedom reflects a general understanding of selfhood as an ongoing process of self-improvement dependent on the capacity for financial rationality and reflexivity (Gershon 2011; Lemke 2011). In Chile, the recovery of freedom from state dependence, *estatismo*, was the ideological foundation behind the restructuring of society designed by the Chicago Boys during Pinochet's military dictatorship. In this particular ideological project, self-realization was ideally achieved only through individual empowerment in the market, a goal that the state could help citizens to achieve by setting the right conditions for the cultivation of financial ingenuity (Cárcamo-Huechante 2006; Silva 2009; Valdés 1995). Among policy makers in Chile, Indigenous rural areas are generally treated as preferred targets for the implementation of social policies aimed at reducing poverty through the mechanisms of microfinance. The implementation of such policies is typically sustained by the articulation of training and educational programs aimed at forming ideal types of citizens characterized by both financial rationality and commercial ingenuity. As seen earlier, the scenario that land endowment has opened for Mapuche beneficiaries is marked by hopes of commercial empowerment, mainly associated with new possibilities of embarking upon entrepreneurial projects enjoying the support of different state programs.[1] Among Mapuche rural residents, becoming entrepreneurs is a prospect animated by a desire for autonomy and independence from non-Indigenous employers (Di Giminiani 2018). Entrepreneurial hopes contrast with the reality of precarious employment and the need to rely on private intermediaries and state support to sustain susceptible commercial activities. Such a faith in entrepreneurship among the residents of the new ancestral territory is not unique to southern Chile but rather follows a global trend toward the indigenization of entrepreneurship, a process consisting in the dual reconfiguration of entrepreneurship as a means for emancipation and indigeneity as a market force (Comaroff and Comaroff 2009). One of the implications of a renewed trust in ethnic entrepreneurship is that self-realization is reoriented from the fields of politics and everyday sociality to that of the market.

With great emphasis placed on entrepreneurship, the new ancestral territories appear at first as the ideal stages from which neoliberal subjects can be formed. Yet social projects made possible by land restoration also motivate critical reflections concerning the moral limits of self-realization as it is conceptualized under neoliberalism. Land claims are not exhausted with property transfer. The consequences of land restoration among the residents of Comunidad Contreras show that the sense of collective responsibility toward the land that they have claimed continues to animate ethical questions on how rightful relations with fellow community members and with the environment can be established. The new businesses made possible by successful land claims tend to be conceived as moral projects centered on values such as respect, upon which Mapuche sociality and environmental engagement is built. Becoming an entrepreneur in this case is not equivalent to neoliberal fantasies of limitless growth and self-made entrepreneurship. A new business should ideally not replicate the social and environmental practices that Mapuche rural residents associate with the patrones (wealthy white landowners). Among residents of Comunidad Contreras, discussions about best entrepreneurial practices in restored territories are centered around the idea of identity (*identidad*) as a morally charged denominator of being Mapuche. Sitting at the dinner table, I once participated in a conversation when a man from Comunidad Contreras clarified to his summer guests from Santiago that land restoration was an unmissable chance to start new commercial enterprises, but the challenge was to run them with "our identity in mind." The conversation quickly moved to the case of commercial forestry as an example of entrepreneurship in stark opposition to Mapuche values. In some areas with low levels of agricultural productivity, Mapuche land beneficiaries often have no other option than to follow the general commercial trend toward commercial forestry. Nonetheless, profiting from timber plantations would hardly be considered a project able to satisfy a desire for self-realization.

The aftermath of ancestral land restoration leaves Mapuche rural residents with invaluable lessons in rethinking the past and the future in terms more consistent with their desires and hopes. Land restoration helps the development of social projects that at once reinforces and challenges neoliberal principles of self-making. This is the case of Indigenous entrepreneurial schemes, which prompt Mapuche claimants to adapt to market-driven ideals of self-improvement, while encouraging them to experiment with the indigenization of their economic practices. Nowhere is the dilemma of reconciling entrepreneurial and Indigenous values more evident than in questions concerning extraction and use of natural resources. We have seen that respect, in particular toward nonhumans, continues to be the leitmotif of hopes and anxieties about the promises of land restoration. Key here is the question of how ancestral land connections can be maintained in the future. The continuance of land connections necessarily requires ongoing vigilance against the threats of environmental degradation. As we know by now, environmental degradation, which has reduced Mapuche farmers' productivity and forced them to depend more heavily on selling their labor on agricultural estates, is associated with agribusiness expansion. Land restitution programs, in my opinion, are insufficient if they disregard questions concerning ongoing threats to land productivity in the new ancestral territories. Such threats are strictly related to the consequences of neoliberal environmental governance and, in particular, its emphasis on natural resource commodification and large-scale extraction. Here, I would like to propose a possible way forward to rethink Indigenous land claims in Chile in ways more attuned to environmental concerns among Mapuche rural residents. I propose that the land claims review process should address all prospective threats to the continuity of land connections, especially those coming from the effects of environmental degradation. In practical terms, this means that the review process should tackle questions such as whether nearby timber plantations do or could contribute to soil and water depletion in the new ancestral territories. Consequently, reparatory measures, including programs of reforestation or subsidies to be invested in soil regeneration, should be added to the land transference package. The focus on environmental threats to new ancestral territories I discuss here is inspired by a broad movement within political theory addressing environmental sustainability as a key factor in the legitimation of territorial claims (see Mansilla 2014).

Avery Kolers (2009, 3) has recently proposed a political theory of territorial rights that places environmental sustainability, particularly stewardship of the climate and of ecosystem services, at the core of legitimate claims. An environmental stance to territorial rights theory, such as Kolers's, works to frame land demands as legitimate only inasmuch as territorial connections are established in ways that they can endure in the future and eventually flourish. The introduction of environmental sustainability in normal frameworks of land justice is clearly not extraneous to shortcomings. Undoubtedly, it would be a gross misstatement to claim that Mapuche land beneficiaries are guided by a preservationist stance in working on their new land. New ancestral territories can be, in some cases, subject to deforestation and soil depletion at the hands of the same Mapuche beneficiaries, and in others, the setting for new conservation initiatives. As discussed in chapter 3, Mapuche rural residents are torn between the desire to make the most out of agricultural land and anxieties over its future standing. Furthermore, legitimizing territorial demands on the grounds of their environmental sustainability could reinforce models of conservation that have historically elicited the exclusion and expulsion of colonized groups in the name of protection of areas understood as wild and pristine (see Brockington 2002). Nonetheless, concern over environmental sustainability in territorial justice should not be easily dismissed as yet another imposition of external parameters of judgment on colonized groups. A further positive implication of this approach might come from the possibility that it could eventually promote the establishment of new alliances between Mapuche and Chilean populations in advancing the recognition of Indigenous rights. Substantive changes in governmental responses to land restitution demands need not only pressure from international human rights groups and Mapuche organizations, but also the strengthening of antiracist coalitions, especially to the greater inclusion of non-Indigenous citizens (Richards 2013, 206). An emphasis on the environmental dimension of Mapuche land demands can help non-Indigenous people in southern Chile recognize the potential positive impact of land restoration in their lives, rather than seeing this process as a privilege for specific people, as many in Chile do now. Ultimately, land claims can offer new directions in thinking about a more sustainable common future for Mapuche and non-Indigenous people. Environmental concerns are also central to the other image of the future surfacing from the new ancestral territories, one drawn in opposite terms with the optimistic tones of neoliberal prospects of self-realization and increasingly linked to the buzzword *Anthropocene*.

## Indigenous Politics and Sentient Lands in the Anthropocene

The Anthropocene has a recent history. While this notion builds on references to anthropogenic changes in earth systems circulating as early as the late nineteenth century, the first scientific use of this term dates to the 1980s with the work of biologist Eugene Stoermer. A couple of decades later, in a time when global climate change was becoming a political concern, the term *Anthropocene* was popularized by the Nobel Prize winner in chemistry Paul Crutzen and gradually made its way in the geoscience community (Steffen et al. 2011, 843).[2] The Anthropocene is a new proposed geological epoch, in which humans have converted from actors influencing ecological relations to full geological forces embedded in earth history and capable of affecting the earth's functioning in its entirety; in this new epoch, the human species "rivals some of the great forces of Nature in its impact on the functioning of the Earth system" (844). The threat of global warming is the most alarming of the many geological effects caused by our species. Humans have become able to alter biogeochemical and water cycles and have driven a large number of species to extinction. Unlike other geological ages that were named retrospectively according to the fossil record, the Anthropocene is the history of an epoch (the present) in which the dominant species (humanity) is not yet extinct (Kersten 2013, 40).

At first glance, the Anthropocene appears as the culmination of a Western narrative of human transcendence from nature made possible by industrial and technological progress. This notion rewrites the end of this particular teleology, replacing its optimistic tone with a darker depiction of human hubris, which, in attempting to achieve mastery over nature, ultimately becomes the instrument of our self-destruction. However, a closer look at the theoretical implications of the Anthropocene reveals that human exceptionalism is a status both denied and reasserted therein (see Haraway et al. 2016). For Latour (2014), the usefulness of the term stems from the fact that "it gives another definition of time, it redescribes what it is to stand in space, and it reshuffles what it means to be entangled within animated agencies" (16). By raising awareness of the embeddedness of social, political, and material processes affecting the earth system, the Anthropocene prompts us to revisit customary assumptions about human and geological history. One such assumption—perhaps the most important—is that social history as we know it has unfolded autonomously from the deeper time of geohistory as the latter was nothing more than a neutral backdrop for human processes. This point has been eloquently raised by Dipesh Chakrabarty (2009), who found in the Anthropocene the occasion for rethinking some of the premises behind globalization and postcolonial theory, largely inspired by a suspicion toward any universal history of life: "The crisis of climate change calls for thinking simultaneously on both registers, to mix together the immiscible chronologies of capital and species history. This combination, however, stretches, in quite fundamental ways, the very idea of historical understanding" (220).

Once placed under critical scrutiny, as in the case of Chakrabarty's appraisal, the Anthropocene can be the occasion for recognizing the entanglement of human and geological history not simply as a universal history but as geographically and historically diverse. Albeit envisaging a common telos for our species, the Anthropos responsible for the geohistorical crisis we are presently facing is not equivalent to humankind in its totality. Human groups should not be held equally accountable for anthropogenic change. We owe to the global social movement against climate warming the awareness that negative effects on the carbon cycle are concentrated into a handful of corporations and allied governmental actors, who have been contributing to carbon emission and working to prevent necessary changes in industrial and consumption practices. While we can single out specific governmental and market actors in this very moment, the earth system alteration we are witnessing is built on a longer history of environmental engagement. Two processes in particular, capital accumulation and modern colonial dispossession, are at the very core of the Anthropocene. Their onset largely coincides with the proposed starting date for this new geological epoch. Among geoscientists the identification of temporal boundaries for the Anthropocene is a much-debated topic, since the strength of a new epoch proposal is bound to its chronological delimitation. Despite evident difficulties in chronologically delimiting the Anthropocene, many would agree that industrialization in the nineteenth century could be taken as a starting point for this epoch for bringing about an unprecedented qualitative change in environmental history. Industrial modernity in all its forms, including socialism, constitutes the economic structure of the Anthropocene because of its dependence on fossil fuel, the primary reason for the alteration in the carbon cycle (Chakrabarty 2009, 217). Within all expressions of industrial modernity, capitalism can be said to have played a key role not only for quantitatively impacting earth systems but also for establishing a dominant perspective of the world as one of infinite resources and constant growth. This is the reason why Capitalocene, a term introduced by Jason Moore (2015, 43), might be a more precise denomination for our current geo-historical moment.

The impact of capitalism on geo-history cannot be fully appreciated if not thought of in conjunction with colonial dispossession, a theme to which much of this book has been dedicated. Like capitalism, colonialism is characterized by two entrenched dimensions—social and ecological. The former refers to the material and conceptual dispossession suffered by colonized groups stripped of their means of subsistence and the legitimacy of their understandings of the world. The latter centers on the domestication and transformation of supposedly wild and empty spaces into agrarian landscapes, a process that has anticipated the current exhaustion of natural resources. Especially in societies built upon the socioecological effects of settler colonialism, the two dimensions are often thought of separately, with Indigenous dispossession being treated as a phenomenon of the past subject to politics of reparation and transitional justice and ecological transformation provoked by settler expansion being praised as the ground for national development. The Anthropocene makes even more evident the fact that these two dimensions cannot be thought of in separation. Dispossession affects at once the terms of engagement with the world of the colonized groups and the very world they inhabit. Colonialism entails the erasure of ontologies centered on a relational view of the world in order to make space for liberal modernity, an ontology that, as defined by Arturo Escobar (2010, 4), is built around isolation between nature and culture, individual and community. Liberal modernity is the background for those economic practices that have led to the emergence and consolidation of the Anthropocene.

Connection between the Anthropocene and Indigenous land politics looks like a long stretch to say the least. What, then, are the effects that local histories of land dispossession and restoration, like the one explored in this book, might have on a geo-history shared among all humanity? Clearly, it would be naïve to assume that an increase in land restoration benefiting Indigenous groups can effectively contribute to the reversal or deceleration of earth cycle change. While in places like the Amazon rainforest, demarcation of Indigenous territories could help in the reduction of deforestation rates, processes of ancestral land restoration largely unfold independently from local and global processes of industrialization and agrarian production taking place around reclaimed territories and necessarily affecting them. Besides, it is often the case that economic life in the new ancestral territories mirrors the depletive agrarian production practices taking place all across the southern Chilean countryside. For instance, cereal cultivation carried out by land beneficiaries is inserted in the same market that agribusiness companies and estate owners capitalize. Despite an undeniable contiguity between Mapuche and winka agricultural practices carried out in the new ancestral territories, land claims cannot be reduced to a mere petition for resources—land, in this case—achieved through the rhetorical tactics of identity politics. Throughout this book, I have proposed that land claims are best approached as instances of world making, operating along with other practices, often less overtly political, aimed at establishing intersubjective relations with sentient elements of the ancestral land. The world made through land claims is not remarkably different than the one imagined and experienced by most farmers in southern Chile. Yet land claims can sustain hopes and practices to reactivate the land connections on which Mapuche land ontologies are built, as well as develop new ones.

Albeit firmly grounded in a shared history of land and agrarian politics across Latin America, Indigenous mobilizations for territorial rights have brought a new way of doing politics to the national arenas. As seen in this chapter, land claims can help the activation of social projects inspired by ideas questioning modernist assumptions about development and environmental engagement. This is the case of *buen vivir* (living well), a notion that has acquired visibility over the last twenty years in Latin America as a culturally sensitive alternative to modernist approaches to development. *Buen vivir* borrows Indigenous notions of well-being and good life, such as the Quechua expression *sumak kawsay*, to emphasize ecological sustainability, democratic participation, and inclusion of local values as the necessary conditions for the development of a truly holistic model of human development (Escobar 2010, 21). Although *buen vivir* has gradually become a rhetorical strategy for the legitimation of new left governments in Latin America in the face of their extractivist policies, its ramifications are still evident in Indigenous social projects across the region. In southern Chile, the influence of this notion has come to be captured by the Mapudungun expression *küme mongen* (good life). This expression is now popular among NGOs and Mapuche communities, and despite its inevitable rhetorical and strategic uses, it has contributed to the promotion of development projects inspired by ideas such as respect toward nonhumans, discussed at length in this book. *Buen vivir* is just one rhetorical example of a larger phenomenon—namely, the emergence of Indigenous social action as a critical intervention against the promises of modernist development.

Indigenous social action epitomizes a type of political engagement defined by Ghassan Hage (2015) as "alter-politics." Unlike the more traditional way of doing politics in oppositional terms, alter-politics coalesces around the search for "alternative economies, alternative modes of inhabiting and relating to the earth, and alternative modes of thinking and experiencing otherness" (4). Key to alter-politics is the emergence of practices questioning the very premises of liberal modernity. As argued by Mario Blaser (2010), "Modernist assumptions about what is at stake in politics (e.g., recognition of subjects and redistribution of objects) . . . cannot grasp those aspects of Indigenous mobilization that do not fit with modern categories (of subjects and objects for instance) because they express a different ontology" (2). Indigenous territorial mobilizations reveal the ontological limits of liberal modernity by advancing an alternative image of how human-environmental relations could take place. To think of lands as sentient in the context of land claims helps us to recognize Indigenous mobilizations as both novel political phenomena and actions built on historically grounded ontological understandings of people and the environment. Significant to the present discussion, the ontological principles both animating and activated by contemporary Indigenous politics warn us against the dangers of acting on the environment, as human and nonhuman agents do not belong to a common history. Indigenous ontologies and the Anthropocene therefore share a sense of dissatisfaction with the chasm between earth and species histories. In different ways, they both prompt us to ecologize our understanding of politics (Kohn 2015, 312).

A central feature of Indigenous ontologies and politics is the significance that environmental destruction plays in conceptions of the future. The thought of a future world without our species, definitely not a prerogative of the Anthropocene, is present also in Indigenous South America. For Danowski and Viveiros de Castro (2017, 74–78), the future depicted in some Amerindian eschatologies presupposes an anthropomorphic world where humanity is consubstantial to the world itself, since all beings were originally humans and could be again. This particular anthropomorphic pluriverse contrasts with the anthropocentric universe depicted by modernist thought, which assigns humans the ability to transcend existing conditions of existence. In the future projected by Amerindian eschatologies, the end of the human species does not correspond to the end of the word, as other beings—all of them potential humans—will continue to inhabit it. Amerindian eschatologies warn us against the dangers of anthropocentrism by embedding human actions within a common history for all entities on the planet. This idea is very much attuned to the reconfiguration of history implicit to the Anthropocene. There is more to it though, as Amerindian projections of the future also help to question the continuity of the idea of human transcendence from nature characterizing certain technocratic versions of the Anthropocene narrative, since such versions present an inversion, rather than a rebuttal, of modernist accounts of nature/culture.

The Anthropocene inevitably brings emotions of grief and hope together (Head 2016). One of the most recurrent critiques of this notion is that it is politically disabling because of its apocalyptic nuance, which renders human actions useless in the face of unavoidable disaster. Yet the apocalypse imagined through the Anthropocene can also be seen as a call for action, one raised in terms different than modern politics have accustomed us. In fact, it forces us to rethink human presence in the earth's future by questioning the collective myth of progress centered on a resolute faith in rational management (Ginn 2015, 7), an idea around which the economic practices responsible for earth cycle alterations have been developed. Grief and hope are also very much present in the future imagined from the new ancestral territories in southern Chile. In the rural areas of southern Chile that I became familiar with, apocalyptic images of the future are ubiquitous among chilenos and Mapuche alike. Deforestation, summer droughts, and loss of land fertility are all thought to have increased dramatically over the years. The current ecological crisis converges on one particularly recurrent anxiety: that water will eventually dry out. In Indigenous southern Chile, as we have seen, water circulation is the movement that makes possible all life processes. Many residents of comunidades fear that the land is destined to lose its vitality as a consequence of increasing water loss caused by global warming, a phenomenon that many have learned about on TV and through meetings with different types of grassroots organizations, as well as from local energy projects, such as the many hydroelectric plants being built throughout Chile. Farmers in southern Chile already have a sense of what the future anticipated by the Anthropocene might look like: an image of a barren land with no water. For the past forty years, they have learned to recognize the terracotta color of the soil and the yellow tones of grass as the main indicator of soil erosion and water depletion, generally caused by commercial timber plantations and overgrazing. Some of them find further confirmation of a waterless future in evangelical predictions of a soon-to-come end of the world. In a few circumstances, I was told about the existence of numerous verses in the Old Testament that predict droughts. In spite of the widespread pessimism for the future to come, land claims have offered a chance to rethink how one could live justly in times of environmental crisis. After decades of imposed distancing from "superstitions" associated with past generations, Mapuche people are reconsidering lessons that the ancient ones might offer for living in a present assailed by environmental crisis. The value of respect might not be lost forever. Land claims give hope that respect can be activated if one is to survive in a future of inevitable droughts and soil depletion.

Concluding a book with hope is an easy cliché, especially when I have portrayed a history of struggle and deception such as that of Mapuche land loss and reclamation. Yet hope in this case might be more than a rhetorical device to conclude a story. From its start, the very idea of sentient lands is one imbued with hope. Thinking of lands as sentient opens the prospect for humans to feel for the land and recognize how land would be responsive to them. Such a prospect contains a hope—that of humans' ability to perceive how their actions do not unfold against a neutral backdrop. Not all land is sentient. Some lands might have lost their sentience, and thus their ability to affect human life. Some others might be sentient, but we fail to perceive it as we might have lost our ability to feel for the land. In the Mapuche lived world, at least the one I have the privilege to know, land contains within it the present and past relations that make a person unique. The land thus actively participates in those life projects through which the self is built in relation to human and nonhuman others. Colonialism has undoubtedly eradicated many of those material and conceptual conditions of existence that made the ancient ones able to feel for the land. Through land claims, many Mapuche people are today attempting to rewrite a history with an apparently ineluctable ending, one framed by the image of a dry, barren land. The new ancestral territories embody a hope for a different future, one where respect can be its motto.

# GLOSSARY

**Awinkado**  A Mapuche person acting as a winka, showing signs of possible assimilation.

**Cacique**  Chief and legal representative of a reducción.

**Chao Ngenchen**  Literally, "the father and owner of people"; the main deity to which appeals and gratitude are expressed. For some Mapuche people in my area of study, there would be no difference between ngenchen and the Christian God. This is the reason why it is frequently referred to as Chao Dios in my area of study.

**Chileno**  Non-Indigenous person from Chile. In Mapuche rural areas, it is used as a less derogatory synonym for winka.

**Colono**  Settler. *Colonos* from Chile are usually labeled as national settlers, *colonos nacionales*.

**Comunidad indígena**  Indigenous community; the legal unit representation of a group of Indigenous residents introduced by the 1993 Indigenous Law. It does not correspond necessarily to a reducción.

**CONADI**  National Corporation for Indigenous Development (Corporación Nacional de Desarrollo Indígena).

**Dirigente**  Delegate, typically elected by the local board of an Indigenous community.

**Fundo**  Agricultural estate, typically equipped with workers' houses.

**Gringo**  A foreigner and Chilean individual of European descent, in most cases an estate owner and descendant of settlers.

**Kalku**  Witch (*brujo* in Spanish). A dangerous person with skills in sorcery.

**Kimün** Wisdom, knowledge. Wise people are typically designated as *kimche*.

**Küpal** Descent; a term referring to the matrilineal and patrilineal influence on the individual physical and spiritual predispositions.

**Lamngen** Sister; also used figuratively to refer to another woman as sister and, if used by a woman, to refer to a man figuratively as brother.

**Lof** The customary social unit of Mapuche society under the authority of lonko. It does not necessarily correspond to a comunidad.

**Lonko** Literally, "head." The headman of a lof. This position is customarily inherited by men belonging to one lineage within a lof according to the principle of primogeniture.

**Los antiguos** The ancient people, or ancestors (*kuifikeche* in Mapudungun).

**Mawida** Hill or forest, most likely used to refer to forested hills.

**Menoko** Literally, "the eye of the water"; a source of underground water similar to a bog.

**Newen** An invisible force that can be exchanged among humans and nonhumans.

**Ngen** Spirit masters, associated with nonhuman animals and topographic features.

**Machi** Shaman, healer.

**Ngillatun** The largest collective ritual in Mapuche society, typically lasting between two and three days.

**Patrón** Boss, a term usually employed in reference to estate owners.

**Peñi** Brother, also used figuratively to refer to another man as brother.

**Reducción** Collective land properties endowed to Mapuche population after the occupation of Araucania (1861–1883).

**Rewe** Ritual congregation and the altar standing in the middle of a ngillatun field (*ngillatuwe*).

**Temporero** Seasonal agricultural worker.

**Toma** Occupation, such as a land takeover.

**Tuwün** Place of origin.

**Werken** Spokesperson of a lof or comunidad indígena.

**Winka** Non-Mapuche person, used in particular to refer to invaders. Non-Mapuche women are more typically referred to as chiñuras.

**Yewen** Respect, a value concerning ecological and social relations.

# NOTES

## Introduction

1. While learning some Mapudungun during my stay in Traiguen, I have conducted fieldwork research for this book in Spanish, the first language for my collaborators. In Indigenous areas of southern Chile, Spanish is enriched by numerous Mapudungun terms. There are several proposed orthographies for the Mapudungun language. The reason for such a variety is the historical nature of Mapudungun as a vocal language and regional variety in pronunciation. For instance, in other areas of southern Chile, the term *Mapudungun* is generally found as the variant Mapuzungun. In this book, I will follow the conventions established by the *Diccionario lingüístico-etnográfico de la lengua Mapuche* by Maria Catrileo (1998).
2. Throughout this book, I use the term *Indigenous* in uppercase following the recommendations of the Native American Journalists Association, for which *Indigenous* is a noun rather than an adjective.
3. For Latour, the difference between anthropology and sociology concerns the exclusive interest of the former in accounting for a plurality of metaphysics, and the focus of the latter on the ontological question of what constitutes a common world (Goldman 2009, 112).
4. Chile is made up of fifteen regions that act as administrative territories with little autonomy. The Araucania region (Región de la Araucanía) is also known as Novena Región (IX region).
5. The Chilean state legally recognizes nine Indigenous groups: the Mapuche, Aymaras (the second largest group), Quechuas, Lickanantay, Collas, and Diaguitas in the northern highland region; the Rapa Nui of Easter Island; and the Kawashkars and Yagan in Patagonia. According to the 2017 census, 1,745,147 Chileans self-identify as Mapuche. The Mapuche population has steadily increased through the last census as a likely consequence of successful cultural revitalization and antidiscriminatory actions carried

6. According to the 2002 census, 15.1 percent of Traiguen's population self-identify as Mapuche, which is lower than the average for Araucania, 23.5 percent. Twenty-one reducciones can be identified within the borders of this municipality. Available at http://www.memoriachilena.cl/archivos2/pdfs/MC0055471.pdf.
7. An *inquilino* is a laborer living in agricultural estates. Before the introduction of labor rights for agricultural work in the 1960s, *inquilinos* worked under a debt peonage system, or in some cases they were compensated with vouchers to be spent within the same agricultural estate.
8. Among medium landholders are individuals who inherited small portions of estate land and those very few beneficiaries of the land reforms of the 1960s and 1970s who did not sell or were forced to return their properties during the counteragrarian reform of the military dictatorship (1973–1990).
9. Additional sources of income include pensions, welfare benefits, and skilled manual labor (e.g., carpentry) offered by some residents within and around their community.
10. The customary role of the *werken* consisted in arranging visits and invitations between different rewe ritual congregations. In the last few decades, the rise in political activism has led to a resignification of this role as a spokesperson for Indigenous communities.
11. Reducción Contreras is located four kilometers from the village of Quino and twenty-five kilometers from Victoria, the main commercial hub in the area.
12. During fieldwork, I was only able to gain a working knowledge of Mapudungun, since in my area of study Mapudungun is rarely used in domestic conversations. Elder residents with whom I became good friends were kind enough to teach me basic Mapudungun.
13. All Spanish nouns have a lexical gender, and when they are expressed in their plural person, the masculine version is conventionally applied. In this book, including in the glossary, I use the masculine convention, as I wanted to reproduce local categories and their grammatical expressions among people involved in this research as faithfully as possible. However, I am aware that such reproductions in this book are gender biased.

## Chapter 1

1. Discurso de S.E. la Presidenta de la República, Michelle Bachelet Jeria, en la firma de proyecto de ley que crea el Ministerio de Pueblos Indígenas y el que crea el Consejo Nacional y Consejos Indígenas, January 11, 2016. Available at https://prensa.presidencia.cl/discurso.aspx?id=26681.
2. The framing of Indigenous demands as human rights was encouraged by, among many international organizations, the United Nations through different actions, such as the Declaration on the Rights of Indigenous Peoples (UNDRIP) in 2007.

3. For the presence of regional groups in the Mapuche political arena, see Le Bonniec 2002.
4. The etymology of *Araucania* is uncertain. For some, it derives from the Quechua term *purum awqa*, "brutal enemy," while for others it is a Spanish modification of the Mapuche term *rag ko*, "water with clay" (Zuñiga 2006, 29). The term *Araucanian* was immortalized by Alonso de Ercilla y Zúñiga ([1569] 1981), a young soldier during the Arauco war who portrayed the Araucanians as honorable fighters in his epic poem *La Araucana*.
5. The most notorious of prewar coalitions was undoubtedly that established among a group of war leaders led by the French lawyer and explorer Orélie-Antoine de Tounens. In 1860 he assumed the title of king of Araucania and Patagonia. He was arrested and deported by the Chilean government two years later (Bengoa 2000, 188).
6. A fort was erected only three kilometers from the area occupied by the ancestors of today's Comunidad Contreras inhabitants. In 1881 a local newspaper reported the killing of fifteen soldiers by Mapuche fighters (Bengoa 2000, 290). The fort would later become a village named Quino.
7. The November 18, 1845, law titled "Colonias de naturales i extranjeros" established colonization concessions to both Native people and foreigners. This law paved the way for the arrival of German migrants in the southern sections of the Mapuche region.
8. In the Mapuche region, agricultural land clearing through fire was practiced as early as the 1850s. Colonization by German settlers around the towns of Valdivia and Llanquihue was overseen by government agent Vicente Pérez Rosales with the assistance of Mapuche guides. In his notes, Vicente Pérez Rosales describes how fires could last for over three months. He believed not only that forest burning could help with clearing fields but also that it would reduce rainfall (Klubock 2014, 60–62).
9. At the beginning of the twentieth century, a small number of Mapuche individuals who settled in mountainous areas with difficult access had been allocated individual land properties, just as settlers were later.
10. In 2000, economic figures indicated that 32.3 percent of the Indigenous population in Chile lived in poverty versus 20.1 percent for non-Indigenous people (Valenzuela 2003).
11. The event was reported in the regional newspaper *El Diario Austral*. However, local accounts of the incident differ from the newspaper version, according to which land reform activists ran away from FLNF members who carried only wooden clubs, not guns (Correa, Molina, Yánez 2005, 203).
12. A few cases of torture suffered by local residents have been recorded in the 2005 National Commission on Political Imprisonment and Torture Report, also known as the Valech Report, from the name of Bishop Ricardo Valech, who headed the commission (Comisión Nacional Sobre Prisión Política y Tortura 2005). I was once shown the book in which the report appears by one of the members of Comunidad Contreras, who appeared in the list of human rights victims.

13. Local Mapuche settlements could participate in the Ad Mapu association by appointing a representative. A resident from Comunidad Contreras held this position throughout the 1980s.
14. Villalobos (1995) has questioned the violent nature of Spanish-Mapuche interactions by drawing attention to the extensive commercial exchanges across the Bio-Bio River, which resulted in the establishment of a mestizo population, the *fronterizos*, or "frontier people."
15. Pewenche (literally, "people of the Araucaria tree") is the common denominator for Mapuche people living in the mountainous areas bordering Argentina.
16. The largest action organized by the Paz en la Araucanía was the coordination of a road blockade in August 2015 led by the Confederación Nacional de Transporte de Carga (CNTC), a guild composed of truck drivers (*camioneros*) and transport entrepreneurs (Baeza 2015).
17. Recent surveys indicate an overall disagreement with radical methods of mobilization among the Mapuche population (De Cea et al. 2016).

## Chapter 2

1. The 2002 census indicated that roughly 60 percent of the Mapuche population lives in cities, primarily Santiago. Data on urban and rural residence among Indigenous population from the 2017 census have yet to be released at the time of writing.
2. For more on the relation between phenomenological approaches in anthropology and the "ontological turn," please see Holbraad and Pedersen 2017, 282–85.
3. *Kupalme* is a common variant for the term *küpal*.
4. In Mapuche society, the only hypothetical possibility for consubstantiation is given by the practice of *lakutun*, a ceremony in which a child receives the name of an elder resident who is expected to guide and helps his or her homonym for their rest of their life. *Laku* is a reciprocal term attributed to both name giver and receiver. In my area of study, *lakutun* are rarely celebrated. As those residents of Comunidad Contreras with firsthand experiences of this ritual explained to me, during their lifetime *laku* can become increasingly similar and even describe each other as close relatives. Yet the emergence of similarities between *laku* never collapses the categories of affines and consanguines. This is because consubstantiality in Mapuche society remains anchored to the persistence of behavioral and physical features along descent lines. For more on *lakutun*, see Faron (1961) and Course (2011).
5. For a discussion of blood as a substance able to make and unmake social relations, see Bonelli 2014.
6. The appearance of the ethnic category "Mapuche" in seventeenth-century chronicles has been interpreted by Boccara (1999) as an instance of ethnogenesis. This thesis has generated an intense debate in Mapuche historiography focused on the nature itself of ethnogenesis, a notion that, in itself, implies a process of dramatic social change understanding a possible context of both continuity and ongoing transformations (see Dillehay 2014, 83). Here, I do not intend to contribute to this particular debate. Rather, as I will discuss

in the next chapter, I am interested in the connection between the category "Mapuche" with ideas about autochthony and colonization, a point firstly raised by Boccara.
7. *Torrantear* is a colloquial term in Chilean Spanish. It can also be found as *atorrantear*.
8. During fieldwork, I was told that many residents with the surname Contreras belonged to a patrilineage known as Achureo, originally from an area located in the proximity of the Ñielol hill in Temuco. In order to differentiate different patrilineages corresponding to the surname Contreras, residents apply nicknames. For instance, one of these patrilineages is known as the Contreras gringos, since a few members of this lineage were born into poor European and Chilean families and were later adopted into this lineage at the beginning of the twentieth century.
9. The most significant phase of any *eluwün* is the *amulpüllün*, in which members of the deceased's matrilineage and patrilineage engage in a biographical speech in which the life of their relative is recounted in both its negative and positive aspects (see Course 2011). Another significant element is the long wake (*velorio*), when the family of the deceased is expected to receive guests in their house at any time. Funerals entail high costs for the family, as guests have to be served meals. In my area of study, funerals continue to be characterized by long wakes, but ceremonial biographies are no longer performed. References to the deceased's life are incorporated into Christian eulogies, accompanied by the recital of Bible verses and the chanting of prayers.
10. *Eltuwe* is the main variant for the term *eltun*.
11. Nowadays only a few ancient *chemamüll* are preserved in archaeological museums, while several reproductions can be found as artworks throughout southern Chile.

## Chapter 3

1. In some rural areas, crickets are also referred to colloquially as machi (Course, personal communication).
2. Another example of the affective character of environmental knowledge in Mapuche society comes from the connection of lunar phases with patterns of plant growth. Customarily, a crescent moon (*luna creciente*) signals a period of slow growth, for which agricultural activities should be limited. In contrast, a waning moon (*luna menguante*) is associated with abundance in water and, generally, ideal conditions for farming. The association of the moon with fertility is also reflected in the traditional belief of lunar deities known as *meli küyen* (literally, "the four moons"), unknown in my area of study and recorded only in a few rural areas. The name of these deities is generally invoked by machi for their ability to influence animal and human procreation and plant germination (Grebe, Pacheco, and Segura 1972, 62).
3. Viveiros de Castro's emphasis on the body as a site of subjectivity is integral to his notion of Amerindian and his critique of metaphorical interpretations of animism such as Bird-David's (1999) proposal and Descola's (1996) earlier formulation of this phenomenon,

whereby the social character of the nonhuman world would be a projection of human society.
4. The quadripartite nature of ngenchen is represented in *kültrun* drums (Marileo in Foerster 1993, 210).
5. There are four periods of the year in the Mapudungun language: *pukem* (winter), *pewü* (spring), *walüng* (summer), and *chomüngen* (fall) (Catrileo 1998).
6. The restricted water supply experienced that year led the local community board to campaign for the construction of a deep community well, which the regional government eventually built in 2015.
7. In the early 1980s, the forest industry was in the hands of three financial groups (Cruzat-Larrain, Matte-Alessandri, and Vial). The three combined owned 75 percent of plantations, 78 percent of industrial production, and 73 percent of export. They received 85 percent of state subsidies (Klubock 2014, 244). At the time of the writing of this book, the Chilean Senate was discussing the renewal of the law known as Decree 701, which is opposed by activists and scholars who question the supposed economic benefit of the timber industry for the rural population.
8. See Citarella 1995 and Ladio and Lozada 2001 for ethnobotanical studies in the Mapuche region.
9. Today *wetripantu* tend to be performed in institutional settings, including schools and cultural centers, as part of the culture revitalization model. For this reason, the morning baths that once concluded this celebration are becoming less and less frequent.
10. In some rural areas, floating skin entities are called *trülke* (Course 2011, personal communication).
11. Ngenko are also symbolically invoked during rituals such as ngillatun, where they are represented by a black bull and a black cock (*kürü achawall*) tied to a pole located in the proximity of the ngillatuwe ritual ground.
12. Timber is collected at the end of the summer so as to have enough time for it to dry and be used efficiently for heating during the winter months.
13. In seminars and meetings about Mapuche culture in Chile, I have often heard from both Indigenous and non-Indigenous researchers that, similarly to good life, *ñuke mapu* might be a translation of the pan-Indigenous notion of mother earth put forward by Indigenous activists in Latin America in the last three decades.

## Chapter 4

1. We have previously seen the term *owner* associated with ngen spirit masters.
2. This excerpt is part of a public correspondence between the Argentinean general Justo José de Urquiza and the cacique Mañil Bueno, written in 1860 and published by the southern newspaper *El Meteoro* in 1869. My translation in English (see Pavez 2008).

3. The introduction of property law in southern Chile and the later introduction of ID documents were instrumental in the eradication of Mapuche naming practices, a process described in chapter 2.
4. Members of a patrilineage known as Achureo, who were originally from the distant area of Cierro Ñielol near Temuco, reached Comunidad Contreras at the beginning of the twentieth century and soon changed their surname.
5. The first agency overseeing the allotment of individual land title was the Tribunal Especial, established by the 1927 law, which was later renamed Juzgado de Indios.
6. Land tenure has been a key issue in anthropology since the earliest stages of the discipline, when an alliance with the colonial enterprise research focused on the cartography of the political structure of colonized groups (Hann 2002).
7. In the first paragraph of Decree 2.568, the law was justified on the ground of the "necessity to end discrimination, to which Indigenous people have been subject, a situation that the current legislation has failed to overcome" (see Ministerio de Agricultura 1979).
8. Child circulation and adoptions were common practices in the Chilean countryside at the turn of the nineteenth century. The enactment of the debt bondage system implied that landless peasants were forced to move across agricultural estates in search of employment and residence, without being able to settle down in owned houses. It was common that Chilean parents who could not take care of their children left them in adoption with Mapuche families, who were more sedentary. For a Mapuche family, the adoption of Chilean children was an indicator of prestige and economic status.
9. A large number of evangelical churches in my area of study belong to Pentecostal congregations. Differences among churches, which partly determine converts' preferences, primarily concern the organization's functions. For instance, Pentecostal churches are known locally for the performance of dances in their meetings.
10. In his analysis of ritual clowns known as *koyong*, who embody many of the stereotypical features of white men, Course (2013) has argued that rather than an example of a "positive mimetic co-option of the potency of white others," this phenomenon constitutes an instantiation of Mapuche people's potential to become white (773–74).
11. Consubstantiation refers to transformation of nonrelated individuals into consanguineal kin members—in other words, people sharing the same substance through proximity, intimate living, commensality, mutual care, and the desire to become kin (Viláça 2002, 352).
12. In the Amazonian region, mythological accounts, shamanic practices, and ideas about death highlight the possibility for humans to transform into different entities, including animals and divinities (Fausto 1999; Viveiros de Castro 2004). These transformations largely depend on power relations among beings structured around the principle of predation, whereby humans can be either prey or predator in relation to different beings (Viveiros de Castro 1998). Interbeing transformations observed in the Amazon resonate

only partially in Mapuche cosmology. Agriculture and pastoralism are defining traits of Mapuche ideas about nature/culture, and coexist with animistic principles. The particular hierarchical ordering between humans and nonhumans in Mapuche society explains why, for instance, machi shamans can be possessed by ancestral spirits (*püllü* in Mapudungun) associated with animals, such as bulls or horses (Bacigalupo 2007, 100) but are unable to transform into other species.

13. Among the twenty-one reducciones established in the municipality of Traiguen at the turn of the nineteenth century, eighteen had been divided into individualized properties before the 1979 decree and only three were divided as a consequence of Decree 2.568. These data are held in the General Archive of Indigenous Issues (Archivo General de Asuntos Indígena) of CONADI.

## Chapter 5

1. For a critique of Indigenous representations enforcing a strict dichotomy between rural and urban residence, see Paerregaard 1998.
2. As seen earlier in this book, lonko are customarily the headmen of a dominant lineage; they are in charge of organizing the major activities of a local group (lof). In many Indigenous communities, residents publicly recognized for their knowledge about rituals can be appointed as ritual organizers and named lonko.
3. Manuel Panguilef (1887–1952), one of the earliest Mapuche political activists, was known for incorporating documentation within his own messianic and spiritual political discourse (Crow 2013, 77).
4. As the assembly of the community previously agreed, those residents who were invited to take part in the land claim and decided not to get involved in it were excluded from land redistribution.

## Chapter 6

1. In one circumstance, a few residents organized an occupation (toma) of CONADI's head office by entering the premises in Temuco and locking its entrance, which prevented the normal running of the agency for a few hours.
2. A report on the case of Comunidad Contreras was published by the Observatorio de Derecho de los Pueblos Indígenas, now Observatorio Ciudadano, one of the oldest and most renowned human rights research institutes in Chile (see González, Meza-Lopehandía, and Sánchez 2007).
3. In the past two decades, senior members of the clergy have occasionally acted as mediators in disputes involving Mapuche activists and forces of order, as in the case of the death

of Matias Catrileo, who was killed by a policeman during a land occupation in 2008 (Richards 2013, 235).
4. In other rural areas, the installation of the rewe is named *rewetun*.
5. For thorough descriptions of the ngillatun ritual, see Alonqueo 1979; Course 2011; Foerster 1993; Pereda and Perrotta 1994; and Schindler 2006.
6. Music is performed by a few attendees. The main instruments are *kültrun* drums; *cascahuillas* (small bells); different types of wind instruments such as *trutrukas*—which are made out of bull horns and characterized by a deep, reverberating sound—and *pifülkas*, or small wooden flutes played by alternating lower and higher notes. *Purrun* is not the only style of dance associated with ngillatun. Other types of dance are *masatun*, in which men and women in different lines move longitudinally along the *ngillatuwe* ground, and *choyque purrun*, a dance performed only by young men for the enjoyment of the rest of the attendees. *Choyque purrun*, roughly translatable as the "ostrich dance," consists in the rapid alternation of steps and the simultaneous use of a shawl, opened up to represent the wings of the now barely extant Patagonian ostrich (*Rhea pennata*). The dance is playful and performers can joke around with their audience, in some cases to draw the attention of young women.
7. During the *misawun*, food is exchanged among households gathered in different *ramadas*. Food offerings are never refused. Leftovers can be saved in bags according to the practice of *rokin*, described earlier in this book. Wine drinking is strictly forbidden during the entire ngillatun except in the final meal, where small quantities accompany the meal. In other Mapuche settlements, alcohol use can range from total prohibition to large consumption.
8. Other phases of the ngillatun are the *awün*, in which several horsemen gallop along a north-south axis meant as a form of protection toward the ngillatun field, and the *choyacal*, a term that friends at Comunidad Contreras translated in Spanish as the presentation of food, during which attendees leave pots full of food and jars of *muday*, a traditional corn beer, around the rewe. In the ngillatun held at Comunidad Contreras, a game called *palin* is played with mixed teams comprising both hosts and guests. The game starts with the two teams distributing their players along the longer lines of a rectangular field (*paliwe*). Each player faces their team counterpart and cannot swap position around the field during the game. Their main objective is to hit a wooden ball (*pali*) toward their opponent's goal (*raya*) with a wooden stick known as *wüño*, a space at the end of the field marked by small branches of the *maki* tree. In other rural areas, *palin* games are played independently from ngillatun.
9. The role of water in healing practices is a phenomenon observed in numerous religious traditions (Strang 2004, 91).
10. The most notable exception concerns the Pewenche regional group located in southern Andean areas, among whom the centre of the *ngillatuwe* ground can be an araucaria tree.

11. Certain sites, such as the *kuel* burial grounds, which consist of large mounds artificially leveled, are believed to be the location of ancestral spirits (Dillehay 2007, 168–69). *Kuel*, however, represent only a small minority of sacred sites in Indigenous southern Chile, and the assumption of the presence of ancestral spirits cannot be automatically extended to other sacred places, such as rewe.
12. The controversial construction of the Ralco Dam discussed in chapter 1 exemplifies this point. The then director of CONADI, Mapuche activist Mauricio Huenchulaf, was removed from this position due to his resolute opposition to this development project, which eventually resulted in the forced relocation of several Mapuche-Pewenche families.

## Chapter 7

1. Deeply inspired by the microfinance movement, welfare programs in Chile emphasize the initiation of small businesses as a foundational step to overcome extreme property. Through programs such as Yo Emprendo (I make business) run by the Solidarity and Social Investment Fund (FOSIS), state credit schemes previously available only to established companies are extended toward impoverished sectors of society.
2. The official designation of the Anthropocene as the geological era that should follow the Holocene is under review by the International Union of Geological Science (A. Moore 2015, 32).

# REFERENCES

Abercrombie, Thomas. 1998. *Pathways of Memory and Power: Ethnography and History Among an Andean People*. Madison: University of Wisconsin Press.

Abrams, Philip. 1977. "Notes on the Difficulty of Studying the State." *Journal of Historical Sociology* 1 (1): 58–89.

Abramson, Allen. 2000. "Mythical Land, Legal Boundaries: Wondering About Landscape and Other Tracts." In *Land, Law and Environment: Mythical Land, Legal Boundaries*, edited by Allen Abramson and Dimitrios Theodossopoulos, 1–30. London: Pluto Press.

Abramson, Allen, and Martin Holbraad. 2014. "Introduction: The Cosmological Frame in Anthropology." In *Framing Cosmologies: The Anthropology of Worlds*, edited by Allen Abramson and Martin Holbraad, 1–29. Manchester: Manchester University Press.

Agamben, Giorgio. 2005. *La potenza del pensiero: Saggi e conferenze*. Vicenza: Neri Pozza.

Agrawal, Arun. 1995. "Dismantling the Divide Between Indigenous and Scientific Knowledge." *Development and Change* 26 (3): 413–39.

Alberti, Benjamin, and Tamara L. Bray. 2009. "Animating Archaeology: Of Subjects, Objects and Alternative Ontologies." *Cambridge Archaeological Journal* 19 (3): 337–43.

Alonqueo, Martín. 1979. *Instituciones religiosas del pueblo mapuche*. Santiago: Editorial Nueva Universidad.

Alonso, Ana Maria. 1994. "The Politics of Space, Time and Substance: State Formation, Nationalism and Ethnicity." *Annual Review of Anthropology* 23:379–405.

Ancán, José. 2005. "Mapuche rurales v/s mapuche urbanos en el Chile del siglo XXI. Una contienda imaginaria." *Boletín IFP, Mundo Indígena y Lenguas Originarias*, January 2005.

Anderson, David. 2000. *Identity and Ecology in Arctic Siberia: The Number One Reindeer Brigade*. Oxford: Oxford University Press.

Antileo, Enrique. 2010. *Urbano e Indígena: Dialogo y Reflexión en Santiago Warria.* Working Paper Series, 31. Gothenberg: Ñuke Mapuforlaget.

Argyrou, Vassos. 2005. *The Logic of Environmentalism: Anthropology, Ecology and Postcoloniality.* Oxford: Berghahn Books.

Astuti, Rita. 1995. *People of the Sea: Identity and Descent Among the Vezo of Madagascar.* Cambridge: Cambridge University Press.

Aylwin, José. 2002. *El acceso de los indígenas a la tierra en los ordenamientos jurídicos de América Latina: Un estudio de casos.* Volumes I and II. Documento borrador. Santiago: Cepal-Naciones Unidas, División de Desarrollo Productivo y Empresarial.

Bacigalupo, Ana Mariella. 1996. "Ngünchen, El concepto de Dios Mapuche." *Historia* (29): 43–68.

———. 2007. *Shamans of the Foye Tree: Gender, Power and Healing Among Chilean Mapuche.* Austin: University of Texas Press.

Bauer, Kelly. 2018. "Not-So-Neoliberal Governance: Chile's Response to Mapuche Territorial Demands." *Latin American and Caribbean Ethnic Studies* 30:1–23. https://doi.org/10.1080/17442222.2018.1457007.

Baeza, Angelica. 2015. "Camioneros amenazan con llegar hoy a Santiago y dormir frente a La Moneda." *La Tercera*, August 26, 2015. Accessed March 31, 2016. http://www2.latercera.com/noticia/camioneros-amenazan-con-llegar-hoy-a-santiago-y-dormir-frente-a-la-moneda/.

Basso, Keith H. 1988. "Speaking with Names: Language and Landscape Among the Western Apache." *Cultural Anthropology* 3 (2): 99–130.

Battaglia, Debbora. 1995. "Problematizing the Self: a Thematic Introduction." In *Rhetorics of Self-Making*, edited by Debbora Battaglia, 1–15. Berkeley: University of California Press.

Bender, Barbara. 1993. "Introduction: Landscape—Meaning and Action." In *Landscape: Politics and Perspectives*, edited by Barbara Bender, 1–17. Oxford: Berg.

———. 2002. "Time and Landscape." *Current Anthropology* 43 (S4): S103–12.

Bengoa, José. 1999. *Historia de un conflicto.* Santiago: Ediciones Planeta.

———. 2000. *Historia del pueblo mapuche: Siglo XIX y XX.* Santiago: Lom Ediciones.

———. 2007. *El Tratado de Quilín: Documentos adicionales a la historia de los antiguos mapuches del sur.* Santiago: Catalonia.

Bengoa, José, and Eduardo Valenzuela. 1983. *Economía mapuche: Pobreza y subsitencia en la sociedad mapuche contemporánea.* Santiago: PAS.

Bennett, Jane. 2010. *Vibrant Matter: A Political Ecology of Things.* Durham: Duke University Press.

Berdichewsky, Bernardo. 1980. "Etnicidad y Clase Social en los Mapuches." *Araucaria de Chile* 9:65–86.

Bird-David, Nurit. 1999. "'Animism' Revisited: Personhood, Environment, and Relational Epistemology." *Current Anthropology* 40 (S1): 67–91.

Blaser, Mario. 2009. "The Threat of the Yrmo: The Political Ontology of a Sustainable Hunting Program." *American Anthropologist* 111 (1): 10–20.

———. 2010. *Storytelling Globalization from the Chaco and Beyond*. Durham: Duke University Press.

Bloch, Maurice. 1984. "Property and the End of Affinity." In *Marxist Analyses and Social Anthropology*, edited by Maurice Block, 203–28. London: Routledge

Bloch, Maurice, and Jonathan Parry, eds. 1982. *Death and the Regeneration of Life*. Cambridge: Cambridge University Press.

Boccara, Guillaume. 1999. "Etnogénesis mapuche: Resistencia y restructuración entre los indígenas del centro-sur de Chile (siglos XVI-XVIII)." *Hispanic American Historical Review* 79:425–61.

———. 2007. "Etnogubernamentalidad: La formación del campo de la salud intercultural en Chile." *Revista de Antropología Chilena* 39 (2): 185–207.

Bonelli, Cristóbal. 2014. "What Pehuenche Blood Does: Hemic Feasting, Intersubjective Participation, and Witchcraft in Southern Chile." *HAU: Journal of Ethnographic Theory* 4 (1): 105–27.

———. 2015. "Eating One's Worlds: On Foods, Metabolic Writing and Ethnographic Humor." *Subjectivity* 8 (3): 181–200.

Bourdieu, Pierre. 1990. *The Logic of Practice*. Stanford: Stanford University Press.

Brightman, Marc, Vanessa Elisa Grotti, and Olga Ulturgasheva, eds. 2014. *Animism in Rainforest and Tundra: Personhood, Animals, Plants and Things in Contemporary Amazonia and Siberia*. Oxford: Berghahn Books.

Briones, Claudia. 2007. "Our Struggle Has Just Begun: Experiences of Belonging and Mapuche Formations of Self." In *Indigenous Experience Today*, edited by Marisol De la Cadena and Orin Starn, 99–121. Oxford: Berg.

Brockington, Dan. 2002. *Fortress Conservation: The Preservation of the Mkomazi Game Reserve*. Tanzania: Indiana University Press.

Caniuqueo, Sergio. 2011. "Reconstrucción intraétnica: Reflexiones acerca de los procesos de reconstrucción territorial en Koliko, en la comuna de Carahue, IX Región." *Cultura, Hombre, Sociedad* 21 (1): 105–27.

Cárcamo-Huechante, Luis E. 2006. "Milton Friedman: Knowledge, Public Culture, and Market Economy in the Chile of Pinochet." *Public Culture* 18 (2): 413–35.

Carneiro da Cunha, Manuela. 2009. *"Culture" and Culture: Traditional Knowledge and Intellectual Rights*. Chicago: Prickly Paradigm Press.

Casey, Edward. 1996. "How to Get from Space to Place in a Fairly Short Stretch of Time: Phenomenological Prolegomena." In Feld and Basso 1996, 13–52.

———. 1997. *The Fate of Place: A Philosophical History*. Berkeley: University of California Press.

Catrileo, Maria. 1998. *Diccionario lingüístico-etnográfico de la lengua mapuche*. Santiago: Editorial Andrés Bello.

Catriquir, Desiderio, and Teresa Durán. 2007. "Mapun üy: El nombre personal en la sociedad y cultura mapunche. Implicancias étnicas y sociales." In *Patrimonio cultural mapuche. Volumen 3*, edited by Teresa Durán, Desiderio Catriquir, and Roberto Hernandez, 371–93. Temuco: Universidad Católica de Temuco.

Cayuqueo, Pedro. 2014a. "El racismo que no da tregua." *La Tercera*, November 13, 2014. Accessed March 29, 2016. http://www2.latercera.com/voces/el-racismo-que-no-da-tregua/.

———. 2014b. "El sueño de la autonomia Mapuche." *La Tercera*, October 12, 2014, R12.

Chakrabarty, Dipesh. 2009. "The Climate of History: Four theses." *Critical Inquiry* 35 (2): 197–222.

Chihuailaf, Elicura. 1999. *Recado Confidencial a los Chilenos*. Santiago: Lom Ediciones.

———. 2008. *Sueños de luna azul*. Santiago: Cuatro Vientos.

Citarella, Luca. 1995. *Medicinas y Culturas en la Araucania*. Santiago: Editorial Sudamericana.

Clammer, John, Sylvie Poirier, and Eric Schwimmer, eds. 2004. *Figured Worlds: Ontological Obstacles in Intercultural Relations*. Toronto: University of Toronto Press.

Clapp, Roger. 1995. "Creating Competitive Advantage: Forest Policy as Industrial Policy." *Economic Geography* 71 (3): 273–96.

Clarke, Sandra, and Sarah Greer. 2012. *Land Law Directions*. Oxford: Oxford University Press.

Clastres, Pierre. 1987. *Society Against the State*. New York: Zone Books.

Clifford, James. 1988. *The Predicament of Culture: Twentieth-Century Ethnography, Literature, and Art*. Cambridge: Harvard University Press.

Cohn, Bernard. 1996. *Colonialism and Its Forms of Knowledge: The British in India*. Princeton: Princeton University Press.

Cohn, Bernard, and Nicholas Dirks. 1988. "Beyond the Fringe: The Nation State, Colonialism, and the Technologies of Power." *Journal of Historical Sociology* 1:224–29.

Comaroff, John L., and Jean Comaroff. 1999. *Civil Society and the Political Imagination in Africa: Critical Perspectives*. Chicago: University of Chicago Press.

———. 2009. *Ethnicity, Inc.* Chicago: University of Chicago Press.

Comisión Nacional Sobre Prisión Política y Tortura. 2005. *Informe*. Santiago: La Nación.

Coña, Pascual. (1930) 2010. *Testimonio de un cacique mapuche*. Originally published under the name of Wilhelm de Moesbach. Santiago: Pehuen.

Correa, Martin, Raúl Molina, and Nancy Yánez. 2005. *La Reforma Agraria y la Tierra Mapuche: Chile 1962–1975*. Santiago: Lom Ediciones.

Corrigan, Philip, and Derek Sayer. 1985. *The Great Arch: English State Formation as Cultural Revolution*. Oxford: Basil Blackwell.

Cosgrove, Denis E. 1984. *Social Formation and Symbolic Landscape*. Madison: University of Wisconsin Press.

Course, Magnus. 2010a. "Of Words and Fog Linguistic Relativity and Amerindian Ontology." *Anthropological Theory* 10 (3): 247–63.

———. 2010b. "Los Géneros Sobre el Pasado en la Vida Mapuche Rural." *Revista Chile de Antropologia* 21:39–58.

———. 2011. *Becoming Mapuche: Person and Ritual in Indigenous Chile*. Urbana: University of Illinois Press.

———. 2012. "The Birth of the Word: Language, Force, and Mapuche Ritual Authority." *HAU: Journal of Ethnographic Theory* 2 (1): 1–26.

———. 2013. "The Clown Within: Becoming White and Mapuche Ritual Clowns." *Comparative Studies in Society and History* 55 (4): 771–99.

Craib, Raymond. 2004. *Cartographic Mexico: A History of State Fixations and Fugitive Landscapes*. Durham: Duke University Press.

Cresswell, Tim. 2005. *Place: A Short Introduction*. New York: Blackwell Publishing.

Crow, Joanna. 2013. *The Mapuche in Modern Chile: A Cultural History*. Gainesville: University Press of Florida.

Cruikshank, Julie. 2005. *Do Glaciers Listen? Local Knowledge, Colonial Encounters, and Social Imagination*. Vancouver: UBC Press.

Cuminao, Clorinda. 2007. "Ensayo en torno a los escritos mapuche." In *Intelectuales Indígenas Piensan América Latina*, edited by Claudia Zapata, 151–68. Quito: Ediciones Abya Yala.

Dalsheim, Joyce. 2011. *Unsettling Gaza: Secular Liberalism, Radical Religion, and the Israeli Settlement Project*. Oxford: Oxford University Press.

Danowski, Déborah, and Eduardo B. Viveiros de Castro. 2017. *The Ends of the World*. Cambridge: Polity Press.

Davis, John. 1973. *Land and Family in Pisticci*. London: Burns & Oates.

Davidson, Donald. 1984. *Inquiries into Truth and Interpretation*. Oxford: Clarendon Press.

De la Cadena, Marisol. 2015. *Earth Beings: Ecologies of Practice Across Andean Worlds*. Durham: Duke University Press.

De la Cadena, Marisol, and Orin Starn. 2007. "Introduction." In *Indigenous Experience Today*, edited by Marisol De la Cadena and Orin Starn, 1–32. Oxford: Berg.

De Cea, Maite, Berta Teitelboim, Gabriel Otero, Camila Peralta, and Claudio Fuentes. 2016. "Resultados de la Encuesta de Opinión Pública en la Araucania de la UDP." Universidad Diego Portales. Accessed December 19, 2016. http://www.icso.cl/noticias/divididos-en-la-solucion-2.

De Certeau, Michelle. 1984. *The Practice of Everyday Life*. Berkeley: Berkeley University Press.

Deleuze, Gilles. 1990. *Expressionism in Philosophy: Spinoza*. Cambridge: MIT Press.

Deleuze, Gilles, and Felix Guattari. 1987. *A Thousand Plateaus: Capitalism and Schizophrenia*. Minneapolis: University of Minnesota Press.

———. 1994. *What Is Philosophy?* New York: Columbia University Press.

Descola, Philippe. 1996. "Constructing Nature: Symbolic Ecology and Social Practice." In *Nature and Society: Anthropological Perspectives*, edited by Philippe Descola and Gisli Pálsson, 82–102. London: Routledge.

———. 2013. *Beyond Nature and Culture*. Chicago: University of Chicago Press.

Desjarlais, Robert, and Jason Throop. 2011. "Phenomenological Approaches in Anthropology." *Annual Review of Anthropology* 40:87–102.

Di Giminiani, Piergiorgio. 2016. "How to Manage a Forest: Environmental Governance in Neoliberal Chile." *Anthropological Quarterly* 89 (3): 721–48.

———. 2018. "Entrepreneurs in the Making: Indigenous Entrepreneurship and the Governance of Hope in Chile." *Latin American and Caribbean Ethnic Studies*, 1–23 https://doi.org/10.1080/17442222.2018.1463891.

Di Giminiani, Piergiorgio, and Martin Fonck. 2015. "El paisaje como proceso de vida: Experiencias de domesticación del bosque en el sur de Chile." *Revista de Geografía Norte Grande* 61:7–24.

Dillehay, Tom D. 1990. "Mapuche Ceremonial Landscape, Social Recruitment and Resource Rights." *World Archaeology* 22 (2): 223–41.

———. 2007. *Monuments, Empires, and Resistance: The Araucanian Polity and Ritual Narratives*. Cambridge: Cambridge University Press.

———. 2014. "Data, Methods and Background." In *The Teleoscopic Polity: Andean Patriarchy and Materiality*, edited by Tom D. Dillehay, 77–99. New York: Springer.

Dillehay, Tom D., and José Manuel Zavala. 2013. "Compromised Landscapes: The Protopanoptic Politics of Colonial Araucanian and Spanish Parlamentos." *Colonial Latin American Review* 22 (3): 319–43.

Dominy, Michèle D. 2001. *Calling the Station Home: Place and Identity in New Zealand's High Country*. Lanham: Rowman & Littlefield

Dove, Michael R. 2006. "Indigenous People and Environmental Politics." *Annual Review of Anthropology* 35 (1): 191–208.

Dreyfus, Hubert L. 1991. *Being-in-the-World: A Commentary on Heidegger's Being and Time, Division I*. Cambridge: MIT Press.

Durán, Teresa. 1998. "Comunidad mapuche y reducción: Factores de continuidad y cambio." In *Gente de carne y hueso: Las tramas de parentesco en los Andes*, edited by Denise Arnold, 139–55. La Paz: CIASE/ILCA.

Eliade, Mircea. 1961. *Images and Symbols: Studies in Religious Symbolism*. Princeton: Princeton University Press.

Ercilla y Zúñiga, Alonso de. (1569) 1981. *La Araucana*. Barcelona: Ramón Sopena.

Escobar, Arturo. 2008. *Territories of Difference: Place, Movements, Life, Redes*. Durham: Duke University Press.

———. 2010. "Latin America at a Crossroads: Alternative Modernizations, Post-liberalism, or Post-development?" *Cultural Studies* 24 (1): 1–65.

Esposito, Roberto. 2015. *Persons and Things: From the Body's Point of View*. Cambridge: Polity Press.

Fabian, Johannes. 1983. *Time and the Other: How Anthropology Makes Its Object*. New York: Columbia University Press.

Fausto, Carlos. 1999. "Of Enemies and Pets: Warfare and Shamanism in Amazonia." *American Ethnologist* 26 (4): 933–56.

Faron, Louis. 1961. *Mapuche Social Structure: Institutional Reintegration an a Patrilineal Society of Central Chile*. Urbana: University of Illinois Press.

———. 1964. *Hawks of the Sun: Mapuche Morality and its Ritual Attributes*. Pittsburgh: University of Pittsburgh Press.

Fay, Derrick, and Deborah James. 2009. "'Restoring What Was Ours': An Introduction." In *The Rights and Wrongs of Land Restitution: Restoring What Was Ours*, edited by Derrick Fay and Deborah James, 1–24. London: Routledge.

Feld, Steven, and Keith H. Basso, eds. 1996. *Senses of Place*. Santa Fe: School of American Research Press.

Ferguson, James. 2010. "The Uses of Neoliberalism." *Antipode* 41 (s1): 166–84.

Foerster, Rolf. 1993. *Introducción a la religiosidad mapuche*. Santiago: Editorial Universitaria.

———. 2002. "Sociedad mapuche y sociedad chilena: La deuda histórica." *Polis* 2, November 23, 2012. Accessed July 20, 2016. http://polis.revues.org/7829.

———. 2010. "Acerca de los nombres de las personas (üy) entre los mapuches. Otra vuelta de tuerca." *Revista Chilena de Antropología* 21 (1): 81–110.

Foerster, Rolf, and André Menard. 2009. "Futatrokikelu: Don y autoridad en la relación mapuche-wingka." *Atenea* 499:33–59.

Foerster, Rolf, and Sonia Montecino. 1988. *Organizaciones, líderes y contiendas mapuches: 1900–1970*. Santiago: CEM.

Foucault, Michel. 1982. "The Subject and Power." *Critical Inquiry* 8 (4): 777–95.

———. 1986. "Of Other Spaces." *Diacritics* 16 (1): 22–27.

———. 2008. *The Birth of Biopolitics: Lectures at the Collège de France, 1978–1979*. New York: Palgrave Macmillan.

Fraser, Nancy. 1995. "From Redistribution to Recognition? Dilemmas of Justice in a 'Postsocialist' Age." *New Left Review* 212:68–94.

Fredes, Ivan. 2008. "Mapuches culpan al Gobierno de enfrentamiento por un fundo." *El Mercurio*, September 16, 2008. Accessed August 1, 2015. http://www.mapuche.info/news/merc080916.html.

Gal, Susan. 2015. "Politics of Translation." *Annual Review of Anthropology* 44:225–40.

Gell, Alfred. 1998. *Art and Agency: An Anthropological Theory*. Oxford: Clarendon.

Gershon, Ilana. 2011. "Neoliberal Agency." *Current Anthropology* 52 (4): 537–55.

Ginn, Franklin. 2015. "When Horses Won't Eat: Apocalypse and the Anthropocene." *Annals of the Association of American Geographers* 105 (2): 351–59.

Gledhill, John. 2004. "Neoliberalism." In *A Companion to the Anthropology of Politics*, edited by David Nugent and Joan Vincent, 332–48. Oxford: Wiley-Blackwell.

Gobierno de Chile. 2016. *Así será la nueva institucionalidad para los pueblos indígenas*. Accessed April 4, 2016. http://www.gob.cl/2016/01/11/ministerio-de-pueblos-indigenas/.

Goodale, Mark, and Nancy Postero. 2013. "Revolution and Retrenchment: Illuminating the Present in Latin America." In *Neoliberalism, Interrupted: Social Change and Contested*

*Governance in Contemporary Latin America*, edited by Mark Goodale and Nancy Postero, 1–21. Stanford: Stanford University Press.

Goldman, Marcio. 2009. "An Afro-Brazilian Theory of the Creative Process: An Essay in Anthropological Symmetrization." *Social Analysis* 53 (2): 108–29.

———. 2013. *How Democracy Works: An Ethnographic Theory of Politics*. Canon Pyon: Sean Kingston Publishing.

González, Marcelo. 2015. "The Truth of Experience and its Communication: Reflections on Mapuche Epistemology." *Anthropological Theory* 15 (2): 141–57.

———. 2016. *Los mapuche y sus otros: Persona, alteridad y sociedad en el sur de Chile*. Santiago: Editorial Universitaria.

González, Karina, Matías Meza-Lopehandía, and Rubén Sánchez. 2007. *Política de Tierras y Derechos Territoriales de los Pueblos Indígenas en Chile: el caso de las Comunidades "Carimán Sánchez y Gonzalo Marín" y "Comunidad Manuel Contreras."* Temuco: Observatorio de Derechos de los Pueblos Indígenas.

Gordillo, Gastón. 2006. "The Crucible of Citizenship: ID-Paper Fetishism in the Argentinean Chaco." *American Ethnologist* 33 (2): 162–76.

———. 2011. "Longing for Elsewhere: Guaraní reterritorializations." *Comparative Studies in Society and History* 53 (4): 855–81.

Gow, Peter. 1991. *Of Mixed Blood: Kinship and History in Peruvian Amazonia*. Oxford: Oxford University Press.

———. 2001. *An Amazonian Myth and Its History*. Oxford: Oxford University Press.

Grebe, María Ester. 1986. "Algunos paralelismos en los sistemas de creencia mapuche: Los espíritus del agua y la montaña." *Cultura, Hombre y Sociedad* 3:143–54.

Grebe, María Ester, Sergio Pacheco, and José Segura. 1972. "Cosmovisión mapuche." *Cuadernos de la realidad nacional* 14:46–73.

Guevara, Tomás. 1910. *Folklore Araucanos*. Santiago: Imprenta Cervantes.

———. 1913. *Las últimas familias y costumbres araucana*. Tomo VII. Santiago: Imprenta Barcelona.

———. 1925. *Historia de Chile: Chile prehispano*. Santiago: Balcells & Co.

Gupta, Akhil. 1995. "Blurred Boundaries: The Discourse of Corruption, the Culture of Politics, and the Imagined State." *American Ethnologist* 22 (2): 375–402.

———. 2012. *Red Tape: Bureaucracy, Structural Violence, and Poverty in India*. Durham: Duke University Press.

Gupta, Akhil, and James Ferguson. 1992. "Beyond 'Culture': Space, Identity, and the Politics of Difference." *Cultural Anthropology* 7 (1): 6–23.

Hage, Ghassan. 2012. "Critical Anthropological Thought and the Radical Political Imaginary Today." *Critique of Anthropology* 32 (3): 285–308.

———. 2015. *Alter-Politics: Critical Anthropology and the Radical Imagination*. Melbourne: Melbourne University Publishing.

Hale, Charles R. 1997. "Cultural Politics of Identity in Latin America." *Annual Review of Anthropology* 26:567–90.

———. 2006a. *Mas Que Un Indio (More than an Indian): Racial Ambivalence and Neoliberal Multiculturalism in Guatemala*. Santa Fe: School of American Press.

———. 2006b. "Activist Research v. Cultural Critique: Indigenous Land Rights and the Contradictions of Politically Engaged Anthropology." *Cultural Anthropology* 21 (1): 96–120.

Hale, Charles R., and Rosamel Millaman. 2005. "Cultural Agency and Political Struggle in the Era of the 'Indio Permitido.'" In *Cultural Agency in the Americas*, edited by Doris Sommer, 281–304. Durham: Duke University Press.

Han, Clara. 2012. *Life in Debt: Times of Care and Violence in Neoliberal Chile*. Berkeley and Los Angeles: University of California Press.

Handelman, Don. 2008. "Afterword: Returning to Cosmology. Thoughts on the Positioning of Belief." *Social Analysis* 52 (1): 181–95.

Hanks, William F., and Carlo Severi. 2014. "Translating Worlds: The Epistemological Space of Translation." *HAU: Journal of Ethnographic Theory* 4 (2): 1–16.

Hann, Chris M. 1998. "Introduction: The Embeddedness of Property." In *Property Relations: Renewing the Anthropological Tradition*, edited by Chris Hann, 1–47. Cambridge: Cambridge University Press.

———. 2002. "Land Tenure." In *Encyclopedia of Social and Cultural Anthropology*, edited by Alan Barnard and Jonathan Spencer, 321–23. London: Routledge.

Haraway, Donna. 2008. *When Species Meet*. Minneapolis: University of Minnesota Press.

Haraway, Donna, Noboru Ishikawa, Scott F. Gilbert, Kenneth Olwig, Anna L. Tsing, and Nils Bubandt. 2016. "Anthropologists Are Talking–About the Anthropocene." *Ethnos* 81 (3): 535–64.

Harris, Olivia. 2000. *To Make the Earth Bear Fruit: Essays on Fertility, Work and Gender in Highland Bolivia*. London: Institute of Latin American Studies.

Harvey, David. 2005. *A Brief History of Neoliberalism*. Oxford: Oxford University Press.

Hassler, Willy. 1979. *Ngillatunes del Neuquén: Costumbres Araucanas*. Neuquén: Editorial Siringa.

Haughney, Diane. 2006. *Neoliberal Economics, Democratic Transition, and Mapuche Demands for Rights in Chile*. Gainesville: University Press of Florida.

Head, Lesley. 2016. *Hope and Grief in the Anthropocene: Re-conceptualising Human-Nature Relations*. London: Routledge.

Heidegger, Martin. (1927) 1996. *Being and Time: A translation of* Sein und Zeit. New York: SUNY Press.

———. 2001. *Poetry, Language, Thought*. New York: Harper Collins.

Henare, Amiria, Martin Holbraad, and Sari Wastell. 2007. "Introduction: Thinking Through Things." In *Thinking Through Things: Theorising Artefacts Ethnographically*, edited by Amiria Henare, Martin Holbraad, and Sari Wastell, 1–31. London: Routledge.

Hertz, Robert. (1907) 2013. *Death and the Right Hand*. London: Routledge.

Herzfeld, Michael. 1992. *The Social Production of Indifference: The Symbolic Roots of Bureaucracy in Western Europe*. Chicago: University of Chicago Press.

Hetherington, Kregg. 2011. *Guerrilla Auditors: The Politics of Transparency in Neoliberal Paraguay*. Durham: Duke University Press.

Hilgers, Mathieu. 2011. "The Three Anthropological Approaches to Neoliberalism." *International Social Science Journal* 61:351–64.

Hirsch, Eric. 1995. "Landscape: Between Place and Space." In *The Anthropology of Landscape: Perspectives on Place and Space*, edited by Eric Hirsch and Michael O'Hanlon, 1–30. Oxford: Oxford University Press.

———. 2010. "Property and Persons: New Forms and Contests in the Era of Neoliberalism." *Annual Review of Anthropology* 39:347–60.

Hirt, Irene. 2009. "Cartographies autochtones: Éléments pour une analyse critique." *L'Espace Géographique* 38 (2): 171–86.

Holbraad, Martin. 2012. *Truth in Motion: The Recursive Anthropology of Cuban Divination*. Chicago: University of Chicago Press.

Holbraad, Martin, and Morten Axel Pedersen. 2017. *The Ontological Turn: an Anthropological Exposition*. Cambridge: Cambridge University Press.

Hubert, Jane. 1994. "Sacred Beliefs and Beliefs of Sacredness." In *Sacred Sites, Sacred Places*, edited by David Carmichael, Jane Hubert, Brian Reeves, and Audhild Schanche, 1–19. London: Routledge.

Huenchulaf, Ernesto, Prosperino Cárdenas, and Gladys Ancalaf. 2004. *Nociones de Tiempo y Espacio en la Cultura Mapuche. Guía didáctica para el profesor*. Temuco: Centro de Desarrollo sociocultural Mapuche, Corporación Nacional de Desarrollo Indígena.

Hugh-Jones, Stephen. 1992. "Yesterday's Luxuries, Tomorrow's Necessities: Business and Barter in Northwest Amazonia." In *Barter, Exchange and Value: An Anthropological Approach*, edited by Caroline Humphrey and Stephen Hugh-Jones, 42–74. Cambridge: Cambridge University Press.

Human Rights Watch. 2010. *World Report 2010: Events of 2009*. Seven Stories Press, New York.

Hunt, Sarah. 2014. "Ontologies of Indigeneity: The Politics of Embodying a Concept." *Cultural Geographies* 21 (1): 27–32.

Ingold, Tim. 2000. *The Perception of the Environment: Essays on Livelihood, Dwelling and Skill*. London: Routledge.

———. 2001. "From the Transmission of Representations to the Education of Attention." In *The Debated Mind: Evolutionary Psychology Versus Ethnography*, edited by Harvey Whitehouse, 113–53. Oxford: Berg.

———. 2014. "Religious Perception and the Education of Attention." *Religion, Brain & Behavior* 4 (2): 156–58.

Ingold, Tim, and Jo Vergunst, eds. 2008. *Ways of Walking: Ethnography and Practice on Foot*. London: Ashgate Publishing.

Inostroza, Iván. 2011. "El concepto de propiedad de la tierra en la tradición mapuche." *Educación y Humanidades* 2 (1): 101–33.

James, Deborah. 2007. *Gaining Ground? Rights and Property in South African Land Reform*. London: Routledge.

Kay, Cristobal. 2002. "Chile's Neoliberal Agrarian Transformation and the Peasantry." *Journal of Agrarian Change* 2 (4): 464–501.

Kelly, José Antonio. 2005. "Notas para uma teoria do 'virar branco.'" *Mana* 11 (1): 201–34.

———. 2011. *State Healthcare and Yanomami Transformations: A Symmetrical Ethnography*. Tucson: University of Arizona Press.

Kersten, Jens. 2013. "The Enjoyment of Complexity: A New Political Anthropology for the Anthropocene." *RCC Perspectives* 3:39–55.

Kirsch, Stuart. 2006. *Reverse Anthropology: Indigenous Analysis of Social and Environmental Relations in New Guinea*. Stanford: Stanford University Press.

Klubock, Thomas M. 2014. *La Frontera: Forests and Ecological Conflict in Chile's Frontier Territory*. Durham: Duke University Press.

Koessler-Ilg, Bertha. 2006. *Cuenta el pueblo Mapuche*. Santiago: Mare Nostrum.

Kohn, Eduardo. 2013. *How Forests Think: Toward an Anthropology Beyond the Human*. Berkeley: University of California Press.

———. 2015. "Anthropology of Ontologies." *Annual Review of Anthropology* 44:311–27.

Kolers, Avery. 2009. *Land, Conflict, and Justice: A Political Theory of Territory*. Cambridge: Cambridge University Press.

Kopytoff, Igor. 1986. "The Cultural Biography of Things: Commoditization as Process." In *The Social Life of Things: Commodities in Cultural Perspective*, edited by Arjun Appadurai, 64–91. Cambridge: Cambridge University Press.

Ladio, Ana, and Mariana Lozada. 2001. "Nontimber Forest Product Use in Two Human Populations from Northwest Patagonia: A Quantitative Approach." *Human Ecology* 29 (4): 367–80.

Langer, Erick D., and Elena Muñoz, eds. 2003. *Contemporary Indigenous Movements in Latin America*. Wilmington: SR Books.

Latcham, Ricardo. 1924. *La organización social y las creencias religiosas de los antiguos araucanos*. Santiago: Imprenta Cervantes.

*La Tercera*. 2011. "Conadi cierra negociación para compra de tierras." *La Tercera*, March 4, 2011. Accessed June 9, 2016. http://www2.latercera.com/noticia/conadi-cierra-negociacion-de-compra-de-4-mil-hectareas-para-familias-mapuches/.

Latour, Bruno. 2005. *Reassembling the Social: An Introduction to Actor-Network Theory*. Oxford: Oxford University Press.

———. 2014. "Anthropology at the Time of the Anthropocene: A Personal View of What Is to Be Studied." Distinguished lecture delivered at the American Anthropological Association annual meeting, Washington, D.C., December 2014.

Le Bonniec, Fabien. 2002. "Las identidades territoriales o Como hacer historia desde hoy día." In *Territorialidad Mapuche en el siglo XX*, edited by Roberto Morales, 31–49. Temuco: Ediciones Escaparate.

Lemke, Thomas. 2011. "Critique and Experience in Foucault." *Theory, Culture and Society* 28 (4): 26–48.

Levi-Strauss, Claude. 1995. *The Story of Lynx*. Chicago: University of Chicago Press.

Li Murray, Tania. 2007. *The Will to Improve: Governmentality, Development, and the Practice of Politics*. Durham: Duke University Press.

———. 2014a. *Land's End: Capitalist Relations on an Indigenous Frontier*. Durham: Duke University Press.

———. 2014b. "What Is Land? Assembling a Resource for Global Investment." *Transactions of the Institute of British Geographers* 39 (4): 589–602.

Liffman, Paul. 2011. *Huichol Territory and the Mexican Nation: Indigenous Ritual, Land Conflict, and Sovereignty Claims*. Tucson: University of Arizona Press.

Little, Christian, Antonio Lara, James McPhee, and Sebastián Urrutia. 2009. "Revealing the Impact of Forest Exotic Plantations on Water Yield in Large Scale Watersheds in South-Central Chile." *Journal of Hydrology* 374 (1): 162–70.

Lovell, Nadia, ed. 1998. *Locality and Belonging*. London: Routledge.

Low, Setha M., and Denise Lawrence-Zúñiga. 2003. "Introduction." In *The Anthropology of Space and Place: Locating Culture*, edited by Setha M. Low and Denise Lawrence-Zúñiga, 1–47. Oxford: Blackwell.

Luhrmann, Tanya M. 2010. "What Counts as Data?" In *Emotions in the Field: The Psychology and Anthropology of Fieldwork Experience*, edited by James Davies and Dimitrina Spencer, 212–38. Stanford: Stanford University Press.

Mallon, Florencia E. 2005. *Courage Tastes of Blood: The Mapuche Community of Nicolás Ailío and the Chilean State, 1906–2001*. Durham: Duke University Press.

Malpas, Jeff. 2006. *Heidegger's Topology*. Cambridge: MIT Press.

Mansilla, Alejandra. 2014. "Review Article: The Environmental Turn in Territorial Rights." *Critical Review of International Social and Political Philosophy*, 19 (2): 1–21. https://doi.org/10.1080/13698230.2013.868981.

Marimán, José. 2000. *El nacionalismo asimilacionista chileno y su percepción de la nación mapuche y sus luchas*. Centro de Documentación Mapuche, Ñuke Mapu. Accessed March 2015. http://www.mapuche.info/mapuint/mariman001011.html.

———. 2012. *Autodeterminación: Ideas políticas mapuche en el albor del siglo XXI*. Santiago: Lom Ediciones.

Marimán, Pablo. 1999. "Coñuepán en el Parlamento de 1947." *Liwen* 5:157–75.

———. 2006. "Los Mapuche antes de la Conquista Militar Chileno-Argentina." In *¡ . . . Escucha, winka . . . ! Cuatro ensayos de Historia Nacional Mapuche y un epílogo sobre el futuro*, edited by Pablo Marimán, Sergio Caniuqueo, José Millalén, and Rodrigo Levil, 53–127. Santiago: Lom Ediciones.

Maureira, Ramón, and Javier Quidel. 2003. "Principios básicos presente en el derecho propio del pueblo nación mapuche." In *Informe final de la Comisión Autónoma Mapuche*, 1121–74. Santiago: Ministerio de Planificación.

Melucci, Alberto. 1989. *Nomads of the Present: Social Movements and Individual Needs in Contemporary Society*. London: Hutchinson Radius.

Merlan, Francesca. 2009. "Indigeneity." *Current Anthropology* 50 (3): 303–33.

Merleau-Ponty, Maurice. 1962. *Phenomenology of Perception*. Routledge: London.

Millalén, José. 2006. "La sociedad mapuche prehispanica: kimün, arqueología y etnohistoria." In ¡... *Escucha, winka*... ! *Cuatro ensayos de Historia Nacional Mapuche y un epilogo sobre el futuro*, edited by Pablo Marimán, Sergio Caniuqueo, José Millalén, and Rodrigo Levil, 17–52. Santiago: Lom Ediciones.

Ministerio de Agricultura. 1979. "Modifica Ley No. 17.729 sobre protección de indígenas y radica funciones del Instituto de Desarrollo Indígena en el Instituto de Desarrollo Agropecuario." Biblioteca del Congreso Nacional de Chile. https://www.leychile.cl/Navegar?idNorma=6957&idVersion=1979-03-28.

Miyazaki, Hirokazu. 2004. *The Method of Hope: Anthropology, Philosophy, and Fijian Knowledge*. Stanford: Stanford University Press.

Mol, Annemarie. 2002. *The Body Multiple: Ontology in Medical Practice*. Durham: Duke University Press.

Monet, Don, and Skanu'u. 1991. *Colonialism on Trial: Indigenous Land Rights and the Gitksan-We'Suwet'En Sovereignty Case*. Gabriola Island, Canada: New Society.

Moore, Amelia. 2015. "Anthropocene Anthropology: Reconceptualizing Contemporary Global Change." *Journal of the Royal Anthropological Institute* 22 (1): 27–46.

Moore, Jason W. 2015. *Capitalism in the Web of Life. Ecology and the Accumulation of Capital*. London: Verso.

Moran, Anthony. 2002. "As Australia Decolonizes: Indigenizing Settler Nationalism and the Challenges of Settler/Indigenous Relations." *Ethnic and Racial Studies* 25 (6): 1013–42.

Morphy, Howard. 1993. "Colonialism, History and the Construction of Place: The Politics of Landscape in Northern Australia." In *Landscape, Politics and Perspectives*, edited by Barbara Bender, 205–43. Oxford: Berg.

Murray, Marjorie, Sofia Bowen, Nicole Segura, and Marisol Verdugo. 2015. "Apprehending Volition in Early Socialization: Raising 'Little Persons' Among Rural Mapuche Families." *Ethos* 43 (4): 376–401.

Nadasdy, Paul. 2002. "'Property' and Aboriginal Land Claims in the Canadian Subarctic: Some Theoretical Considerations." *American Anthropologist* 104 (1): 247–61.

———. 2003. *Hunters and Bureaucrats: Power, Knowledge, and Aboriginal-State Relations in the Southwest Yukon*. UBC Press: Vancouver.

———. 2005. "Transcending the debate over the ecologically noble Indian: Indigenous peoples and environmentalism." *Ethnohistory* 52 (2): 291–331.

Nahuelhual, Laura, Alejandra Carmona, Antonio Lara, Cristian Echeverría, and Mauro E. González. 2012. "Land-Cover Change to Forest Plantations: Proximate Causes and Implications for the Landscape in South-Central Chile." *Landscape and Urban Planning* 107 (1): 12–20.

Nahuelpan, Héctor, Herson Huinca, Pablo Marimán, Luis Cárcamo-Huechante, Maribel Mora, José Quidel, Enrique Antileo et al. 2012. "Introducción: Ta iñ fijke xipa rakizuameluwün." In *Ta iñ fijke xipa rakizuameluwün. Historia, colonialismo y resistencia desde el país Mapuche*, edited by Comunidad de Historia Mapuche, 11–24. Temuco: Ediciones Comunidad de Historia Mapuche.

Ñanculef, Juan. 2003. "La cosmovisión y la filosofía mapuche: Un enfoque del Az-Mapu y del Derecho Consuetudinario en la cultura Mapuche." *Revista de Estudios Criminológicos y Penitenciarios* 6:38–57.

Nichols, Robert. 2014. *The World of Freedom: Heidegger, Foucault, and the Politics of Historical Ontology*. Stanford: Stanford University Press.

Nugent, Daniel, and Ana María Alonso. 1994. "Multiple Selective Traditions in Agrarian Reform and Agrarian Struggle: Popular Culture and State Formation in the Ejido of Namiquipa, Chihuahua." In *Everyday Forms of State Formation*, edited by Joseph Gilbert and Daniel Nugent, 3–24. Durham: Duke University Press.

Nujten, Monique. 2003. *Power, Community and the State: The Political Anthropology of Organization in Mexico*. London: Pluto.

Nujten, Monique, and David, Lorenzo. 2009. "Dueños de todo y de nada (Owners of All or Nothing): Restitution of Indian Territories in the Central Andes of Peru." In Fay and James 2009, 185–207. London: Routledge.

Ong, Aihwa. 2006. *Neoliberalism as Exception: Mutations in Citizenship and Sovereignty*. Durham: Duke University Press.

Occhipinti, Laurie. 2003. "Claiming a Place: Land and Identity in Two Communities in Northwestern Argentina." *Journal of Latin American Anthropology* 8 (3): 155–74.

Orlove, Benjamin. 1991. "Mapping Reeds and Reading Maps: The Politics of Representation in Lake Titikaka." *American Ethnologist* 18:3–38.

———. 1998. Down to Earth: Race and Substance in the Andes. *Bulletin of Latin American Research* 17 (2): 207–22.

Paerregaard, Karsten. 1998. "The Dark Side of the Moon: Conceptual and Methodological Problems in Studying Rural and Urban Worlds in Peru." *American Anthropologist* 100 (2): 397–408.

Pairicán, Fernando. 2014. *Malón. La rebelión del movimiento mapuche. 1990–2013*. Santiago: Editorial Pehuén.

Paley, Julia. 2001. *Marketing Democracy: Power and Social Movements in Post-dictatorship Chile*. Berkeley: University of California Press.

Painemal, Millaray. 2008. "El velo de la mujer mapuche." *AZ Domingo*, March 9, 2008. Accessed May 4, 2016. https://www.mapuche-nation.org/espanol/html/articulos/art-75.htm.

Park, Yun-Joo, and Patricia Richards. 2007. "Negotiating Neoliberal Multiculturalism: Mapuche Workers in the Chilean State." *Social Forces* 85 (3): 1319–39.

Patton, Paul. 1984. "Conceptual Politics and the War-Machine in Mille Plateaux." *SubStance* 45:61–80.

Pavez, Jorge. 2008. *Cartas mapuche. Siglo XIX*. Santiago: Colibris Ediciones.

Pels, Peter. 1997. "The Anthropology of Colonialism: Culture, History, and the Emergence of Western Governmentality." *Annual Review of Anthropology* 26:163–183.

Peluso, Nancy L. 1995. "Whose Woods Are These? Counter-Mapping Forest Territories in Kalimantan, Indonesia." *Antipode* 27 (4): 383–406.

Pereda, Isabel, and Elena Perrotta. 1994. *Junta de hermanos de sangre: Un ensayo de analisis del nguillatun a traves de tiempo y espacio desde una vision huinca*. Buenos Aires: Sociedad Argentina de Antropología.

Pérez, Patrick. 2012. "Elements of an Amerindian Landscape: The Arizona Hopi." In *Landscapes Beyond Land: Routes, Aesthetics, Narratives*, edited by Arnar Árnason, Nicolas Ellison, Jo Vergunst, and Andrew Whitehouse, 83–97. Oxford: Berghahn Books.

Pichinao, Jimena, Ernesto Huenchulaf, and Fresia Mellico. 2003. "Kisu Güneluwün Zugu Mapunche Rakizuam Mew Gülu Ka Pwel Mapu Mew." In *Informe final de la Comisión Autónoma Mapuche*, 602–706. Santiago: Ministerio de Planificación.

Pilleux, Mauricio, and María Eugenia Merino. 2004. "El prejuicio étnico desde una perspectiva del análisis del discurso." *Onomázein* 9:169–86.

Pinto, Jorge. 2003. *La formación del Estado y la nación, y el pueblo mapuche. De la inclusión a la exclusión*. Santiago: Dibam.

Postero, Nancy. 2007. *Now We Are Citizens: Indigenous Politics in Postmulticultural Bolivia*. Stanford: Stanford University Press.

Povinelli, Elizabeth A. 1993. "'Might Be Something': The Language of Indeterminacy in Australian Aboriginal Land Use." *Man* 28 (4): 679–704.

———. 1995. "Do Rocks Listen?" *American Anthropologist* 97 (3): 505–18.

———. 2001. "Radical Worlds: The Anthropology of Incommensurability and Conceivability." *Annual Review of Anthropology* 30:319–34.

———. 2002. *The Cunning of Recognition: Indigenous Alterities and the Making of Australian Multiculturalism*. Durham: Duke University Press.

———. 2011. *Economies of Abandonment: Social Belonging and Endurance in Late Liberalism*. Durham: Duke University Press.

———. 2016. *Geontologies: A Requiem to Late Liberalism*. Durham: Duke University Press.

Power, Michael. 1997. *The Audit Society: Rituals of Verification*. Oxford: Oxford University Press.

Praet, Istvan. 2014. *Animism and the Question of Life*. London: Routledge.

Prieto, Manuel, and Carl Bauer. 2012. "Hydroelectric Power Generation in Chile: An Institutional Critique of the Neutrality of Market Mechanisms." *Water International* 37 (2): 131–46.

Protevi, John. 2009. *Political Affect: Connecting the Social and the Somatic*. Minneapolis: University of Minnesota Press.

Quidel, José. 2016. "El quiebre ontologico a partir del contacto Mapuche Hispano." *Chungará* 48 (4): 713–19.

Quilaqueo, Daniel, and Segundo Quintriqueo. 2010. "Saberes educativos mapuches: Un análisis desde la perspectiva de los kimches." *Polis* 9 (26): 337–60.

Radcliffe, Sarah A., and Andrew J. Webb. 2015. "Subaltern Bureaucrats and Postcolonial Rule: Indigenous Professional Registers of Engagement with the Chilean State." *Comparative Studies in Society and History* 57 (1): 248–73.

Rappaport, Joanne. 1998. *The Politics of Memory: Native Historical Interpretation in the Colombian Andes*. Durham: Duke University Press.

Reimán, Alfonso. 2001. "Expansión Forestal: La visión desde el movimiento Mapuche." In *Territorio Mapuche y Expansión Forestal*, edited by Sara McFall, 33–40. Temuco: Ediciones Escaparate.

Reuque Paillalef, Rosa Isolde. 2002. *When a Flower Is Reborn: The Life and Times of a Mapuche Feminist*. Durham: Duke University Press.

Richards, Paul. 1993. "Cultivation: Knowledge or Performance?" In *An Anthropological Critique of Development*, edited by Mark Hobart, 61–78. London: Routledge.

Richards, Patricia. 2004. *Pobladoras, Indígenas, and the State. Conflicts over Women's Rights in Chile*. New Brunswick: Rutgers University Press.

———. 2013. *Race and the Chilean Miracle: Neoliberalism, Democracy and Indigenous Rights*. Pittsburgh: University of Pittsburgh Press.

Robbins, Joel. 2004. *Becoming Sinners: Christianity and Moral Torment in a Papua New Guinea Society*. Berkeley: University of California Press.

Rodman, Margaret. 1992. "Empowering Place: Multilocality and Multivocality." *American Anthropologist* 94:640–56.

Rosaldo, Renato. 1989. "Imperialist Nostalgia." *Representations* 26:107–22.

Rose, Nikolas. 1999. *Powers of Freedom: Reframing Political Thought*. Cambridge: Cambridge University Press.

Saavedra, Alejandro. 2002. *Los Mapuche en la sociedad chilena actual*. Santiago: Lom Ediciones.

Santos-Granero, Fernando. 1998. "Writing History into the Landscape: Space, Myth and Ritual in Contemporary Amazonia." *American Ethnologist* 25 (2): 128–48.

Sauer, Jacob J. 2015. *The Archaeology and Ethnohistory of Araucanian Resilience*. New York: Springer International Publishing.

Schild, Verónica. 2007. "Empowering Consumer Citizens or Governing Poor Female Subjects? The Institutionalization of 'Self-Development' in the Chilean Social Policy Field." *Journal of Consumer Culture* 7 (2): 179–203.

Schindler, Helmut. 2006. *Acerca de la Espiritualidad Mapuche*. Berlin: Martin Meidenbauer Verlagsbuch.

Schlosberg, David, and David Carruthers. 2010. "Indigenous Struggles, Environmental Justice, and Community Capabilities." *Global Environmental Politics* 10 (4): 12–35.

Scott, James C. 1998. *Seeing Like a State: How Certain Schemes to Improve the Human Condition Have Failed*. New Haven: Yale University Press.

Scott, Michael W. 2007. *The Severed Snake: Matrilineages, Making Place, and a Melanesian Christianity in Southeast Solomon Islands*. Durham: Carolina Academic Press.

———. 2013. "The Anthropology of Ontology (Religious Science?)." *Journal of the Royal Anthropological Institute* 19 (4): 859–72.

Senado de Chile. 1993. "Ley 19.253." Biblioteca del Congreso Nacional de Chile. https://www.leychile.cl/Navegar?idNorma=30620&idParte=0&a_int_=True.

Sillar, Bill. 2009. "The Social Agency of Things? Animism and Materiality in the Andes." *Cambridge Archaeological Journal* 19 (3): 367–77.

Sillitoe, Paul, ed. 2007. *Local Science vs. Global Science: Approaches to Indigenous Knowledge in International Development*. Oxford: Berghahn Books.

Silva, Patricio. 2009. *In the Name of Reason: Technocrats and Politics in Chile*. University Park: Pennsylvania State University Press.

Spencer, Jonathan. 1997. "Post-colonialism and the Political Imagination." *Journal of the Royal Anthropological Institute* 3 (1): 1–19.

Soto, Karen. 2014. "Intendente Huenchumilla: El conflicto Mapuche 'es de naturaleza política.'" *La Tercera*, June 16, 2014. Accessed March 31, 2016. http://www2.latercera.com/noticia/intendente-huenchumilla-el-conflicto-mapuche-es-de-naturaleza-politica/.

Stasch, Rupert. 2009. *Society of Others: Kinship and Mourning in a West Papuan Place*. Berkeley: University of California Press.

Steffen, Will, Jacques Grinevald, Paul Crutzen, and John McNeill. 2011. "The Anthropocene: Conceptual and Historical Perspectives." *Philosophical Transactions of the Royal Society of London A: Mathematical, Physical and Engineering Sciences* 369 (1938): 842–67.

Stengers, Isabelle. 2005. "The Cosmopolitical Proposal." In *Making Things Public: Atmospheres of Democracy*, edited by Bruno Latour and Peter Weibel, 994–1004. Cambridge: MIT Press.

———. 2010. *Cosmopolitics I*. Minneapolis: University of Minnesota Press.

Stewart, J. Pamela, and Andrew Strathern, eds. 2003. *Landscape, Memory and History: Anthropological Perspectives*. London: Pluto.

Stocks, Anthony. 2005. "Too Much for Too Few: Problems of Indigenous Land Rights in Latin America." *Annual Review of Anthropology* 34:85–104.

Strang, Veronica. 2004. *The Meaning of Water*. Oxford: Berg.

Strathern, Marilyn. 1980. "'No Nature, No Culture: The Hagen Case." In *Nature, Culture, and Gender*, edited by Carol MacCormack and Marilyn Strathern, 174–222. Cambridge: Cambridge University Press.

———. 1988. *The Gender of the Gift: Problems with Women and Problems with Society in Melanesia*. Berkeley: University of California Press.

———. 1996. "Cutting the Network." *Journal of the Royal Anthropological Institute* 2 (3): 517–35.

———. 1999. *Property, Substance and Effect: Anthropological Essays on Persons and Things*. London: Athlone Press.

Strathern, Marilyn, ed. 2000. *Audit Cultures: Anthropological Studies in Accountability, Ethics, and the Academy*. London: Routledge.

Strathern, Marilyn, and Eric Hirsch. 2004. "Introduction." In *Transactions and Creations: Property Debates and the Stimulus of Melanesia*. Edited by Eric Hirsch and Marilyn Strathern, 1–18. Oxford: Berghahn Books.

Stuchlik, Milan. 1976. *Life on a Half Share: Mechanisms of Social Recruitment Among the Mapuche of Southern Chile*. New York: St. Martin's Press.

Suzuki, José Joaquín. 2015. "Primera condena por fraude a seguros por 'autoatentado' a camión en La Araucanía." *El Mercurio*, July 19, 2015, C16.

Tilley, Christopher. 1994. *A Phenomenology of Landscape: Places, Paths, and Monuments*. Oxford: Berg.

Thompson, Janna. 2002. *Taking Responsibility for the Past: Reparation and Historical Injustice*. Cambridge: Polity Press.

Toledo Llancaqueo, Victor. 2005. "Las Tierras Que Consideran Como Suyas. Reclamaciones mapuches en la transición democrática chilena." *Asuntos Indígenas IWGIA* 4:39–50.

Toro, Sergio, and Nathalie Jaramillo-Brun. 2014. "Despejando mitos sobre el voto indígena en Chile: Preferencias ideológicas y adhesión étnica en el electorado Mapuche." *Revista de ciencia política* 34 (3): 583–604.

Tuan, Yi-fu. 1974. *Topophilia: A Study of Environmental Perception, Attitudes, and Values*. Englewood Cliffs: Prentice-Hall.

Turnbull, David. 2000. *Masons, Tricksters and Cartographers: Comparative Studies in the Sociology of Scientific and Indigenous Knowledge*. London: Taylor & Francis.

Valdés, Juan Gabriel. 1995. *Pinochet's Economists: The Chicago School of Economics in Chile*. Cambridge: Cambridge University Press.

Valenzuela, Eduardo, and Maria Belén Unzueta. 2015. "Parental Transmission of Ethnic Identification in Mixed Couples in Latin America: The Mapuche Case." *Ethnic and Racial Studies* 38 (12): 2090–107.

Valenzuela, Rodrigo. 2003. *Inequidad, ciudadanía y pueblos indígenas en Chile*. Santiago: CEPAL.

Van Cott, Donna L. 1994. *Indigenous Peoples and Democracy in Latin America*. New York: St. Martin's Press.

Veber, Hanne. 1998. "The Salt of the Montaña: Interpreting Indigenous Activism in the Rain Forest." *Cultural Anthropology* 13:382–413.

Verdery, Katherine, and Caroline Humphrey. 2004. "Introduction: Raising Questions About Property." In *Property in Question: Value Transformation in the Global Economy*, edited by Katherine Verdery and Caroline Humphrey, 1–24. Oxford: Berg.

Vilaça, Aparecida. 2002. "Making Kin out of Others in Amazonia." *Journal of the Royal Anthropological Institute* 8:347–65.

Villalobos, Sergio. 1995. *Vida Fronteriza en la Araucania*. Santiago: Editorial Andrés Bello.

———. 2000. "Araucania: Errores Ancestrales." *El Mercurio*, May 14, 2000, A2.

Viveiros de Castro, Eduardo Batalha. 1998. "Cosmological Deixis and Amerindian Perspectivism." *Journal of the Royal Anthropological Institute* 4 (3): 469–88.

———. 2001. "Gut Feelings About Amazonia: Potential Affinity." In *Beyond the Visible and the Material: The Amerindianization of Society in the Work of Peter Rivière*, edited by Laura Rival and Neil Whitehead, 19–43. Oxford: Oxford University Press.

———. 2004. "Perspectival Anthropology and the Method of Controlled Equivocation." *Tipiti* 1:3–22.

———. 2011. "Zeno and the Art of Anthropology: Of Lies, Beliefs, Paradoxes, and Other Truths." *Common Knowledge* 17 (1): 128–45.

———. 2015. *Cannibal Metaphysics*. Minneapolis: University of Minnesota Press.

Von Baer, Ena. 2003. "La cuestión mapuche: raíces, situación actual y desafíos futuros." In *La cuestión mapuche: Aportes para el debate*, edited by Eugenio Guzmán, 13–41. Santiago: Fundación Libertad y Desarrollo.

Von Benda-Beckmann, Franz, Keebet von Benda-Beckmann, and Melanie Wiber, eds. 2006. *Changing Properties of Property*. Oxford: Berghahn Books.

Wainwright, Joel, and Joe Bryan. 2009. "Cartography, Territory, Property: Postcolonial Reflections on Indigenous Counter-mapping in Nicaragua and Belize." *Cultural Geographies* 16 (2): 153–78.

Wade, Peter. 2005. "Rethinking Mestizaje: Ideology and Lived Experience." *Journal of Latin American Studies* 37 (2): 239–57.

Wagner, Roy. 1981. *The Invention of Culture*. Chicago: University of Chicago Press.

Walker, Harry. 2009. "Baby Hammocks and Stone Bowls: Urarina Technologies of Companionship and Subjection." In *The Occult Life of Things: Native Amazonian Theories of Materiality and Personhood*, edited by Fernando Santos-Granero, 81–104. Tucson: University of Arizona Press.

Walker, Margaret U. 2006. "Restorative Justice and Reparations." *Journal of Social Philosophy* 37 (3): 377–95.

Warren, Kay B., and Jean E. Jackson. 2002. "Introduction: Studying Indigenous Activism in Latin America." In *Indigenous Movements, Self-Representation, and the State in Latin America*, edited by Kay B. Warren and Jean E. Jackson, 1–46. Austin: University of Texas Press.

Webb, Andrew. 2014. "Articulating the Mapu: Land as a Form of Everyday Ethnicity Among Mapuche Youth of Chile." *Latin American and Caribbean Ethnic Studies* 9 (3): 222–46.

———. 2015. "Indigenous Schooling Grants in Chile: The Impacts of an Integrationist Affirmative Action Policy Among Mapuche Pupils." *Race Ethnicity and Education* 18 (3): 419–41.

Weiner, James F. 2001. *Tree Leaf Talk: A Heideggerian Anthropology*. Oxford: Berg.

Willerslev, Rane. 2007. *Soul Hunters: Hunting, Animism, and Personhood Among the Siberian Yukaghirs*. Berkeley: University of California Press.

Winn, Peter. 2004. "Introduction." In *Victims of the Chilean Miracle: Workers and Neoliberalism in the Pinochet Era, 1973–2002*, edited by Peter Winn, 1–13. Durham: Duke University Press.

Wright, Robin, and Neil L. Whitehead. 2004. "Introduction: Dark Shamanism." In *Darkness and Secrecy: The Anthropology of Assault Sorcery and Witchcraft in Amazonia*, edited by Robin Wright and Neil L. Whitehead. Durham: Duke University Press.

Zeitlyn, David. 2012. "Anthropology in and of the Archives: Possible Futures and Contingent Pasts. Archives as Anthropological Surrogates." *Annual Review of Anthropology* 41:461–80.

Zúñiga, Fernando. 2006. *Mapudungun: El habla Mapuche*. Santiago: Centro de Estudios Públicos.

# INDEX

accountability, 20, 34, 53, 175, 194
activism, 12, 52, 97, 176, 178, 181, 214n3
Actor Network Theory (ANT), 16, 17
Ad Mapu, 46, 116, 119, 210n13
affinity, 69
Agamben, Giorgio, 73
agency, 13, 18, 20, 62, 155, 174; Mapuche, 169–75
agribusiness, 4, 46, 47, 50
agricultural estates (*fundos*), 23, 24, 35, 42, 75, 110, 112, 141, 163, 187, 205
agricultural reform, 24, 44
agriculture, 23, 29, 101–2, 109, 110, 135, 178; historical adoption of, 91; winka, 103
Allende, Salvador, 44, 45
Alonqueo, Martin, 92
Amazonian societies, 69, 160, 213
Amerindian societies, 18, 172, 173
*amunrewe*, 168, 172, 174
ancestors (*los antiguos*), 80–81, 83, 148, 206
ancestral land, 147; becoming, 156–61; connections, 17, 58, 78, 82–83, 196; as ontological/ political category, 137; significance of, 73, 78, 83
ancestral spirits (*pullu*), 70, 81, 214n12, 216n11

ancestral territory (*territorio ancestral*), 4, 6–8, 11–13, 19, 57, 141, 161, 190, 191, 194, 200, 203; boundaries of, 148; character of, 164; codification of, 143; conceptualizations of, 159; cultural significance of, 82; demarcation of, 153; land claims and, 30; land grants and, 159; life in, 193; saliency of, 142; transformation of, 150; translation of, 156; veracity of, 154; world making and, 192–93
ancient ones (*los antiguos*), 59, 81, 107–10, 175, 206
Andean societies, 69, 80, 105, 115
Anderson, David, 87
animals, 75, 92, 102, 107; control/domination over, 91; humans and, 106
animism, 11, 89, 91, 92, 211n3
Anthropocene, 30, 193, 197–203
anthropology, 8, 20, 62, 89, 113–14, 134, 180; research in, 15, 16, 60
Araucania, 23, 41, 44, 53, 68, 117, 128
archival knowledge, 152–54
Archivo General de Asuntos Indígenas (AGAI), 151
assimilation, 5, 7, 34, 40–48, 52, 72, 82, 91, 93, 115, 124, 125, 127, 130; colonial, 20,

assimilation (*continued*)
87, 113, 155; culture and, 8, 155; forced, 107; national discourses of, 120; other-becoming and, 128; preventing, 123; processes of, 126; strategy of, 122
Associación Gremial de Pequeños Agricultores y Artesanos Ad Mapu, 46
attachment, 14–19, 191
Aukiñ Wallmapu Ngulam, 49
autonomy, 7, 53, 67, 94; economic, 158; indigenous, 30, 48–55; political, 123; valorization of, 73
awinkado, 28, 63, 124, 180, 205
Aylwin, Patricio, 49

Bachelet, Michelle, 33, 54, 167
Basso, Keith H., 62
behavior, 63, 64, 66, 69, 73, 90, 91, 95, 124, 131, 175, 180; codes of, 127; winka, 13, 57, 133
belonging, 9, 36, 78, 123, 191; descent and, 63–69; land ownership and, 134–37
Bengoa, José, 39
Bio-Bio River, 38, 39, 210n14
Blaser, Mario, 201
body: healing and, 98; physicality of, 91; use/cultural forms of, 16
buen vivir, 201
Bueno, Mañil, 116, 212n2
Bunster, Jose, 75
bureaucracy, 125, 145, 147, 161
burial grounds, 13, 59, 79, 169, 216n11

caciques, 68, 117, 118, 125, 128, 131, 143, 155, 205
Calidad Indígena, 134
canelo (*Drimys winteri/foye*), 3, 8, 149, 150, 151
care, 110, 135; farming and, 101–7
cartography, 152, 153, 154, 155, 213n6
Casey, Edward, 60, 61
Catholic Church, 46, 93, 126, 127, 182
Catrileo, Matias, 215n3

Cayuqueo, Pedro, 47
Centros Culturales Mapuche, 46
cereal production, 102, 188; photo of, 103
Chakrabarty, Dipesh, 198
Cheuque, Nelly, 3, 4, 123, 171
Chicago Boys, 21, 46, 194
Chihuailaf, Elicura, 65, 89
Chilean army, war with, 79, 81
Chilean Senate, 39, 54, 212n7
Christian and Missionary Alliance, 126
citizenship, 48, 55
claimants, 30, 143, 147, 157, 161, 166; Indigenous, 10, 49, 83, 155, 159, 183, 184; Mapuche, 6, 141, 166, 178, 181, 185
class, 46, 48; hierarchy, 188; race and, 67
Clastres, Pierre, 117, 160
climate change, 197–98, 199
collective rights, 5, 22, 51, 53, 144, 183
colonialism, 113, 142–43, 155, 199, 200, 203
colonos, 40, 50, 65, 205
colonization, 40–41, 65, 88, 155, 209n8, 211n6; property law/tenure and, 115–21
Comisión de Verdad Histórica y Nuevo Trato, 151
Comisión Especial de Pueblos Indígenas, 49
Comisión Radicadora de Indígenas, 117
Comisión Repartidora de Terrenos Indígenas, 41
Commission for Historical Truth and New Treatment of Indigenous Peoples (CVHNT), 34
communication, 89, 155, 156, 164, 182, 183
Comunidad Contreras, 3, 12, 24, 27, 39–40, 51, 63, 64, 66, 68, 69, 72, 79–82, 93, 95; agricultural activities in, 101–2, 103, 178; collective responsibility in, 195; customs in, 104–5, 132; economic conditions in, 187–88; history of, 191; land claim of, 24, 147, 148, 151, 156, 158; land grants and, 165–66; life in, 28, 57, 102; mythological ancestors of, 80–81; photo of, 6; school in, 122, 123 (photo); Traiguen and, 74–78

comunidad indígena, 23, 67, 68, 144, 145, 205
CONADI. *See* National Corporation for Indigenous Development
Concertación de Partidos por la Democracia (Coalition of Parties for Democracy), 5, 49, 144
consanguinity, 64, 65, 69, 135, 180
consciousness, 88, 113; diasporic, 57; historical, 122
Consejo de Todas las Tierras (Council of all Lands), 49
Conservador de Bienes Raíces, 145
conservation, 60, 78, 86, 87, 197
constructivism, 8, 9, 10, 11, 58
Consulta Indígena, 33
Contreras, Francisca, 26, 55, 80, 101, 108, 262
Contreras, José, 24, 26, 163, 168, 187
Contreras, Juan, 108, 177
Contreras, Liscán, 26, 27, 73, 81, 82, 96, 101, 104, 105, 106, 108, 126
Contreras, Manuel, 117
Contreras, Miguel, 26, 27, 40, 57, 73, 79, 85, 90, 101, 112, 132, 146, 187
Contreras, Nicolás, 125, 126
Coña, Pascual, 107
Coñuepán, Venancio, 43, 44
Coordinadora Arauko-Malleko (CAM), 50
Corporación Araucana, 43
Corporation of the Agrarian Reform (CORA), 44
cosmology, 105, 110, 128; Indigenous, 127–28; Mapuche, 88, 92, 93, 214n12
Course, Magnus, 64, 74, 91
Crow, Joanna, 45–46
Crutzen, Paul, 198
cultural difference, 165, 183, 184, 194
cultural revitalization, 53, 72, 191
culture, 89; assimilation and, 8, 155; audit, 177; colonial, 76, 93, 111, 115, 124, 126, 128, 133, 138, 155; Indigenous, 28, 48, 112, 144, 183; landscape beyond, 74, 78; Mapuche, 58–59, 63, 80, 86, 107,

123, 180, 188, 191; nature and, 9, 60, 88; society and, 87

Danowski, Déborah, 201
DASIN (Direccion de Asuntos Indígenas), 44
Davidson, Donald, 183
de Ercilla y Zúñiga, Alonso, 209n4
de la Cadena, Marisol, 18
de Tounens, Orélie-Antoine, 209n5
de Urquiza, Justo José, 212n2
Declaration on the Rights of Indigenous Peoples (UNDRIP), 208n2
Decree 2.568 (1979), 119, 120, 129, 213n7, 214n13
Decree 701 (1974), 96, 101, 212n7
Decreto ley No. 4.111 (1931), 118
deforestation, 40, 87, 95, 96, 101, 107, 197, 200, 202
Deleuze, Gilles, 12, 83–84, 143, 159, 160,
democracy, 144, 154; transition to, 48–55
descent, belonging and, 63–69
Descola, Philippe, 88, 91, 211n3
deterritorialization, 159–60
development, 17, 52, 200, 201; agencies, 177; economic, 21; environmental conditions for, 105; language of, 52; Mapuche and, 39, 44; national, 39, 120; policies, 53; process of, 40–41
Dillehay, Tom, 80
discourses, 82; anti-terrorist, 51; moral, 192; reconciliation, 39
discrimination, 29, 30, 43, 63, 72, 123, 124, 191; school, 43
dispossession, 132, 158, 161, 165, 193, 199, 200; colonial, 56; compensation for, 151; historical, 153; memories of, 36–40
diversity, 14, 22, 54, 59, 86, 89
documents, 121, 154, 155
domestication, 127, 164, 182, 184
droughts, 85, 95, 202, 203

ecological relations, 86, 89, 97, 105, 137, 198
economic exclusion, 43, 44, 52

economic practices, 20, 42, 196, 200
education, 22, 23, 42, 53, 105; formal, 122–23, 124
El Huadaco, 3, 4, 5, 141, 166
*El Mercurio*, 39, 163
El Panal estate, 171, 173, 174, 175, 178, 179, 180, 181, 187; ancestral owners and, 177; dispute over, 163, 164, 165–69
Eliade, Mercea, 171
eltun, 59, 79, 80, 169, 211n10
*eluwün*, 77, 79, 80, 211n9
embodiment, 16, 17, 47, 60, 61, 62
emplacement, 29, 59, 60, 62, 83; phenomenological understandings of, 61, 74
employment, 23, 42, 96, 108–9; precarious, 189, 195; seasonal/stable, 24
empowerment, 59–62, 154
entrepreneurs, 51, 53, 188, 195, 196
environment, 72, 88, 110, 193; conflicts over, 18, 199; farming and, 104; issues concerning, 87, 93, 95, 101, 108, 111, 186, 196, 193, 197, 200, 203
environmental notions, 86, 89, 132
environmental relations, 84, 86, 107, 137, 191
Escobar, Arturo, 200
Esposito, Roberto, 14, 16, 60
essentialism, 8, 9, 10, 11, 87
estate owners, 40, 67, 73, 76, 146, 165
Estero Huadaco, 148, 149, 153
ethnic groups, 9, 65, 179, 189
ethnic issues, 29, 45, 54, 180
evangelical churches, 76, 126–27, 171
experiences, 87, 94–95, 137; collective arrangement of, 60; landscape, 82, 83

farmers, 30, 35, 44, 109; Mapuche, 53, 88, 105, 131; vulnerability of, 46, 47
farming, 86, 97, 108, 109; care and, 101–7
Faron, Louis, 80, 92, 116
Fay, Derrick, 5
Federación Araucana, 43
first occupancy, principle of, 42
forestation, 96, 97, 149

forestry: commercial, 101, 196; modernization of, 96
Foucault, Michel, 36, 185, 192
Frei Montalva, Eduardo, 42, 44, 49
Frente Nacionalista Patria y Libertad (FNPL), 45
Friedman, Milton, 21, 46
Fund for Indigenous Land and Water (Fondo Tierras y Aguas Indígenas), 144
Fundación Instituto Indígena, 151, 167
Fundo del Huadaco, 3

Gell, Alfred, 174
genealogy, 13, 23, 55, 64, 72, 83, 124, 135
geographies, 59, 67–68, 142, 192; Indigenous, 7, 10, 17, 20, 30, 159, 160, 185
Gledhill, John: on audit culture, 177
global warming, 202
González, Marcelo, 94
Gordillo, Gastón, 160
governance, 184; autonomous, 53–54, 157; land, 8, 14; multicultural, 164; neoliberal, 22
Gow, Peter, 87
grassroots organizations, 26, 49, 190, 202
Guattari, Félix, 143, 159, 160
Guevara, Tomás, 37, 132

Hage, Ghassan, 201
Hale, Charles, 22, 27
half-share agreements, 108, 146
Han, Clara, 35
Hann, Chris M., 114, 120
Haraway, Donna, 106
healing practices (*machitun*), 64, 108, 150
Heidegger, Martin, 61, 62
Henare, Amiria, 175
Hertz, Robert, 80
Hirsch, Eric, 76, 143, 155, 176, 194
historical debt (*deuda historica*), 5, 33, 34, 35, 56
Holbraad, Martin, 175
housing, 22, 24, 34, 35, 42, 49

## Index

Huadaco Creek, 149, 150
Huenchulaf, Mauricio, 49, 216n12
Huenchumilla, Francisco, 53
human rights, 35, 51, 52, 54, 119, 144, 151
Human Rights Watch, 51
humans, 61, 83, 88–89, 198; animals and, 106; environment and, 87, 110; land and, 104, 105; nonhumans and, 16, 92, 134
Humphrey, Caroline, 114
Hunt, Sarah, 18

identity, 53, 60, 164, 182, 195; ancestral land connections and, 58; collective, 9; ethnic, 72, 130; geographic, 9; Indigenous, 5, 10, 72, 74, 83, 159, 171, 181; Mapuche, 28, 63, 180; national, 22, 29, 159; self-, 28, 38, 43, 63, 65, 127, 181; social, 9, 19
ideologies, 15, 20, 27, 182, 184
incommensurability, problem of, 182–85
indeterminacy, cosmological, 88–95
indigeneity, 5, 43; construction of, 106; perspectives on, 73; transformative nature of, 82
Indigenous and Tribal Peoples Convention, Chilean Senate and, 54
Indigenous groups, 6, 54, 155; exclusion of, 49; majorities and, 182–83
Indigenous Law 19.253 (1993), 49, 134, 144, 158, 188
Indigenous rights, 5, 7, 96, 119, 144; advancement of, 58; recognition of, 22, 197
*Indio insurecto/Indio permitido*, 22
inequality, 35, 44, 74, 103, 122, 143
Ingold, Tim, 71–72, 87, 89, 94, 105
Institute for Agricultural Development, 109
Instituto de Desarrollo Agropecuario (INDAP), 109
Inter-American Development Bank, 52
Invasion of Araucania, 74

James, Deborah, 5
justice, 199; reparative, 34–35; restorative, 34, 53, 56

Juzgados de Indios (Indians' Court), 118, 143, 213n5

kalku, 64, 98, 172, 205
kimün, 70, 89, 90, 107, 175, 206
kinship, 29, 43, 67, 68, 77, 147, 148, 191; cooperative, 72; territorial rights by, 116
knowledge, 16, 61, 123, 175; agricultural, 110; archival, 152–54; cultural, 71; delegitimizing, 154; environmental, 30, 89, 90, 106, 107, 110; modern/primitive, 93; ritual, 150; scientific, 106; shamanic, 93
Koessler-Ilg, Bertha, 66
Kolers, Avery, 196–97
Kolimán, Lorenzo, 116
küpal, 13, 63, 64, 70, 72, 205

*La Araucana* (Ercilla y Zúñiga), 209n4
La Moneda, 33, 45
labor, 24, 102, 131, 208n9; domestic, 42, 135; rights, 44
lamngen, 26, 206
land: access to, 8, 103, 117, 118; acquisition of, 104, 209; agricultural, 104, 197; ceremony celebrating transfer of, 190 (photo); community, 153; compensation, 6, 165–69; concerns about, 95–101; exploitation of, 50, 106; fertility of, 96; individualized, 118–19; jural entitlement to, 133–34; making of, 7–14; mapping, 157; moral entitlement to, 134; productivity of, 105; as property, 15; reclamation of, 203; redistribution of, 41, 48, 116, 129, 189; reservation, 41–42, 114; state-owned, 39, 117, 157
land claims, 14, 17, 27, 79, 82, 138, 142, 157, 171, 180, 185, 188, 189, 190, 191, 192, 197, 200; analysis of, 19; compensation and, 161; documents/maps/transactions in, 151–56; evidentiary production in, 165; impact of, 186, 203; Indigenous, 5–6, 8–9, 10, 115; Mapuche, 6, 22, 142, 143–47, 153, 154, 155, 161, 162; process, 141, 157

land connections, 5, 11, 13, 18, 29, 56, 79, 104, 115, 185, 200; as affective relation, 14; analytical types of, 114; ancestral, 7, 8, 57; articulating, 83, 113; chronological narrative of, 10; configuration of, 137; continuance of, 196; explanation of, 84; Indigenous, 6, 62, 83, 113; metaphorical understanding of, 12; ontological dimension of, 16, 17; phenomenological dimension of, 15, 17; properties of, 138

land disputes, 11, 49, 50, 129, 144, 160, 172; conflictive nature of, 27; proliferation of, 38; resolution of, 162

land division, 120, 125, 129, 130, 131, 133; map of, 130 (fig.)

land formalization, 30, 111, 114, 118, 121, 131, 132, 133; benefits of, 129; celebration of, 115; history of, 189; perceptions on, 120

land grabbing, 51, 118, 143

land grants, 49, 156, 191, 196; allotment of, 117, 143, 158, 159; competing for, 165–66

land loss, 120, 121, 151, 153, 203

land ontologies, Indigenous/legal, 6–7, 14, 15, 17, 55, 114, 137, 138, 142, 143, 161, 185

land ownership, 8, 112, 130, 133–34, 159; as belonging, 134–37; formalization of, 131; geographic markers of, 116; as property, 134–37; recognition of, 118; significance of, 113; social life and, 119

land program, 142, 157, 158, 162, 164, 165

land reforms, 24, 45, 143, 158

land restitution, 3, 7, 150, 156, 196, 197

land shortage, 42, 97, 107, 108, 111, 135

land takeovers (tomas), 45, 49–50, 193, 206

land tenure, 15, 111, 115, 116, 120, 130, 182

land transference, 189; signing agreement for, 179 (photo)

land use, 119, 129, 133, 189; flexible strategies of, 107

landowners, 4, 44, 50, 112, 118; non-Indigenous, 42, 134, 165

landscapes, 16, 98, 101, 186, 187; beings and, 95; beyond culture, 74–78; cultural, 59, 78; experiencing, 13–14, 77, 78, 82, 83; heterogeneous, 58–59; past/present selves in, 78–84; phenomenological approaches to, 15; sentient character of, 13, 93; spiritual forces in, 84

Latcham, Ricardo, 36

Latour, Bruno, 16, 173, 198, 202n3

Lautaro, 37, 154, 155

Law No. 4.169 (1927), 118

Law No. 4.802 (1930), 118

Law No.17.729 (1972), 119, 143

legal reforms, 7, 40, 119, 143

Leintur, 38

Levi-Strauss, Claude, 128

Ley de Seguridad del Estado (2000), 51, 144

Ley del 4 Diciembre 1866, 39, 117

*llellipun*, 4, 150, 170, 172

Locke, John, 115

lof, 37, 68, 206

lonko, 3, 116, 117, 206, 214n2

López de Zúñiga, Francisco, 38

Los Charros de Lumaco, 4

machi (shaman), 64, 70, 170, 206, 211n1

Manquilef, Manuel, 120

maps, 153–54, 155

Mapuche: being, 57, 84; characterization of, 44, 179; dialogic nature of, 66; environmental dimensions of, 197; formation of, 36; as genealogical/topological/performative category, 124; historical process for, 43; historical transformation of, 122; independence of, 38; language, 3–4; marginality of, 19–20; population of, 39, 40, 41, 42, 45, 51, 54; precolonial history of, 36

Mapuche-Pewenche, 49, 216n12

Mapuche society, 67, 71, 74, 80, 107, 128, 150, 173, 210n4, 211n2; anthropological literature on, 68; autonomy in, 94; spiritual aggression in, 172

Mapudungun, 3, 26, 28, 63, 73, 75, 79, 85, 89; learning, 207n1

Marimán, José, 48, 54
marriage, 29; interethnic, 23, 66, 67
*masatun* dance, 3, 4, 215n6
matrilineage, 63, 211n9
mawida, 98, 149, 169, 206
Melucci, Alberto, 9
memory: places of, 59, 78–84, 82; question of, 147–50
*menoko*, 85, 99, 206
Merleau-Ponty, Maurice, 15, 60, 62
*mestizaje*, 47, 123
migration, 5, 24, 43, 88, 124
military dictatorship, 35, 45, 46, 48, 54, 130, 143, 208n8
Millaman, Rosamel, 22
Ministry of Indigenous People (Ministerio de Pueblos Indígenas), 33, 54
Ministry of Social Development (Ministerio de Desarrollo Social), 176
*misawun*, 4, 170, 215n7
Miyazaki, Hirokazu, 154
mobilization, 10, 158, 167, 200; Mapuche, 50–51, 53; precolonial, 142
Moore, Jason, 199
Movimiento de Izquierda Revolucionario (Movement of the Revolutionary Left), 44
multiculturalism, 11, 161; liberal, 182–85; neoliberal, 22, 53, 165
mutual relations, 64, 131, 133

Nadasdy, Paul, 161
National Corporation for Indigenous Development (CONADI), 3, 5, 23, 27, 49, 52, 54, 144, 145, 148, 156, 158, 167, 168, 171, 178, 180, 205; civil servants and, 176; criticism of, 134; discordance within, 177; El Panal and, 163; guidelines from, 151, 152, 153; headquarters of, 146 (photo); land claims and, 141, 157; negotiations with, 165, 166; oversight and, 176
National Forest Corporation (Corporación Nacional Forestal) (CONAF), 101

national society, 8, 56, 107
nationalism, 37, 48, 115
nationhood, 29, 55, 56
natural resources, 6, 49, 196, 199
naturalism, 88, 89, 93
nature, 88, 89; knowledge of, 90, 214n12
nature/culture divide, 15, 17, 18, 60, 88, 89
neoliberalism, 53, 184, 186; land restoration under, 193–97; political imagination under, 19–22; self-making under, 193–97
newen, 13, 85, 95, 98, 100, 172, 173, 206; concentration of, 70, 99; rewe and, 174
ngen, 13, 90, 92, 93, 100, 108, 206; concentration of, 98; conduct toward, 91; encounters with, 94, 95, 100
ngenchen, 4, 71, 81, 92, 105, 169, 172, 205
ngenko, 100, 149, 212n11
ngillatun, 55, 76, 150, 169, 170, 171, 172, 175, 206, 215n5, 215n6, 215n7, 215n8
ngillatuwe, 76, 116, 169, 212n11, 215n6, 215n10
nonhuman agency, 16, 18, 56, 91, 173
nonhumans, 11, 88, 90, 91; humans and, 16, 92, 134
Nueva Mayoria, 33

Observatorio de Derecho de los Pueblos Indígenas, 151, 214n2
occupation: land, 4, 36, 37, 39, 45, 64, 79, 116, 122, 132, 144, 157, 161, 171; markers of, 148
ontology, 14, 15, 16, 19, 30, 62, 93, 110, 173, 174, 182, 201; animist, 91; land, 200; Mapuche, 91, 128; non-Western, 18, 89; nondominant, 17; relational, 89
organizations: environmental, 96; human rights, 151; Indigenous, 33, 147, 151, 157 Mapuche, 4, 43, 49
Orlove, Benjamin, 153–54
otherness, 13, 67, 89, 133, 148; colonial, 115; self-making and, 128
ownership, 16, 136, 137; claims, 39, 119; culture concepts of, 114; rights, 41–42

Pachamama cult, 105
pacification, 36–40
Pairicán, Fernando, 123
Panguilef, Manuel, 214n3
pastoralism, 91, 92, 214n12
patrilineage, 63, 64, 68, 69, 211n9
patrón, 103, 109, 146, 206
Paz en la Araucania (Peace in the Araucania), 50, 210n16
peasants, 40–48
peonage, debt by, 44
Perez Rosales, Vicente, 209n8
personhood, 17, 64, 128; Mapuche, 70, 73, 74; nonhumans and, 91
phenomenology, 15, 18, 60, 62, 83, 88, 89
Piñera, Sebastian, 53
Pinochet, Augusto, 4, 21, 45, 47, 48–49, 96, 194; dictatorship of, 35, 119, 143, 144, 147
place: contentiousness of, 59; notion of, 14, 59, 61, 69; perspectives on, 73; phenomenological approach to, 60, 62; political-economic dimensions of, 59; question of, 147–50; space and, 59, 60–61
place making, 14, 60–61, 62, 78
Plan Araucania, 53
plantations, timber, 24, 87, 96, 100, 101, 112, 196, 202–3
political action, 7, 9, 27, 83, 164
political imagination, 7, 20, 184, 185, 194
politics: alter-, 201; Chilean, 125, 126; class, 48; community, 130; discrimination, 124; ecologically sound, 18; essence/construction and, 7–14; ethnic, 22; grassroots, 190; identity, 7, 10, 18; Indigenous, 4, 8, 10, 142, 197–203; land, 86, 192, 200; multicultural, 56; nonmodern forms of, 18; participation in, 29, 125; reconciliation, 35; reparation, 34, 48–55
potentiality, selfhood and, 69–74
poverty, 40, 42, 43, 53, 209n10; microfinance and, 194; rural, 143; soil, 96
Povinelli, Elizabeth, 21, 183

power: relations, 29, 36, 155, 182; state, 143, 156–61
privatization, 21, 119, 194
production, 105, 147; agricultural, 44, 109, 144, 195, 200; industrial, 44, 199, 212n7
Programa Orígenes, 52
property, 14–19, 131, 189, 194; boundaries, 118; disputes, 118, 178; embodiment and, 16; jural language of, 142, 186; land as, 15, 134–37; language of, 14, 156, 194; ontological principles of, 14, 17; practices/discourses on, 114; private, 112–13, 129; self-contained, 148; sociability of, 129–34; titles of, 119
property law, colonization and, 115–21
property relations, 112, 114, 129, 182; micro levels of, 120; principles of, 132
property rights, 115, 120, 136–37
property theory, 7, 16, 114, 115, 133, 137, 194; key question of, 14; legal, 11, 15, 136
protesters, 45, 50, 51, 189
*purrun* (circular dances), 170, 172, 215n6

Quechuas, 173, 200–201, 207n5
Quidel, Javier, 89
Quidel, José, 73
Quilapán, 122
Quilín treaty, 38
Quino River, 75, 95, 97, 100, 148, 149, 150, 153; crossing, 99 (photo)

race, class and, 67
racism, 125, 134
Ralco Dam, 49, 216n12
Rappaport, Joanne, 153
reciprocity, 12, 13, 92, 104–5
Reducción Contreras, 26, 45, 117, 118, 129, 151, 208n11
*reducciones* (reservations), 4, 23, 26, 41, 42, 49, 60, 64, 107, 117, 118, 119, 129, 131, 132, 206
relatedness, ecological, 88–95
religion, 77, 80, 92, 150, 174, 179; cognitivist interpretations of, 94; decline of, 185

reservation era, Indigenous difference on, 40–48
respect, 82, 98, 133, 206; private property and, 112
restitution, 116, 143–47, 165
restoration, 34, 142; land, 30, 157, 186, 190, 193–97, 200; territorial, 147–50
reterritorialization, 159–60
rewe, 68, 76, 150, 168, 173, 206; agential nature of, 174; installation of, 163, 172; newen and, 172, 174; political implications of, 175; as realpolitik, 175–82; as sacred site, 169–75, 178
ritual congregations, 81, 171–72, 174, 175, 191
rituals, 28, 64, 68, 104, 105, 108, 126; collective, 76, 149, 150; human action in, 174; knowledge of, 124; Mapuche, 79, 81, 127, 149, 163, 191; mortuary, 81; ngillatun, 68, 170, 171; successful, 170
Rivera Cusicanqui, Silva, 22
Rockefeller Foundation, 122
running water (*witrunko*), 98, 173

Saavedra, Cornelio, 39
Saavedra, José, 48
sacred sites, 163–64, 178, 180, 181, 185; rewe, 169–75
schools, 122, 123; photo of, 123
Scott, James, 119, 159
self-defense, 107, 154, 161
self-determination, 9, 29, 53, 72, 88, 111, 138; ancestral land and, 58; cultural/political, 35; land connections in, 115; performative nature of, 63
self-governance, 36, 48, 52, 54, 55
selfhood, 6, 28, 29, 30, 38, 43, 59, 63, 65, 83, 104, 127, 130, 133, 142, 181; ancestral land and, 58; neoliberalism and, 193–97; otherness and, 128; potentiality and, 69–74
sentience, 11, 12, 87
shamans, 64, 70, 126, 128, 170, 172, 206; 211n1, 213n12

signification, 6, 7, 8, 9, 10, 15, 60, 62, 74, 83, 150
sit-in, photo of, 167
smallholders, 100, 109, 112
social policies, 22, 151, 157, 176, 178
sociality, 12, 106, 112, 115, 119, 130, 131, 133, 137, 155, 192, 210n5
Sociedad Caupolicán, 43
soil depletion, 87, 95, 96, 101, 107, 197, 202, 203
soil fertility, 96, 100, 111
space: culture and, 59; phenomenological approaches to, 61; place and, 59, 60–61; semiotic approaches to, 60; theoretical developments on, 59
Spinoza, Baruch, 12
spirit masters, 91
spiritual forces, 84, 150, 175
state actors, analogies/misunderstandings by, 175–82
statecraft, 159, 164, 182–85
Stengers, Isabelle, 18, 174
stereotypes, racial, 29, 43, 47, 51, 113, 168
Stoermer, Eugene, 197
Strathern, Marilyn, 134, 143, 155
subjectivity, 10, 15, 73, 88, 91, 181
subsidies, 96, 101, 109, 184; agricultural, 22, 189; housing/welfare, 35; land, 146, 157, 158
superstitions, 13, 71, 81, 82, 93, 100, 154, 203
Supreme Being, 92
sustainability, environmental, 86, 196, 197, 201
symbolism, 60, 86, 174

technology, 95, 103, 109, 129, 160; agriculture, 15, 101, 157; environmental, 101; property, 115, 121
temporary workers (*temporeros*), 24, 102, 189, 206
Temuco, 24, 26, 43, 135, 145, 167, 211n8, 213n4, 214n1; organizations in, 151; photo of, 146
tenure, colonization and, 115–21

territoriality, Indigenous, 5, 159, 162
territory, 144, 160, 196; demarcation of, 200
Thompson, Janna, 34
Tilley, Christopher, 61, 78, 150
timber companies (*forestales*), 24, 50, 96, 97, 193
Título de Merced 18-B, 117, 152, 152 (map), 153
Traiguen, 24, 25 (map), 26, 28, 39, 97, 126, 135, 187; Comunidad Contreras and, 74–78; described, 23; Mapuche in, 24, 208n6; photo of, 41, 75; raid on, 40
transactions, 41, 121, 134, 135, 151–56
transformations, 48, 122, 128, 150, 156, 210n6; agrarian, 78; ecological, 19; interbeing, 213–14n12
translations, 80, 181, 156–61
Tratado de las Paces de Quilín, 38
Tren Tren myth, 71
trilla, 102; photo of, 103
tuwün, 13, 58, 59–74, 104, 113, 134, 137, 138, 148, 157, 206; conceptual/practical principles of, 64; influence of, 68, 72, 73; notion of, 69, 73, 83, 136, 150

Unidad Popular (UP) government, 44, 45, 48, 119, 143
Unión Demócratica Independiente (UDI), 146
United Nations, 52

Valdivia, Luis de, 116
Valdivia, Pedro de, 37, 154, 155
Valdivia earthquake (1960), 71
Valech, Ricardo, 209n12
values, 129, 191, 196; customary, 108; environmental, 29, 30, 84, 86, 87, 88, 89, 101, 107, 110; market, 165; moral, 15; neoliberal, 193
Verdery, Katherine, 114
Villalobos, Sergio, 48, 210n14
violence, 27, 39, 40, 51, 88
Viveiros de Castro, Eduardo Batalha, 91, 181, 201, 211n3

Wagner, Roy, 180
Wallmapu, 37, 49, 54
War of Arauco, 37–38
Wastell, Sari, 175
water, 90; concerns about, 95–101; cosmological significance of, 99, 100; cycle, 198; rights, 95–96; sources, 86, 100, 212n6; timber plantations and, 202–3
Water Code (1981), 95
water loss, 95, 101, 202
welfare, 22, 42, 52, 53, 110, 144, 208n9, 216n1
*werken*, 24, 26, 163, 168, 187, 206, 208n10
winkas, 4, 28, 56, 57, 63, 65, 67, 73, 82, 87, 88, 94, 103, 111, 113, 115, 120–21, 136, 155, 172; acting like/against, 121–29; adoption of, 29–30, 138; assimilation and, 72; interethnic marriages and, 66; nature of, 66, 104; necessity of, 128; power asymmetries with, 133; representation of, 104; self-defense against, 121–22; tricks of, 154; ways of, 107–10
world making, ancestral territory and, 192–93

# ABOUT THE AUTHOR

**Piergiorgio Di Giminiani** obtained his Ph.D. at University College London in 2011. Upon completing his degree, he took a lectureship at the Pontificia Universidad Católica de Chile, where he is currently associate professor. His latest research focuses on forest conservation, a phenomenon ethnographically approached through the analysis of relationships linking settlers, Indigenous farmers, state officials, NGO workers, and scientists imbricated in conservation initiatives in southern Chile. He has recently started a new research project on sheep farming, localism, and liberal globalism in southern Italy.